Plone
Live

March 2006

SourceBeat

Plone Live
by Michel Pelletier and Munwar Shariff

Published by SourceBeat, LLC, Highlands Ranch, Colorado.

Managing Editor: James Goodwill
Technical Editor: Jean Jordaan
Copy Editor: Amy Kesic
Layout Designer: Sarah Hogan
Cover Designer: Max Hays

ISBN: 0-9765534-0-6

To the loving memory of my daughter Naureen Sultana (1996-2005) — Munwar Shariff

People complain that open source doesn't have good documentation. Usually they are correct, but occasionally the reverse is true. Sometimes an open source project produces a documentation success story that is not just thorough and professional, but is as innovative and exciting as the software itself.

Plone Live is such an example. This mammoth effort, produced by Michel Pelletier and Munwar Shariff, is a tremendous addition to the world of Plone and one of the best values on the market. Written by people who are involved in the development of Plone, *Plone Live* is up-to-date, comprehensive, and well-organized.

This book captures the spirit of Plone as it continues its rise as the leading open source content management system. Nobody asked Michel and Munwar to write it. They saw a market, had interest, and showed initiative. They know all the people involved, go to conferences, give speeches, and have fun. In fact, CIGNEX hosts development activities and employs several of the top Plone developers. *Plone Live* feels like Plone itself, both in spirit and in execution.

I first encountered Plone while still at Zope Corporation. It was a relief to see a project doing the specific thing that CMF tried to avoid: focus on an out-of-the-box experience. It wasn't until I moved to Europe that I saw the real attraction, best summarized by *Martin Aspeli* at a recent conference:

"Plone values you and your efforts; come join us and have fun."

Even when the world of Plone is frustrating, there remains a sense that you matter and your efforts count.

Similarly, my experiences with Michel go back some time, when Zope Corporation was called Digital Creations. Michel is in a unique position; he is an early chronicler of both Zope and Plone.

With Michel and now with Munwar, I see the same "Let's make it happen!" approach that encourages others and generates even broader participation.

Plone Live will be your guidebook on your journey. As Plone grows, *Plone Live* will grow with it. Thanks, Michel and Munwar, for showing that open source can be a leader in documentation.

— *Paul Everitt*

Paul Everitt is the Executive Director of Plone Foundation, a Co-founder of Zope Corporation, the Founder of Zope Europe Association, and a Board member of OSCOM.

TABLE OF CONTENTS

Chapter 1: Introduction to Plone Development 1

Chapter 2: Anatomy of Plone 15

Chapter 3: Getting Started with Plone 61

Chapter 4: Basic Customizations 97

Chapter 5: Membership and Security 141

Chapter 6: Creating Portal Types 181

Chapter 7: Archetypes 215

Chapter 8: Advanced Plone Features
and Products 245

Chapter 9: Plone and Relational Databases 275

Chapter 10: Membership Using LDAP 301

Chapter 11: Integrating with Non-Plone Systems 339

Appendix A: Mind Maps 359

Appendix B: Page Template Reference 373

Appendix C: Useful Resources 387

Index 393

Michel Pelletier

Michel is the co-author of *The Zope Book* and *The Zope Developer's Guide*, and he has written numerous articles on Zope and ZODB. Michel worked for *CIGNEX Technologies* (http://www.cignex.com) as an architect. He has written various books and articles about Zope, Python, and other leading web technologies.

He has been working on Python and Zope for over five years. He also worked at Zope Corporation, helping them develop Zope versions 1.0 to 2.2 and creating features such as ZCatalog and MIME encoding support. Michel lives in Portland, Oregon, where he spends time hiking in the nearby Cascade Mountains.

Munwar Shariff

Munwar is CTO and VP of Business Development at *CIGNEX Technologies* (http://www.cignex.com). He is a Board Member of *Plone Foundation* and a sponsor of the *Goldegg* initiative (http://www.goldeggstack.org). He has extensive experience in managing engineering teams and acting as chief architect of several large-scale projects in open source and J2EE Technologies. His experience spans three continents — North America, Europe, and Asia.

Since co-founding CIGNEX in late 2000, he worked on more than 50 web applications using Zope, CMF, Plone, MySQL, and LDAP technologies. He has written a number of articles on open source, and he is a frequent speaker at conferences related to this topic. He has consulted with clients such as Epson, Lawrence Livermore, Broadvision, Wal-Mart, Mitsubishi, and Compaq. He earned his M.S. from REC Surathkal, India.

Jean Jordaan, Technical Editor

Jean studied languages at the University of Stellenbosch in South Africa and spent the first year of his
Masters program in the Netherlands. After he returned
to South Africa in 1996, the Internet had arrived in the
humanities department in Stellenbosch. He started
developing the department's web site, which published
poetry magazines. Jean spent three years developing applications on Linux and
found his home in the open source movement. He is active in the Zope and
Plone community, and he has contributed to online Plone documentation. He
currently works for *Upfront Systems* and does projects of his own. One of his
projects is a book for the tuXlabs project.

Amy Kesic, Lead Editor

Amy worked as a technical writer for four years before
taking time out to be a full-time mom to her three children. In January 2004, Amy joined the *SourceBeat
Publishing* editorial team, and in June 2004, she became
the Lead Editor. Currently, she is also involved in a
volunteer position as a Girl Scout Troop Leader. Her
interests include reading (of course!), working on her personal web site, home
improvement projects, traveling, and much more. Amy lives in sunny Colorado
and enjoys "getting away from it all" in the Rocky Mountains.

Plone Live is the result of a year of work of the two authors, Michel Pelletier and Munwar Shariff, our technical editor, Jean Jordaan, and our copy editor, Amy Kesic. But this book is more than what you are holding (or reading on the screen), because this book is *live*; every month, the authors add new content and fix typos, responding to the feedback our readers leave on our site, http://plonelive.com.

Over the next year, this book will tackle one of the greatest challenges for any book about modern, open source software: remaining current. Using the traditional publishing method, books quickly become out-of-date and irrelevant, rather than remaining up-to-date, useful references. By updating this book every month, *SourceBeat* has created a unique publication format that solves these problems with traditional publication methods.

First, it's hard to get a book about a complex piece of open source software 100% correct; in fact, almost impossible when one or two authors and one technical reviewer must often document a system built by dozens or perhaps hundreds of programmers. By creating orderly, feature-based releases each month, the book can evolve over time to cover more and more complex features of the software, and we can catch errors quickly in the first few updates.

Second, open source software, like Plone, often does not follow a hard-and-fast feature plan, but instead adds new, innovative features as they are thought up by creative developers trying to solve real-world problems. By updating the book each month, the book can quickly adapt to cover any new technologies or trends that emerge from the community of users. Books that are released once every year or two cannot follow or easily adapt to these trends.

Third, like open source software, books have communities. However, traditional books have a large disconnect between the readers and the author because there is no way for the readers to provide feedback to the author. Even if they could, there are seldom clear, easy-to use-channels for redistributing books or errata. By creating the "live" book format, *SourceBeat* is creating a new way for readers and authors to make better books cooperatively.

Finally, *SourceBeat's* format of shipping books as electronic additions saves a lot of paper from being wasted, and for those who must absolutely have a book in print, *SourceBeat* can print the most recent version of the book on demand. You can choose whether you want electronic or paper editions of any of the various revisions the book goes through throughout the year.

So, welcome to *Plone Live*. We hope that you take advantage of our web site, http://plonelive.com, by contributing to it. You can contribute by reporting any errors you find in the book, making suggestions for new content that you'd like to see in future updates, and commenting and blogging in our readers' blog. See you online!

Sincerely,

— Michel Pelletier and Munwar Shariff

This book is written for Zope, CMF, Plone, and Python developers familiar with web frameworks. The main purpose of this book is to help people develop Content Management Systems using Plone. Readers should have a beginner's understanding of Python and intermediate experience with HTML and web technologies. Many good books cover the Python language and Zope framework, so we are not going to repeat them in this book. This book focuses on concepts, customization, and advanced development using Plone.

Chapters 1 through *6* cover the basics of Plone and various customization techniques. *Chapters 7* and *8* cover advanced development with Archetypes and ATCT types. *Chapters 9* through *11* cover the powerful integration features of Plone.

Chapter Summaries

Chapter 1: Introduction to Plone Development

This chapter introduces you to Plone, Zope, and Python in the context of web applications. It includes instructions on how to download and install them. It also provides you with several online resources, including the PloneLive.com web site, other Plone resources, and the source code for the examples in this book.

Chapter 2: Anatomy of Plone

This chapter describes how the major components of a Plone system relate to each other. It also describes the major features of Zope. This chapter is essential reading for anyone not already familiar with Plone's tools and features.

Chapter 3: Getting Started with Plone

This chapter introduces you to some of Plone's basic features, such as creating content, editing content, the underlying fundamentals of the object database and acquisition, and how to use and edit workflow.

Chapter 4: Basic Customizations

This chapter explains Plone's many features, which you can customize to make Plone look and behave the way you want. It describes all of those customizable options and their possible values. It also explains the differences between file system development and Zope Through The Web development.

Chapter 5: Membership and Security

This chapter explains the framework behind the membership and security system. Zope has a powerful security system that prevents users from calling methods or accessing objects for which they do not have permission. Plone uses this security system to provide a flexible and configurable membership system for controlling the content, workflow, search, and security policies.

Chapter 6: Creating Portal Types

This chapter explains how to create new types in Python that work with Plone. Eventually, you are going to need functionality that Plone's default types don't provide. For this, you will create your own types that work according to your specifications.

Chapter 7: Archetypes

This chapter introduces you to Archetypes. New in Plone 2.1, Archetypes is a type system to replace the CMF type system described in *Chapter 5*. This new, schema-driven type system was initially a third-party product, but it became so popular that the Plone developers decided to adopt it as the new type system for Plone 2.1.

Chapter 8: Advanced Plone Features and Products

This chapter covers the techniques for advanced development and functional testing.

Chapter 9: Plone and Relational Databases

This chapter highlights how Plone supports external databases to provide an enterprise-scale content management system. Relational databases are widely used in medium to large enterprises. Zope supports almost all the relational databases available in the market.

Chapter 10: Membership Using LDAP

This chapter explains how to leverage the Lightweight Directory Access Protocol (LDAP) to implement a highly scalable membership system on Plone.

Chapter 11: Integrating with Non-Plone Systems

This chapter covers integration with non-Plone systems, such as WebDAV, Syndication, Web Services, and XML-RPC.

Appendix A: Mind Maps

This appendix represents the key features of Zope and Plone as Mind Maps, so readers can remember them easily.

Appendix B: Page Template Reference

This appendix provides a quick reference to the three components of Zope's dynamic presentation language: the Tag Attribute Language (TAL), the TAL Expression Syntax (TALES), and Macro Expansions for TAL (METAL).

Appendix C: Useful Resources

This appendix provides Plone-, Zope-, and Python-related resources and links to some useful Plone products that you can install and customize.

ACKNOWLEDGEMENTS

I would like to thank my friends and family, the developers of Plone, Zope, and Python, and the many people I have met, both online and face-to-face, who share my passion for cutting-edge, socially enabled software. I would also like to thank the editors, proofreaders, and all the rest of the staff at *SourceBeat* for their effort in making this book a reality. I would like to thank the team members at *CIGNEX*, who have helped make the book possible and providing real world problems to solve. Finally, I would like to thank *Jean Jordaan*, this book's technical editor, who has a keen eye for fact and error.

— *Michel Pelletier*

I would like to thank my friend *Rajesh Setty*, Chairman of *CIGNEX*, for his encouragement and great support; without him, this book would not have existed. Thanks to *Matt Filios*, President and CEO of *SourceBeat*, who is dedicated to providing amazing documentation to the open source software community. I would like to thank the editors, *Jean Jordaan* and *Amy Kesic*, who made my chapters more sensible. My special thanks to all my team members at *CIGNEX* for making this book a reality. My sincere thanks to *Paul Everitt* for supporting me on *Goldegg* (http://www.goldeggstack.org) project, which helped the Plone community significantly. Thanks to *Alan Runyan*, *Joel Burton*, and all other Plone gurus for providing us with great feedback. I would like to thank my wife, *Nafeesa*, who encouraged me with hot Indian tea and took care of our kids. She is a great mother.

— *Munwar Shariff*

## CHAPTER 1

Introduction to Plone Development

This chapter introduces you to Plone, Zope, and Python in the context of web applications. It includes instructions on how to download and install them. It also provides you with several online resources, including the PloneLive.com website, other Plone resources, and how to download the source code for the examples in this book.

Overview

The Internet provides amazing possibilities for people to interact and communicate in ways they have never done before. This new form of communication is changing the way people socialize and do business.

These new concepts and ideas are driving the need for a new set of web tools, including Plone. The tools are too many and varied to describe here, but many tools share the following high-level concepts:

▶ **Community:** Old-generation web tools were a way for an organization to communicate to a broad audience. This unidirectional approach works only for broadcasting information, not for true two-way communication. New tools offer the ability for users within a community to collaborate, using organizational concepts like *managers*, *groups*, and *teams*.

▶ **Content Management:** Content is a broad term that describes any kind of digital information that is managed by a community of users. Content typically includes documents, images, files, and other data, or it may represent real-world objects like people, inventories, and so forth.

▶ **Workflow:** The rules by which a community manages content are called workflow. It defines the various states of content, how those states can change, and who can change them.

▶ **Scripting:** Scripting is another broad term, but it usually means the ability for users to create small programs, called scripts and expressions, that customize the behavior of their sites in some way. Scripts can be an integral part of the framework, or they can be "one-off" scripts that achieve a one-time purpose. Expressions are tiny, one-line scripts that return a computed result.

▶ **Extensibility:** A key feature for many frameworks is the ability to bolt on new functionality from other parties and to package your own functionality to give to others. This extensibility improves production by eliminating the need to duplicate work and provides a way for many developers to access a wider market of users.

Plone is all of these things and more. This book addresses these needs by showing you how to design and develop an extensible, community-driven content management system with workflow and scripting tools.

Introducing Plone

Plone is a simple, powerful, well-designed content management system for the Windows, UNIX, and Macintosh OS X platforms. Plone provides ready-to-use content management for documents, images, files, site templates, news, and events. It also allows you to create your own types of content or add third-party content to your site.

Numerous third-party products are available to add to Plone and Zope to extend your Plone site's functionality. Sometimes, using these products can be simple, but Plone/Zope/Python programming expertise is often required to customize or extend these products to suit your needs.

This book provides you with the expertise needed to "jump the gap" from simply manipulating content in Plone to actually developing those objects in Python and using frameworks like Archetypes. By reading this book, you will acquire a firm understanding of the various layers of Plone: the skins, Archetypes, the Content Management Framework (CMF), Zope, and Python.

Figure 1.1 shows Plone's default front page:

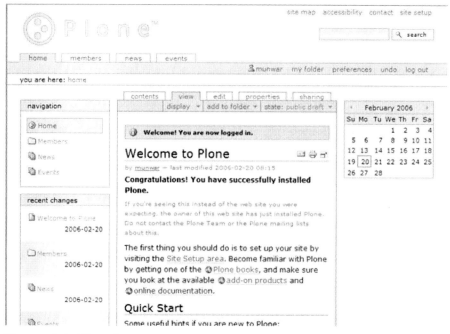

Figure 1.1: Plone home page

Plone provides many features on one well-designed page, like search, navigation, recent items, calendar, membership access, and much more. This compact, clean, and powerful interface is one of Plone's greatest features.

Another wonderful aspect of the interface, which is not visible, is the HTML encoding, which helps to enable effective DHTML and styling. Besides respecting standards, it uses classes to describe areas, it assigns ids to all widgets, it contains a listing of all the tabs on the screen, and it defines many variables and points where you can customize.

After reading this book, you will understand not only how the interface works, but also how the underlying Plone and Zope applications work to create it.

Content Management Systems

A content management system (CMS) is a software framework that manages digital content and information about that data. Content can include documents, images, files, and folders. Information about the content can include the author, the date it was written, whether it is private or public, and so forth. In fact, a CMS is often more than just managing data; it is also about managing data *about* data. This is called *metadata*, and the remainder of this book contains much more discussion on that topic.

Many content management systems are available, but what sets Plone and Zope apart are the following features:

▸ **A Through the Web (TTW) interface:** Plone and Zope do not have a special GUI front-end or require any special programs. Anyone can work with a Plone site using only a browser, because Zope and Plone's GUI *is* a web browser.

▸ **An Object-Oriented design:** From its object database to its simple publication method of turning URLs into rendered objects, Plone and Zope are object-oriented from the ground up.

▸ **Internationalization:** Plone is fully internationalized, currently available in more than 40 languages.

▸ **A Scriptable Language:** Plone and Zope are written in Python, a powerful, rapid-prototyping, cross-platform, and high-level object-oriented language. You can quickly compose site logic using Python's clean syntax.

▸ **An HTML Presentation Language:** The Zope Page Template (ZPT) language is one of the cleanest and best presentation languages available. Page templates are always valid XHTML, and they involve no custom tags or proprietary markup languages. ZPT also lets you store macros of HTML that you can reuse throughout your site, maintaining a common look and feel.

CMS functionality varies widely, depending on its goals and its design. When you compare Plone to other systems, feature for feature, Plone provides an amazingly complete suite of tools and software to create easy-to-use, productive web sites.

Introducing Zope

Plone is built on top of Zope and the Zope Content Management Framework (CMF). Zope and the CMF constitute the "guts" of many Plone components.

Another way to put it is that Plone is an application and Zope is the web operating system that provides many of the underlying features.

The CMF provides a framework of services for content management systems. These services include content type management, workflow, users, membership, cataloging, and many other features. Plone is an application that uses these underlying CMF services to accomplish much of its functionality.

One of Plone's key features is the way that it stores your content on the server. Like most other platforms, Plone uses a database, but instead of the more common relational database where data is stored in columns and rows, Plone uses the Zope Object Database (ZODB), which allows you to manage web content in a persistent, object-oriented way. This unique object database uses data objects like *Files*, *Folders*, *Images*, and *News Items* to manage your site content.

Object databases are a different concept than relational databases. For example, with a relational database, you would query sets of tables using the SQL database language to retrieve information that you have previously stored there. An object database needs no special queries. Objects are transparently and efficiently stored in the database for you, and you only need to follow a few simple rules outlined in the ZODB documentation.

As previously mentioned, Zope provides a low-level extension mechanism called **Products,** which allows third-party extensions to plug in to Zope. Many of these extensions are available publicly, provided by many developers from the Zope community. Products are the basis for turning a plain Zope site into a fully dynamic web site that provides complex components and behavior specifically tailored to your application. Some of these products require you to install other products or frameworks like Plone or the CMF in order to work.

Introducing Python

Zope and all CMF and Plone components are written primarily in the Python programming language. Therefore, Python's features have a heavy influence on the object-oriented nature of Plone. Python is a high-level, dynamic, object-oriented programming language with a clear, simple syntax. An understanding of the basics of Python programming is a prerequisite for this book.

The Python developers have a short and simple online tutorial on the Python web site (http://www.python.org). After reading this tutorial, you will know enough to be able to start with this book.

Installing Plone

The current version of Plone is 2.1.2. This pack provides all of the advanced Archetype and content translation features that are used in this book.

Windows

On Windows, install Plone by double-clicking on the Plone installer that you downloaded from http://plone.org/products/plone/releases/2.1.2. This will launch the Plone Windows installation tool, as shown in Figure 1.2.

Figure 1.2: The Plone installer

The installer will ask where you want to install Plone. Keep in mind that while the Plone installer is a good way to start, you will need to install the following source instructions if you want to do more serious configuration for development or with multiple sites. You do not require any special Windows compilers to install Plone from the source.

Linux and Other UNIX Platforms

On Linux, install Plone either by downloading a pre-compiled binary package from http://plone.org/products/plone/releases/2.1.2 or by installing the source distribution as described in the following section. Binary packages for Linux and other UNIX platforms like BSD are available.

Source Installation

Plone comes bundled as a "source distribution." This comes with all of the Plone source files, but it does not include an installation program; you must install Zope and Plone yourself. Zope also comes with a Windows and Linux binary installation and a source installation. For more information, see *The Zope Book, Edition 2.7* (http://www.plope.com/Books/2_7Edition).

Download Plone 2.1.2 for all platforms from http://plone.org/products/plone/releases/2.1.2. This is the Plone product package, which requires Zope 2.7.8 or 2.8.5 and Python 2.3.5 already installed.

To install Plone from the source, unpack the source distribution file and copy all of its contents into the *Products* directory of your Zope instance home. Restart your Zope site, and you're ready to begin using Plone!

Note: If you're having trouble, make sure your underlying Zope system works before you begin installing Plone. This will help you narrow the problem down much faster. If all goes well, the option **Plone Site** will appear in your Zope **Add** menu, and the Control Panel will show that the Plone products have been successfully installed.

Plone and Zope Configuration

Regardless of which OS you run or how you installed Plone, all Plone setups have the same basic structure and configuration. First, you need to know a little about how Plone is installed and run on your system.

Every Plone site is inside of a directory or folder on your computer that is referred to as the *instance home*. You will often see this concept capitalized as INSTANCE_HOME, because that is the name of the variable inside Zope that holds this information. Your instance home is where all of the configuration files and data for your site are stored.

The actual Plone software is stored in a different location, called the *software home*. Plone installs into two different locations to support multi-hosting, which is running two or more Plone instances on the same machine (this is very different from *virtual hosting*, which is running two or more Plone sites inside the same Plone instance).

It is possible to have many Plone sites running on the same server with the same software home, but each site has its own distinct instance home. An instance home has an *etc/* folder that contains the *zope.conf* file for the site, and a *var/* folder that contains the ZODB database file and logging information from the site. Each instance also has a *bin/* folder containing scripts to start or stop that particular site.

Configuring Zope

To customize the way your Plone site runs on your computer, you can edit the underlying Zope configuration file. You can configure Zope by editing the *zope.conf* file for a particular instance home. This file contains various configuration options that you can tweak to change the way the Zope server starts up. For a complete description of this file, read the comments inside the file itself and look at http://www.plope.com/Books/2_7Edition/InstallingZope.stx. You can configure Zope to listen for requests on either the default development port (8080) or another port, such as the well-known HTTP port 80. In order to access low ports such as 80, you may require administrative privileges on your machine. Another popular way of running Plone is behind a proxy (like Squid), a firewall, or a web server (like Apache or Microsoft t IIS).

The *Plone Live* CVS Server

The code examples in this book are hosted on CIGNEX's SVN server under the *Plone Live* section (https://svn.cignex.com/public/PloneLive).

SVN is a source code repository tool that manages large code projects as they evolve over time. Instead of keeping your files in a private directory where they can be lost and where you have no information about how they were developed, the SVN keeps your files "checked in" to a code repository.

The repository keeps track of more than just your files; it keeps track of every change made to those files over their entire history. In the case of the *Plone Live* SVN repository, as the book and the code evolve, you will be able to update your code to get the most recent version. Additionally, you will be able to browse the history of each file so that you can understand how that file evolved, or why a certain change was made a certain point in the file's 's evolution.

Note: You can also download the code examples of this book from Plone Live blog site (http://www.plonelive.com/downloads)

SVN Checkout

If you are interested in developing with Plone or finding out the latest "bleeding edge" feature, then checking Plone out of its subversion revision control system may be a good choice for you. The SVN code (specifically, the trunk and the tips of branches) are almost always experimental and unstable, and you should not use it for production environments unless you are prepared to mitigate the risks associated with using untested software.

Tip: If you check out a release tag, it's the same as running the release.

To check Plone out of SVN, you must first install a subversion client. For more information on subversion, go to the subversion web site (http://www .subversion.org).

Note: The SVN URL for checking out a copy of Plone is https://svn.plone .org/svn/plone. Keep in mind that you are downloading code that is still in development, so if it breaks you don't have much recourse but to keep all the pieces and fix it yourself. However, this is a great way to gain experience if you are a serious code developer.

Online Resources

Many online resources are available for beginner Plone users and developers, which are listed here. A more exhaustive list of sites and products is available for Zope and Plone in *Appendix C: Useful Resources*.

▶ **Plone** (http://www.plone.org): The Plone site is where it all starts. Here you will find lots of information about Plone, including Plone itself, third-party products, documentation, information about the community and how to get involved, and links to outside Plone resources.

▶ **Demo Plone Site** (http://plone.net): The demo site allows you to create a test Plone account so that you can experiment with Plone before installing it yourself. If you do not have access to a Plone site, this may be a good option for you to get started.

▶ **Zope** (http://www.zope.org): The Zope.org site is one of the largest Plone sites in the world. On this site, you will find a lot of information about the Zope community and links to Zope books and documentation.

▶ **Planet Plone** (http://planet.plone.org): This is a syndicated blog site of all Plone gurus. Serious Plone developers should visit this site on a daily basis.

Summary

This chapter introduced you to Plone, Zope and Python. It showed you how to install and configure these elements to set up a Plone site so you can begin learning about Plone. It also gave you several online resources that will aid you as you learn about and work with Plone. *Chapter 2: Anatomy of Plone* is a thorough introduction to Plone and its various components.

Summary

## CHAPTER 2

Anatomy of Plone

Plone can seem to have a bewildering array of features, interfaces, screens, tools, and objects right out of the box. This chapter describes the major components of a Plone system and how they relate to each other. It also describes the major features of Zope. This chapter is essential reading for anyone not already familiar with Plone's tools and features.

Creating a Plone Site

When you install Plone using the source distribution, you usually copy the Plone-related products to the Zope instance's *Products* folder as specified in *Chapter 1*. When you start Zope, you must create your Plone site.

Since Plone is a content management system developed on a Zope framework, you can access all the features of Zope. Access the default Zope site by typing the URL http://localhost:8080 (the host name and port number will change, depending upon your installation).

Once you start a Zope instance, the default home page displays, as shown in Figure 2.1. It contains all the pointers and examples related to the Zope server.

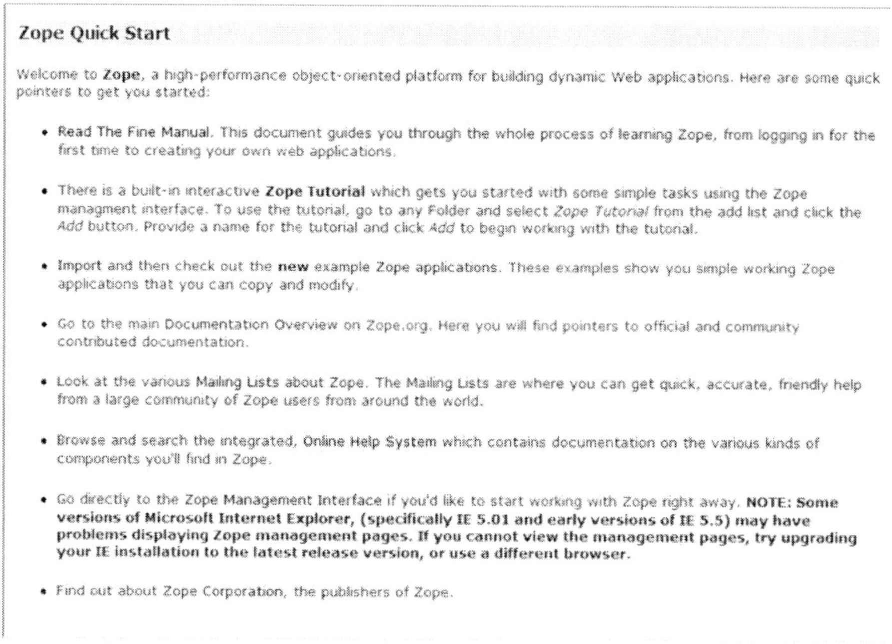

Zope Quick Start

Welcome to **Zope**, a high-performance object-oriented platform for building dynamic Web applications. Here are some quick pointers to get you started:

- **Read The Fine Manual.** This document guides you through the whole process of learning Zope, from logging in for the first time to creating your own web applications.

- There is a built-in interactive **Zope Tutorial** which gets you started with some simple tasks using the Zope managment interface. To use the tutorial, go to any Folder and select *Zope Tutorial* from the add list and click the *Add* button. Provide a name for the tutorial and click *Add* to begin working with the tutorial.

- Import and then check out the **new** example Zope applications. These examples show you simple working Zope applications that you can copy and modify.

- Go to the main Documentation Overview on Zope.org. Here you will find pointers to official and community contributed documentation.

- Look at the various Mailing Lists about Zope. The Mailing Lists are where you can get quick, accurate, friendly help from a large community of Zope users from around the world.

- Browse and search the integrated, Online Help System which contains documentation on the various kinds of components you'll find in Zope.

- Go directly to the Zope Management Interface if you'd like to start working with Zope right away. **NOTE: Some versions of Microsoft Internet Explorer, (specifically IE 5.01 and early versions of IE 5.5) may have problems displaying Zope management pages. If you cannot view the management pages, try upgrading your IE installation to the latest release version, or use a different browser.**

- Find out about Zope Corporation, the publishers of Zope.

Figure 2.1: Default Zope home page

Adding a Plone Site

If you have successfully installed all the Plone products, you will see **Plone Site** in the Add list in the Zope Management Interface (ZMI), as shown in Figure 2.2. In Windows, the Windows installer will automatically add a Plone site

---

titled *Plone*. You must have a *Manager* role in the Zope folder where you want to create the new Plone Site.

Contents
View
Properties
Security
Undo
Ownership
Find
Folder at /
Help!
Plone Site
Add

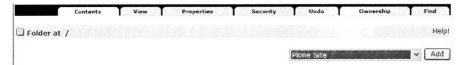

Figure 2.2: Adding a Plone site through the Zope Management Interface

Once you click the **Add** button, the **Add Plone Site** form displays, as shown in Figure 2.3.

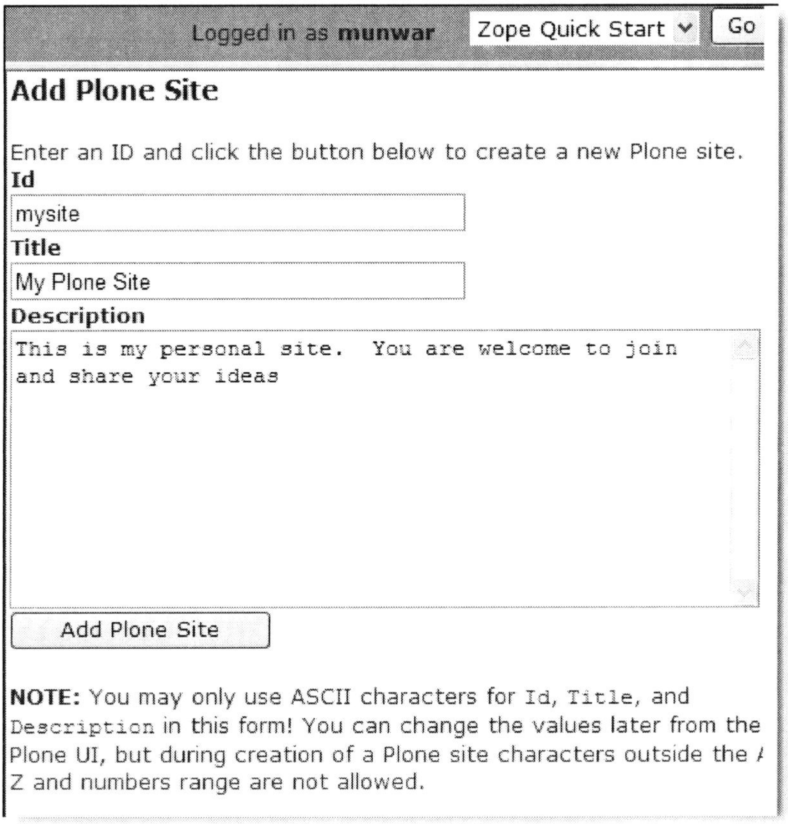
Logged in as munwar
Zope Quick Start
Go
Add Plone Site
Enter an ID and click the button below to create a new Plone site.
Id
mysite
Title
My Plone Site
Description
This is my personal site. You are welcome to join and share your ideas
Add Plone Site
NOTE: You may only use ASCII characters for Id, Title, and Description in this form! You can change the values later from the Plone UI, but during creation of a Plone site characters outside the A-Z and numbers range are not allowed.

Figure 2.3: Add Plone Site form

Table 2.1 provides the field definitions for the Add form.

Table 2.1: Add Plone Site field definitions

Field	Definition
Id	This determines the URL of your new web site (http://localhost:8080/mysite). If you use Virtual Host Monster, Apache, or any other multi-host setting (as explained in *Chapter 1*), the URL for your newly created web site can be different (such as www.mysite.com).
Title	This is the title for the new Plone site object. The title provides a human-friendly label for the site object. Providing a title is optional, but recommended.
Membership Source	This is the source from which Plone draws its user information. The default for this field is "Create a new user folder in the Portal." This option will create a new user folder in the Plone site to be used as the authentication source. You may also select "I have an existing user folder and want to use it instead." In this case, the Plone site will draw its user information from a user folder that exists in the Zope object hierarchy above the new Plone site.
Description	This is a short description of the site. This description may be made available for syndicated content, and it may be used by some of the default user interface elements of the site. Providing a description is optional, but recommended.
Customization Policy Setup	The dialog box itself defines this. A pre-defined site comes with pre-installed products and pre-configured tools. For example, the CMFMember tool needs a separate set of Membership tools in Plone.

Default Plone Site

After providing the appropriate information, click the **Add Plone Site** button to create a new Plone. By default, Plone includes the following features:

▶ Basic content types

▶ Member properties

▶ Simple workflow

▶ Look and feel (layout/templates)

▶ Plone user interface with style sheets

▶ Standard metadata

▸ Real-time search engine

▸ Multi-language support

▸ Security policy

A default Plone site is shown in Figure 2.4. You should customize the default application according to your requirements (*Chapter 4* covers customization in detail).

Figure 2.4: Default Plone site

Plone Site Objects

Refresh the ZMI to see the newly created Plone site (*mysite*). Once you click on the newly created Plone site, all default Plone objects and tools will be listed, as shown in Figure 2.5.

Type	Name
▸▸	HTTPCache
▣	MailHost
▭	Members (Members)
▸▸	RAMCache
▦	acl_users (Group-aware User Folder)
⋮	archetype_tool
◔	caching_policy_manager
▦	content_type_registry
▦	cookie_authentication
✕	error_log
▦	events (Events)
▯	front-page (Welcome to Plone)
⇗	kupu_library_tool (Kupu visual editor)
◈	mimetypes_registry (MIME types recognized by Plone)
▦	news (News)
◔	plone_utils (Various utility methods)
◇	portal_actionicons (Associates actions with icons)
◇	portal_actions (Contains custom tabs and buttons)
∕	portal_atct (ATContentTypes Tool)
▦	portal_calendar (Controls how events are shown)
◉	portal_catalog (Indexes all content in the site)
◔	portal_controlpanel (Control Panel)
◔	portal_css (CSS Registry)
◔	portal_discussion (Controls how discussions are stored)
◔	portal_factory (Responsible for the creation of content objects)
▤	portal_form_controller (Manages form validation and post-validation actions)
▦	portal_groupdata (Handles properties on groups)
▦	portal_groups (Handles group related functionality)
◔	portal_interface (Allows to query object interfaces)
◔	portal_javascripts (JavaScript Registry)
▦	portal_memberdata (Handles the available properties on members)
▦	portal_membership (Handles membership policies)
◉	portal_metadata (Controls metadata like keywords, copyrights, etc)
◔	portal_migration (Handles migrations to newer Plone versions)
◔	portal_properties (Portal)
▦	portal_quickinstaller (Allows to install/uninstall products)
∕	portal_registration (Handles registration of new users)
▥	portal_skins (Controls skin behaviour (search order etc))
▦	portal_syndication (Generates RSS for folders)
◈	portal_transforms (Handles data conversion between MIME types)
▯	portal_types (Controls the available content types in your portal)
∕	portal_uidannotation (CMF portal_uidannotation)
∕	portal_uidgenerator (CMF portal_uidgenerator)
∕	portal_uidhandler (CMF portal_uidhandler)
↺	portal_undo (Defines actions and functionality related to undo)
◔	portal_url (Methods to anchor you to the root of your Plone site)
↻	portal_workflow (Contains workflow definitions for your portal)
▦	reference_catalog (Archetypes Reference Catalog)
◔	translation_service (Provides access to the translation machinery)
▦	uid_catalog (Archetypes UID Catalog)

[Rename] [Cut] [Copy] [Delete] [Import/Export] [Select All]

Figure 2.5: Plone site default objects and tools

The following sections of this chapter explain each component and tool in detail. The tools are grouped by type for the sake of ke of clarity.

Login and Membership Tools

This section briefly explains the user folder, member folder, and the portal tools related to members and groups. *Chapter 5: Membership and Security* provides detailed information about Membership.

acl_users

Zope defines users in user folders. A user folder contains objects that define Zope user accounts. User folder objects always have a **Zope id of acl_users**. More than one user folder can exist within a Zope instance, but more than one user folder may not exist within the *same* Zope folder. *The Zope Book* provides more information about Zope users and security (http://www.plope.com/ Books/2_7Edition/Security.stx).

Plone ships with a Group User Folder (GRUF). By default, GRUF uses two basic Zope user folders: one for users, and one for groups. You can reconfigure GRUF to retrieve users from other types of user folders, but you'll always need a user folder for groups, as well. You may obtain your users from an LDAP directory, MySQL database, and other sources. *Chapter 5: Membership and Security* provides more information about GRUF.

Click on the *Sources* tab to manage sources. Click on the **Groups** tab to create groups. Click on the **Users** tab to create users. If you create users via the GRUF ZMI, Plone won't have a chance to intervene (for example, a ZMI user lacks the Member role). Click on the **Audit** management tab to check how the site security is applied.

cookie_authentication

A cookie is a piece of information sent by a web server to a user's browser. Cookies may include any state information of interest to the server, such as login or registration identification, user preferences, online "shopping cart" information, and so forth. The browser saves the information and sends it back to the web server according to the cookie parameters (the paths to which the cookie should be presented, when it should expire, etc.).

Plone supports cookie-based authentication by default. The cookie authentication mechanism might change based on the type of user folder (for example, MySQLUserfolder).

This tool defines the following:

▶ Cookie for User login name

▶ Cookie for Password

▶ Automated login page (when a secure object is accessed)

▶ Logout page (page that displays after the user logs out)

portal_groups

Groups are a logical categorization of users and often confused with *Roles*. A Role is a collection of permissions. A user with a specific set of Roles has different permissions than another user with a different set of Roles. Groups create a common workspace for a related set of users in the web site. Groups also add sets of roles to users to allow members to share content implicitly with other members by sharing with a group. In fact, in the Plone UI, the only way to associate roles with a member is by creating a group with those roles and putting the member in that group. By default, Plone does not come with any groups. *Chapters 3* and *5* provide more information about groups.

The **portal_groups** tool provides user-group management functions for use in a Plone site. Its interface provides a common front-end to any group implementation. This tool controls the creation of work group spaces and specifies the name of the workspace folder.

portal_groupdata

The **portal_groupdata** tool stores properties on user groups. You can add custom properties (profiles) for a group. You can use these properties to share the group details with others. You can also use them to search groups.

portal_memberdata

The **portal_memberdata** tool stores the member properties (profile information), controls the membership properties, and provides default values for member properties. You can use this tool to add your application-specific member profiles.

For example, the default WYSIWYG editor is Kupu. If you installed the Epoz editor (WYSIWYG), and you want it to be the default editor for every member of your site, then you must set the default value as shown in Figure 2.6.

Figure 2.6: Member properties (profile information)

portal_membership

The **portal_membership** tool handles membership policies. The user sources are managed through GRUF (explained earlier in the *acl_users* section and in *Chapter 5*). Using GRUF, you can configure them to use an external source, such as LDAP (Lightweight Directory Access Protocol). LDAP uses a concept called "groups" to group the users, similar to "roles" in Plone. Using this tool, you can map LDAP groups to Plone roles (such as Member, Reviewer and any other Role defined in the Plone site). *Chapters 9* and *10* provide more information about external user sources and the usage of this tool.

This tool also controls user-specific actions, such as Login, My Folder, and so forth, which are visible on the portal, as shown in Figure 2.7.

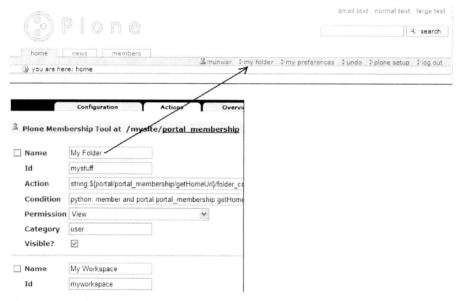

Figure 2.7: Controlling portal members actions using the portal_membership tool

In a Plone web site, the objects that a user may access and the actions that they may perform are based on authorization, the type and state of the object, the location of the object, and more. In a Plone site, these actions are featured in various parts of the user interface (for example, as top menu items, tabs, links, buttons, etc.) based on the *category* of the action. You can configure these actions.

Chapter 4 and the *portal_actions* section of this chapter provide more information about various actions.

Each action has a standard set of properties. Refer to Figure 2.7 for the user actions provided in the portal_membership tool.

Table 2.2 provides field definitions for the portal_membership tool:

Table 2.2: portal_membership field definitions

Field	Definition
Name	The name of the action
Id	Unique identifier for the action
Action	The action to be performed (usually a script in portal_skins or a Python expression, or a URL path to a template)
Condition	The conditions that must be satisfied in order for this action to occur. (The condition is a TALES expression that should evaluate as True.) If this condition is not satisfied, then this action will not be visible.
Permission	Only users who have a role with the specified permission will be able to perform this action. This action will not be visible to the users who do not have this permission.
Category	The categorization of the action. Plone uses the category to create navigational elements such as tabs and links at specific places on the Plone UI. For example, the "user" actions display in the top menu, as shown in Figure 2.7.
Visible	Indicates whether the action may be shown on the web site. If you choose for a certain action to be invisible, this feature will hide the action, but it will not prevent the users from performing the action (if they are permitted, based on the *Condition* and *Permission* properties above).

Members Folder

The **Members** folder contains other folders that are member-specific. You can create and configure this folder using the *portal_membership* tool. By default, Plone members can create content in their individual folders. Once logged in, a member (registered user) will have access to his or her member area. This is a secure area for each member where other members can access it, but cannot create content. Members can share their member areas with others using Local Roles (explained in *Chapter 5* in detail).

Member folders are created based on the *portal_membership* configuration, as shown in Figure 2.8. You can disable this feature by clicking the **Turn folder creation off** button.

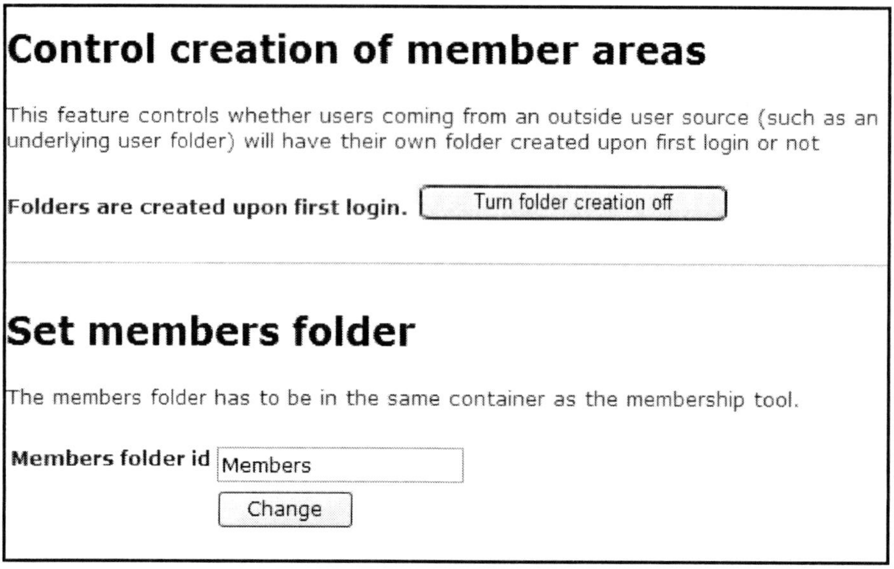

Control creation of member areas

This feature controls whether users coming from an outside user source (such as an underlying user folder) will have their own folder created upon first login or not

Folders are created upon first login. [Turn folder creation off]

Set members folder

The members folder has to be in the same container as the membership tool.

Members folder id [Members]
[Change]

Figure 2.8: Configuring the Member folder using the portal_membership tool

portal_registration

The **portal_registration** tool embodies the new user registration policies of the Plone site. In particular, it does the following actions:

▶ Sets the default policies for allowable member IDs and passwords

▶ Generates passwords (based on the policy)

▶ Mails passwords

▶ Sets member properties

Content Type Tools

This section briefly explains the portal tools as they relate to content type. Once you create a new content type in Plone, other portal tools will detect it and provide default features for it. Some tools iterate over types and provide defaults for all of them. Others, however, are unconcerned with types; for example, portal_skins won't create templates for a new type. The portal_catalog tool won't change its indexes, either.

Figure 2.9 illustrates how the portal tools apply defaults to a new News Item content type in Plone:

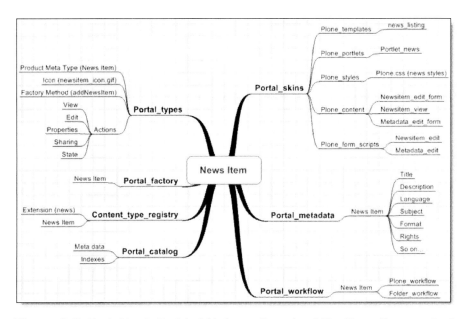

Figure 2.9: Portal tools that hold information about the News Item content type

For example, when you add a News Item content type to Plone, other portal tools detect it and create default features to it.

▸ **portal_types**: contains icon and description. It also links each action to a script in portal_skins, to a Python expression, or to a template URL path.

▸ **portal_factory**: recognizes the news content type for creation

▸ **content_type_registry**: recognizes the news content type for ftp and WebDAV access

▸ **portal_catalog**: indexes the properties or methods of the content. The catalog is set up with a standard set of indexes, according to which it catalogs all Plone content objects. It looks for properties or methods that correspond to these indexes on every object cataloged.

▸ **portal_skins**: holds scripts, templates, images, style sheets, and properties related to forms, view, and edit. It also composes everything in the hierarchy under portal_skins into a flat namespace based on the skin definition in use.

▸ **portal_metadata**: contains metadata information about the News Item. All content types share the same metadata.

▸ **portal_workflow**: provides a "default" workflow for newly created News Items.

content_type_registry

The **content_type_registry** tool maps MIME Types and File Extensions to existing content types. This tool provides a sequence in which to look for these MIME types and file extensions.

With WebDAV support, you can drag and drop files into Plone sites using Windows Explorer or another WebDAV client. If the Content Type Registry contains information that allows Plone to recognize the dropped file (by examining its MIME type or file extension), Plone can create an object of the appropriate type to represent the file.

This feature is very useful for bulk uploads from your local file system into the Plone content management system. For example, you may want a custom content type called *Office File* to handle files differently than the default *File* content type. When you drag and drop specific files (such as Word or Excel files) from your local file system into the Plone site, you want them to upload to the site automatically as *Office File* content type. In this case, you must map your content type to the application, as shown in Figure 2.10.

Figure 2.10: Mapping content to content type using the Content Type Registry

portal_factory

The **portal_factory** tool initiates object creation in such a way that if a user does not complete an Edit form, no object is created in the ZODB.

By default, the portal_factory tool is *not* used in the creation of any content type. When the user creates a document (by clicking on the **Add new item** link and choosing the **Document** type), a new document type object is created in ZODB with a default id. An Edit form displays with a URL similar to the one shown here:

http://localhost:8080/mysite/Members/munwar/document.2005-01-02 .3814312101/document_edit_form

If the user does not complete the Edit form by clicking the **Save** button, the object will still be created in ZODB with no information. Over time, your web site will contain many such dummy objects that weren't saved by the users. The portal_factory tool is an attempt to eliminate this problem.

You can use the portal_factory's **Factory Types** tab to specify the types that should be created using portal_factory. For example, if you allow users to only create *Document* types using portal_factory, the object will not be created in ZODB until user completes the Edit form and clicks the **Save** button. The Edit form will then have a different URL, similar to the one shown here:

http://localhost:8080/mysite/Members/munwar/portal_factory/Document/ document.2005-01-02.3228371090/document_edit_form

---

Chapter 2: Anatomy of Plone

This URL traverses the portal_factory object, which consumes the rest of the URL, using it to create a temporary instance dynamically with the properties submitted with the Edit form. This temporary instance is only finally written to the ZODB when the user clicks **Save**.

Warning: The portal_factory *does not work* with References in Plone. If you will be using References, don't use portal_factory.

Types must be portal_factory aware for this to work. In Plone 2.0, the stock CMFDefault types (Document, News Item, Event, etc.) are all portal_factory aware. Most types in Archetypes 2.0 are also portal_factory aware.

portal_types

The **portal_types** tool manages the set of policies related to the content types that you can create on the Plone site.

These policies include:

▸ The construction mechanism

▸ Whether to allow discussion for the type

▸ What types are allowed to be added as children of instances of this type (significant only for folderish types)

▸ The actions that users can perform on objects of this type. These are the type-specific actions. A variety of other tools provide many other actions that can also be performed on objects of this type.

portal_workflow

▸ The **portal_workflow** tool associates objects of a given content type with a workflow. Workflows are "state machines," each representing the life cycle of a given family of content types, and specifying the workflow actions that are possible in any phase of the life cycle. This tool allows you to perform the following actions:

▸ Link content types with a workflow

- Modify the existing workflow process

- Create a new workflow

- Update the security settings of all workflow-aware objects

portal_metadata

The **portal_metadata** tool embodies site-wide policies concerning required metadata for each content type, as well as default values and controlled vocabularies.

Content objects in Plone support rich metadata. Plone supports the Dublin Core metadata standard, and instances of all of the built-in Plone content types are associated with Dublin Core metadata.

Note: The Dublin Core Metadata Initiative (DCMI) is an organization dedicated to promoting the widespread adoption of interoperable metadata standards and developing specialized metadata vocabularies for describing resources that enable more intelligent information discovery systems.

Content objects provide web forms that allow content creators to enter and maintain metadata for their content. To change the metadata policies for the content types used on your site, go to the ZMI and click on the **portal_metadata** tool to navigate the Metadata Tool.

Change Metadata Policy

To view the current metadata policies for your content types, click the **Elements** tab. This displays the metadata policies form. The top row of the form (labeled "Element") is a set of hyperlinks for each metadata element that is available for configuration. On a normal Plone site, this list includes Subject, Rights, Format, Language, Description, and Title. This top row allows you to select which metadata element you are configuring. The metadata element that is *not* a hyperlink is the one that you are currently working on. To work on a different metadata element, click the name of that element.

When you first visit the metadata policies form, the first metadata element in the top row (Subject) is selected. The rest of the form is divided into sections. The sections represent the current settings for the selected metadata element for different content types in the system.

If you have never changed the settings for a metadata element, you will see two sections. In the first section, the content type is <default>, which means this setting will apply to all content types for which you have not defined explicit settings. At the bottom of the form, the last section (<new type>) allows you to add settings for a specific content type.

To add settings for a content type, select the content type from the **Content Type** drop-down list. The remaining fields in each section allow you to set the policy for the selected metadata element. See Table 2.3.

Table 2.3: Metadata element field definitions

Field	Definition
Required	This determines whether content creators are required to supply a value for the selected metadata element. Check the box to require a value.
Default	This determines the default value for the metadata element.
Supply Default	This determines whether the content edit forms should pre-fill the form field with the defined default value.
Vocabulary	This allows you to offer a set of predefined options for a metadata element. If a vocabulary is defined for a metadata element, the content edit forms will show a drop-down box with the vocabulary items. To supply the vocabulary for a metadata element, enter the possible values in the textboxes provided (one per line).
Enforce Vocabulary	This determines whether the allowed value for the metadata element is restricted to those that are defined in the vocabulary.

Click **Add** to apply your settings to that content type. You may also edit the settings that you have already defined. Make the changes in the sections for each content type you want to change and click **Update** to save these these changes.

Add Custom Metadata

The portal_metadata tool allows you to create custom metadata, which is common for all the content types.

Click on **portal_metadata**, and then click the **Properties** tab. Using this tool, you can add a new metadata element or delete an existing metadata element.

Dublin Core Metadata Query Interface

The Dublin Core Metadata Query Interface provides universal, read-only, textual metadata (suitable for syndication or consumption by external applications). The following interface functions have Anonymous permissions:

▸ **Title:** Content resource name

▸ **Creator:** Content resource author(s)

▸ **Subject:** Content resource keywords (list of strings; should be drawn from a controlled vocabulary)

▸ **Description:** Content resource abstract, summary, or table of contents

▸ **Publisher:** Content resource publisher (normally, the owner of the portal)

▸ **Contributors:** Additional content resource collaborators (list of strings)

▸ **Date:** Default date (effective/created/modified) for content resource (ISO format)

▸ **CreationDate:** Date the content resource was created (ISO format)

▸ **EffectiveDate:** Date the content resource becomes effective (ISO format)

▸ **ExpirationDate:** Date the content resource expires (ISO format)

▸ **ModificationDate:** Date the content resource was last modified (ISO format)

▸ **Type:** Content resource type (for example, Zope meta_type, or a mapping from it)

▸ **Format:** Physical encoding of the content resource (for example, MIME type)

▸ **Identifier:** Content resource URL

▸ **Language:** Content resource language, from RFC list (for example, en-US)

▸ **Rights:** Copyright or other intellectual property pertaining to the content resource

portal_skins

The **portal_skins** tool contains all the existing skins of your site. *Chapter 4: Skins and Layers* provides more information about this tool.

portal_catalog

The **portal_catalog** tool wraps around the standard Zope ZCatalog, supplying additional indexes, metadata, and policies specific to the operation of a Plone site.

This tool allows you to:

▶ Choose the **vocabulary** (English, Japanese, etc.)

▶ Choose the **metadata**: When you catalog objects, the values of any attributes that match a name in the metadata list will get stored in Catalog.

▶ Choose the **indexes**: When you catalog objects, the values of any attributes and methods that match an index in this list will get indexed. This includes names that may be acquired from an object.

▶ Locate and add objects to Catalog

▶ Manually update objects in the Catalog or remove objects from the Catalog.

Content-Specific Tools

Some of the Plone products will provide a content-specific tool to allow users to configure the product. For example, when you install *Archetypes*, a tool will be added to your site called **archetype_tool**. This tool allows users to update schemas, add templates, and so forth.

When you create a Plone site, the following tools will be created automatically.

portal_calendar

The **portal_calendar** tool provides a common interface for rendering calendars and manipulating functions.

By default, only Event content type objects will display in the calendar widget and be listed as upcoming events in the Events portlet. For example, if you want your own content type (such as *Holiday*) to automatically display in the Calendar, you must add your content type using the **Configure** tab provided by this tool. All types that are to display in the calendar must have a **start** and an **end** to return DateTime objects to the Catalog. The Catalog has **start** and **end** indexes, which are cataloged using attribute access as usual.

portal_discussion

The **portal_discussion** tool embodies the policies concerning the storage mechanism for discussion about content. This tool works with content that is enabled for discussion. It controls the "Reply" policy and stores the discussion data as a threaded sub-object of the Plone content. A threaded sub-object is an object with the **talkback** id (stored as an attribute of the discussion item), which stores the discussion as a sequence of posts. Each post contains the information necessary for the **talkback** object to render it as a thread of a discussion. This particular implementation stores the discussion as a sub-object, but the tool exists, in part, that you may change the storage implementation. See Figure 2.11.

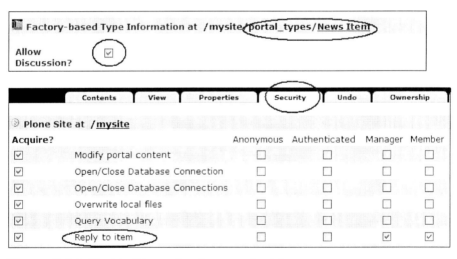

Figure 2.11: Enable Discussion for a content type

To enable discussion for a content type, go to the **portal_types** tool, choose the content type, and select the **Allow Discussion** check box. Also, be sure the users have the **Reply to item** permission.

Utilities

Plone utility tools are useful for content syndication, site control, site migration, installation, and more. This section describes some of these utilities.

MailHost

The **MailHost** utility stores mail information, such as SMTP Host and Port Number. This tool identifies the mail server credentials, which you can use for:

▸ Sending automated mail messages to members regarding issues such as forgotten password, registration confirmation, and so forth.

▸ Notifying members of workflow changes. The PloneCollectorNG (issue tracker) product uses this feature effectively by sending notification mail to all the parties involved.

▸ E-mailing any kind of information based on your application-specific business logic.

Listing 2.1 is some sample code for a Python script to send e-mail:

Listing 2.1

```
# check that we can send email via Mail Host
mailhost=getattr(context, context.portal_url.superValues
    ('Mail Host')[0].id)

# Let's write an email:
mMsg = 'Dear ' + memberName + ',\n\n'
mMsg += 'We thought you\'d be interested
    in hearing about:\n'
mMsg += contentObject.TitleOrId() + '\n\n'
mMsg += 'Description:
    \n' + contentObject.Description() + '\n\n'
mMsg += 'More info at:
    \n' + contentObject.absolute_url() + '\n'
mTo = item.email
mFrom = 'you@yoursite.com'
```

```
mSubj = 'New Content available'

# and send it
mailhost.send(mMsg, mTo, mFrom, mSubj)
```

portal_syndication

Syndication is the process by which a site is able to share information with other sites. For example, the AP news service allows newspapers and other media to receive news stories for publishing with their own presentation without generating the content in-house.

Content syndication in Plone allows you to make content available to other sites. The **portal_syndication** tool allows site managers to control site-wide syndication policy about content. When syndication has been activated for a Plone site, all folders also have a **Syndicate** tab, where you can configure local syndication policy on a per-folder basis.

Syndicated content is available in RSS format for folders where syndication has been enabled. The following DTML method objects that control the RSS formatting for RSS feeds are located in the **cmf_legacy** skin:

▸ RSS

▸ itemRSS

▸ rssBody

Before content can be syndicated from a site, the site manager must enable syndication using the Syndication tool. To access this tool, go to the ZMI of the object that represents your site. From the **Contents** view of the site object, click on the **portal_syndication** tool.

The **Overview** tab of the Syndication tool provides a basic description of the tool. To view the current syndication policy for the site, click the **Properties** tab.

If you have never visited the Syndication tool before, syndication is disabled for the site and you will see a single button: **Enable syndication**. Click this button to enable syndication.

Once you have enabled syndication, the **Properties** form will display the site-wide syndication properties. See Table 2.4.

Table 2.4: Syndication properties

Property	Definition	Default
Update Period	Describes the period over which the channel feed is updated. Acceptable values are hourly, daily, weekly, monthly, and yearly.	Daily
Update Frequency	Describes the frequency of updates in relation to the update period. A positive integer indicates how many times in that period the channel is updated. For example, an Update Period of daily, and an Update Frequency of 2 indicate the channel format is updated twice daily.	1
Update Base	Defines a base date to be used in concert with Update Period and Update Frequency to calculate the publishing schedule.	
Max Syndicated Items	Defines the maximum number of items to include in the syndication feed. The RSS specification recommends that this not exceed 15.	15

Click **Save** to update the site-wide syndication policy. If you later decide you want to disable content syndication, go to the **Properties** tab of the Syndication tool and click the **Disable syndication** button.

To enable syndication for a folder, click on the **Syndication** tab of that folder. For example, you have a news folder in your site containing various News Items. After enabling site-wide syndication, you can enable syndication for the /*news* folder by clicking the **Syndication** tab, then clicking the **Save** button. Visit the URL to your news folder and append *RSS* to obtain the RSS feed: http://www .yourwebsite.com/news/RSS. See Figure 2.12.

Figure 2.12: Portal Syndication

plone_utils

The **plone_utils** tool provides general utility functions for your Plone site. Some of the functions provided by this tool are listed below:

▸ **Sendto**: The *Send this page to somebody* feature on the web site

▶ **validateEmailAddresses**: Validates several e-mail addresses

▶ **editMetadata**: Sets metadata on a content object that implements IDublinCoreMetadata

▶ **changeOwnershipOf**: Changes the ownership of an object

Note: To learn how this tool works, check out the source code at *zopeInstance/ Products/CMFPlone/PloneTool.py*.

portal_controlpanel

The **portal_controlpanel** tool provides actions and scripts for various Plone control panel utilities, as shown in Figure 2.13.

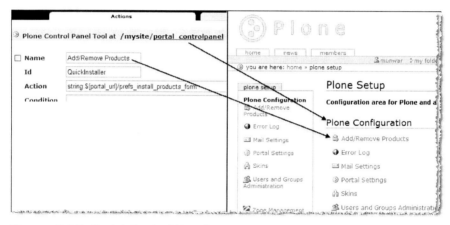

Figure 2.13: Portal Control Panel

portal_form_controller

The **portal_form_controller** tool internally uses the CMFFormController package. The CMFFormController package helps developers by simplifying the process of validating forms. Using Form Controller, things that are likely to change on upgrade (contents of scripts and forms) are separated from things that are less likely to change. In a .metadata file, you can specify the script to be invoked and the page to be displayed by submitting a form. You can override metadata in ZMI. This makes it easier for site administrators to override some of the behavior of packages without modifying the code, making it easier to upgrade packages without disturbing the modifications.

This package is very well documented. To view online documentation from your ZMI, click the *portal_form_controller* tool, and then click the **Documentation** tab.

We also recommend Geoff Davis' *Form Controller Tutorial*, which has the interesting title of "Everything you ever wanted to know but were afraid to ask." You can download this tutorial from http://plone.org/events/conferences/2 /handouts/FormControllerTutorial.pdf.

portal_migration

When you create a Plone site, you also create an instance of a Plone site object. The version of that Plone instance will be the version of Plone code that exists in the file system at that time (instance/Products/CMFPlone). When you upgrade Plone code in the file system, the Plone file system version and the Plone instance version will be different.

This tool handles migrations to newer Plone versions. During migration, if you select *dry run*, the tool prints the result of the migration without actually writing anything to the database. This is a good demonstration of the nature of the ZODB. The migration is executed, all the scripts are run, and objects are updated (allowing you to see any errors that may be triggered). Then the transaction during which all this happened is aborted, preventing the changes from being committed to the database. The nature of transactions in the ZODB is a bad fit for user-facing "undo" functionality (it stops working if any subsequent transaction has changed any of the objects that were involved in the transaction you're trying to undo), but it works well for such things as testing the migration. See Figure 2.14.

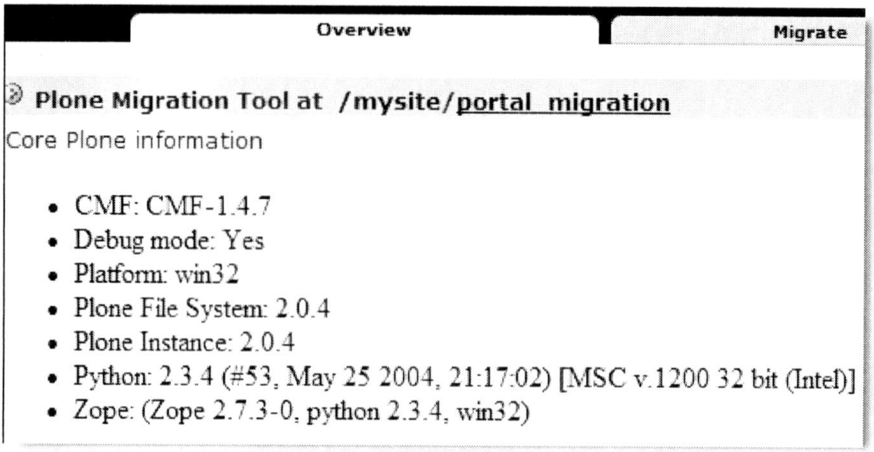

Figure 2.14: Portal Migration Tool

This tool also displays very important information about your Plone instance, such as the CMF version, Plone version, and so forth. For example, you can check whether your Plone instance is running in debug mode or not. See the information provided in Figure 2.14.

Note: For a production Plone instance, we recommend that you switch off the debug mode to improve the performance. Read your *zope.conf* file (at *zope_instance/etc*) for more details.

portal_quickinstaller

The **portal_quickinstaller** tool installs and uninstalls add-on Plone products. You must have the *Manager* role to access this tool. Refer to Figure 2.13, which lists the Quick Installer Tool (under *Add/Remove Products*).

This tool lists all the products available to your Plone instance, both those that are already installed and those that are available but not installed. You can see the **Install Log** of the products that are already installed in your Plone instance. You can also see the errors, if the installation stallation failed.

Caching Tools

Performing some computations in Zope can take a long time or use a lot of resources. One way to deal with expensive tasks is to cache them. The first time the computation is requested, the results are stored in a table, or *cache*. Subsequent requests retrieve the results from the cache. This can result in a dramatic speed increase. This section explains tools that improve the site performance by lessening the workload on Zope. (The tradeoff is that content may be out of date, since Zope doesn't render it freshly every time.) Zope supports the following two types of cache managers:

▸ **RAMCache Managers** allow you to cache the results of calling scripts (such as Page Templates, Python scripts, DTML, and SQL methods) in RAM on the Plone server. This saves the time required for execution or rendering, but it requires a lot of RAM to remain effective. In effect, it trades CPU consumption for RAM consumption, and it still impacts the Plone server.

▸ **Accelerated HTTP Cache Managers** allow you to set caching headers on the content served to browsers (such as Images and Files), so that browsers or intermediate proxies know that they may cache the content, and for how long. This can remove the load of serving these pages completely from the Plone server, but it is less fine-grained than the RAM cache approach, which can cache the result of individual method calls. The HTTP cache generally only allows you to cache entire rendered pages. It is possible to configure caching of parts of pages using ESI (Edge-Side Includes), but the HTTP Cache Manager currently can't assist you with this.

Plone provides an additional cache manager called **Caching Policy Manager (CPM)**, which allows you to cache the content added by users. The CPM sets HTTP cache headers on content objects based on the truth value of a TALES predicate and other parameters.

RAMCache

The RAM cache manager allows you to cache into memory the result of calling Page Templates, DTML methods, Python scripts, and SQL methods. It allows you to cache entire pages as well as parts of pages. It provides access statistics and simple configuration options.

The **Statistics** tab allows you to view a summary of the contents of the cache. Click the column headers once to sort the list, twice to sort backwards. You can use the statistics to gauge the benefit of caching each of your objects. For a given object, if the number of hits is less than or not much greater than the number of misses, you probably need to re-evaluate how that object is cached.

Sometimes, caching might cause problems to content editors, since they cannot see the changes reflected immediately in the web site. One solution is that taken by plone.org, which heavily caches the pages served to the public, but doesn't cache the same site accessed by logged-in members on a different domain.

To add your script (such as Page Template) to RAMCache, follow the steps below:

1. Using ZMI, browse through the site and select the script.

2. Click on the **Cache** tab at the top of the screen.

3. Select **RAMCache** from the drop-down list to cache your script.

See Figure 2.15.

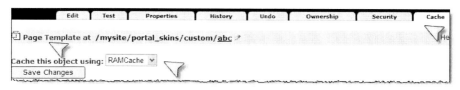

Figure 2.15: Adding a script to RAMCache

HTTPCache

The HTTP protocol provides headers that can indicate to downstream proxy caches, browser caches, and dedicated caches, that certain documents and images are cacheable. For example, most images can safely be cached for a long time. Anonymous visits to most primary pages can be cached as well.

Note: Andy McKay's excellent presentation on Profiling, Benchmarking and Caching in Plone is available at http://www.clearwind.ca/talks/ profiling_and_caching.pdf.

By default, Plone comes with a pre-configured HTTPCache manager. Java scripts, style sheet objects, and images in portal_skins are already cached for you to improve your site performance. See Figure 2.16 for more details.

	Properties	Statistics	Associate	Undo	Ownership	Security

▶▶ Accelerated HTTP Cache Manager at /mysite/HTTPCache

Cache manager hits generally correspond to HTTP accelerator misses. A hit is counted in the "authenticated hits" column even if headers are only set for anonymous requests.

Path	Anonymous hits	Authenticated hits
/mysite/plone_javascript_variables.js	1	4
/mysite/ploneCustom.css	1	4
/mysite/ploneNS4.css	1	4
/mysite/plonePrint.css	1	4
/mysite/plone.css	1	4
/mysite/ploneColumns.css	1	4
/mysite/ploneIEFixes.css	1	4
/mysite/plonePresentation.css	1	4

Figure 2.16: HTTPCache configured for Plone

caching_policy_manager

The **caching_policy_manager** tool works the same as Accelerated HTTP Cache Manager, except it caches the content types.

Miscellaneous Tools

This section explains the remaining objects and portal tools.

error_log

The **error_log** object lists the exceptions that have occurred in the Plone site recently. You can configure how many exceptions to keep and whether to copy the exceptions to Zope's event log file (located at *zope_instance/log/event.log*, depending on the contents of the *zope.conf* file).

One major difficulty in reading the error_log is its lack of clarity when access is denied. During development, site developers need more details. The *VerboseSecurity* product attempts to explain the complete reasoning for failed access. It shows what object was being accessed, what permission is required to access it, what roles map to that permission in that context, the executable object and its owner, the effective proxy roles, and other pertinent information. All of this information appears in the exception message when access is denied.

Unpack the product in your Zope *Products* folder. You can see recent exceptions through the web using the error_log object. Note, however, that in the default configuration, error_log will not display unauthorized exceptions. Just remove "Unauthorized" from the list of ignored exceptions.

index_html

This is the default home page of your portal. You can edit this page and change the home page content.

portal_actionicons

The **portal_actionicons** tool associates portal actions with icons. You can replace the default icons with your own icons by replacing the image file names and clicking the Update button. At the bottom of the page is a form to add your own portal actions and their associated icons.

portal_actions

The **portal_actions** tool assembles the actions that are relevant to the current user (anonymous, member, etc.) and context (content object or folder being viewed).

These actions are drawn from several sources:

▸ The **actions** tool, for "global" actions

▸ The **workflow** tool, for actions that depend on the workflow state of the content object

▸ The **membership** tool, for actions that pertain to the member or user

▶ The **types** tool, for actions that are specific to a given content type

portal_interface

The **portal_interface** tool provides the ability to query object interfaces. Interfaces are one of the major improvements in Zope 2.5 and *especially* in Zope3. Interfaces are used for documentation, unit testing, and asserting implementations. You can find all the interfaces of Plone at *Zope_instance/Products/CMFPlone/interfaces*.

Tip: When you develop a file system based Plone products, provide good documentation for your Application Program Interface. Use the Epydoc tool (http://epydoc.sourceforge.net/) for generating API documentation for Python modules, based on their docstrings.

---

portal_properties

The **portal_properties** tool provides a common interface for accessing portal-wide properties and properties related to custom Plone products. By default, this tool contains the following property sheets and the property sheets for custom Plone products.

▶ form_properties (Form Properties)

▶ navigation_properties (Navigation Properties)

▶ navtree_properties (NavigationTree properties)

▶ site_properties (Site wide properties)

form_properties

This property sheet contains validation properties for all the default controller page template forms in the site.

navigation_properties

This property sheet contains the action argument properties for all the default controller page forms in the site. These properties determine the pages to be displayed when the user clicks on various buttons in the form. Hence, these properties control the navigation.

navtree_properties

This tool holds configurable parameters for the navigation portlet, as shown in Figure 2.17.

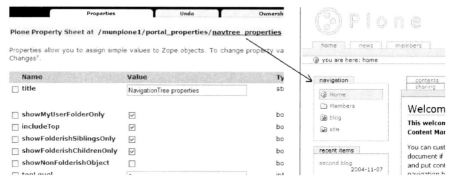

Figure 2.17: navtree_properties

Some of the important options to consider are:

▸ **rolesSeeUnpublishedContent**: By default, only *published* content displays in the navigation portlet. You can list the roles that can see the unpublished content. Be sure those roles are permitted to access to the content. If they aren't, they will be challenged for authentication when they attempt to view it.

▸ **metaTypesNotToList**: Provide a list of content types (in separate lines) that you do not want to list in the navigation portlet.

▸ **showFolderishChildrenOnly**: Show only sub-folders in a selected folder.

site_properties

This property sheet holds important parameters for the entire site, such as the list of default page ids, the default language, the date format, and so forth. If you are creating a new *folderish* content type, then be sure that your installation script adds entries about your product in the *use_folder_tabs*, *use_folder_contents*, and *typesLinkToFolderContentsInFC* property values. This enables the Plone interface to recognize your *folderish* content type and provide appropriate navigation and menu tabs.

YourProduct_properties

If you are writing your own file system-based Plone product, and if you want to have configurable parameters, then you need to write your installation script to create a property sheet in portal_properties. It is a good practice to name your product property sheet as yourProductName_properties. Refer to Figure 2.18, which is a property sheet for a Plone-based discussion forum product called CMFBoard.

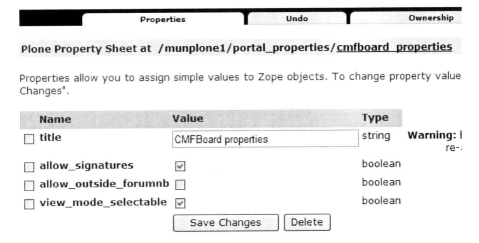

Figure 2.18: Custom Product Properties (cmfboard_properties)

portal_undo

The **portal_undo** tool provides an interface to the Zope undo machinery without requiring access to the ZMI, as shown in Figure 2.19.

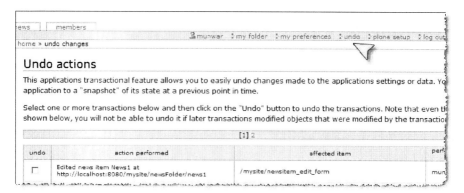

Figure 2.19: Portal Undo Tool

portal_url

The **portal_url** tool provides a common mechanism for finding the "root" object of a Plone site, and for computing paths to objects relative to that root. This tool is used extensively in the Page Templates to compute absolute paths to objects, as shown in Listing 2.2:

Listing 2.2

```
<a href="" tal:attributes="href string:${here/portal_url}
   /folderA/objectA">objectA</a>
```

There is an advantage of using the portal_url tool instead of just using */folderA/ objectA* as a link. Consider the site hierarchy and sample code in Listing 2.3:

Listing 2.3

```
- Zope Root Folder (URL http://www.siteA.com)
|
|-- plonesite (URL http://www.siteB.com)
| |
| |-- FolderC (URL http://www.siteC.com)
| | |
| | |-- FolderD
| | | |-- ObjectE
| | |-- sample_zpt
```

For example, *Zope Root Folder, plonesite,* and *FolderC* have three different URLs (through virtual hosting). The plonesite folder contains *FolderC*. FolderC contains *FolderD* and Page template *sample_zpt*. FolderD contains *ObjectE*. The sample_zpt object contains code as shown in Listing 2.4, to access ObjectE:

Listing 2.4

```
URL1 :
<a href="/FolderD/objectE">objectE</a>
<BR>
URL2 :
<a href="" tal:attributes="href string:${here/portal_url}
    /FolderC/FolderD/objectE">ObjectE</a>
```

If you test *sample_zpt* using the URL http://www.siteA.com/plonesite/FolderC/sample_zpt, then URL1 is rendered as http://www.siteA.com/FolderD/objectE (which is incorrect) and URL2 is rendered as http://www.SiteA.com/plonesite/FolderC/FolderD/objectE (which is correct).

If you test *sample_zpt* using the URL http://www.siteB.com/FolderC/sample_zpt, then URL1 is rendered as http://www.siteB.com/FolderD/objectE (which is incorrect) and URL2 is rendered as http://www.SiteB.com/FolderC/FolderD/objectE (which is correct).

If you test *sample_zpt* using the URL http://www.siteC.com/sample_zpt, then URL1 is rendered as http://www.siteC.com/FolderD/objectE (which is correct) and URL2 is rendered as http://www.SiteC.com/FolderC/FolderD/objectE (which is correct).

In all the three examples, the *portal_url* tool always provided the root object of the Plone site and helped compute the path to *ObjectE* relative to that root.

Online Help System

Zope comes with an Online Help System. You can read help information by clicking the *Online Help System* link (see Figure 2.1), or by typing the URL http://localhost:8080/HelpSys as shown in Figure 2.20.

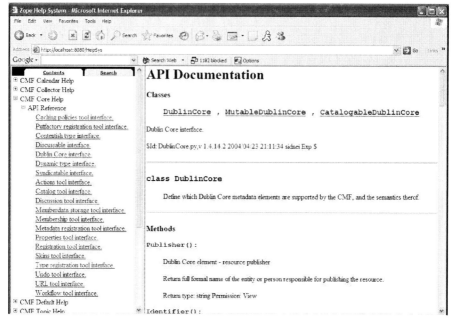

Figure 2.20: Online Help Documentation

The Online Help System contains the following information:

▸ Zope API Reference

▸ Zope Page Templates Reference

▸ DTML Reference

▸ Zope Tutorial

▸ CMF Documentation

▸ DC Workflow Documentation

▸ Plone Custom Product Specific Documentation

You can register any third-party add-on or Product in the Zope online help system.

Tip: For more documentation, install the DocFinder product. It analyzes any Zope object inside a running Zope instance, determines which classes have been used in the object's makeup, and provides information about their class level attributes: name, allowed roles, arguments, and documentation strings. More details are available at http://www.dieter.handshake.de/pyprojects/zope/DocFinder.html.

Context-Sensitive Help

Online Help is context-sensitive. For example, from the ZMI Page Template edit window, the page template-related help displays if you click the Help link, as shown in Figure 2.21.

Figure 2.21: Context-Sensitive Help

Online Help for the Plone Product

It is a good practice to provide online documentation for any Plone Product you create. For a file system-based Plone product, provide online help documentation in a folder titled **help**, as shown in Figure 2.22. The Online Help System will recognize these help files and automatically display as the online documentation, as shown in Figure 2.23. You can format the files as structured text, plain text, or HTML.

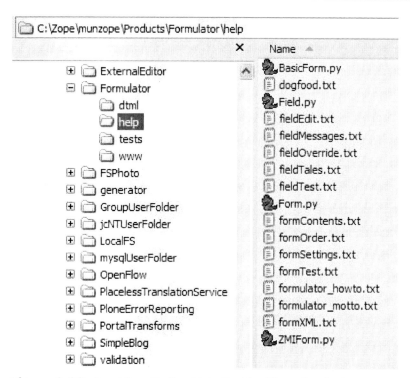

Figure 2.22: Providing Online Help for the Plone Product

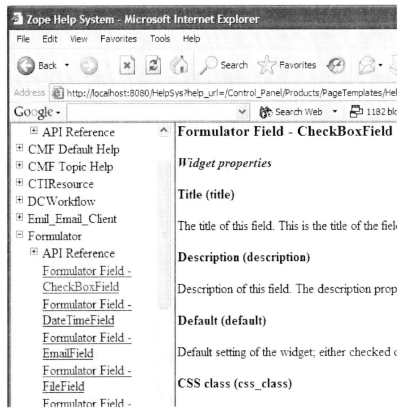

Figure 2.23: Accessing Online Help for the Plone Product

Plone 2.1 Additions

If you have been using Plone 2.0 and are new to Plone 2.1, then it is worth going through the following tools and services added to the Plone 2.1 release.

Content-Specific Tools

Prior to the Plone 2.1 release, CMF content types were the basis for the default content types (such as document and news item). You could add Archetypes-based content types as additional content types. Archetypes provides a flexible way of defining the content, forms, storage, and so forth. A translation service (Linguaplone pack) enabled you to translate Archetypes content type attributes.

To make this transition easy in Plone 2.1, Archetypes content types (ATCT) are the basis for the default content types (such as document and news item). The Plone 2.1 release includes the following tools and services related to ATCT. Refer to *Chapter 7* for more details about Archetypes.

portal_atct

The ATContentTypes tool operates as a front-end to several important functions such as:

▸ **Version migration**: Migrates ATContentTypes to a newer version, just like the plone_migration tool

▸ **Image scales**: Recreates image scales

▸ **Type migration**: Migrates old CMF style types to new ATCT types

▸ **Recatalog**: Recatalogs CMF and ATCT content types. Types migration requires an up-to-date portal_catalog.

▸ **Properties**: Sets certain properties for migration, album view, and more

archetype_tool

This tool installs and uninstalls Archetypes content types and binds the content types with specific templates. You can use it to specify the database connections for the content storage (if the content is not stored in ZODB).

mimetypes_registry and portal_transforms

MIME types are classifications of content. For example, the text/html type represents HTML content, while the text/structured type represents Structured-Text. The MimetypesRegistry, bundled with Archetypes, keeps track of the various MIME types available to Plone in the mimetypes_registry tool.

PortalTransforms, also bundled with Archetypes, provides the portal_transforms tool, which transforms data between two MIME types. For example, if you enter StructuredText in a Page, it is transformed to HTML via the structured text transform called *st_to_html*, when the object displays.

portal_uidgenerator

The portal_uidgenerator tool generates unique IDs. The portal_uidannotation tool attaches unique IDs to a content object. The portal_uidhandler tool manages registering and accessing unique IDs.

portal_uidannotation

This tool sets policies for UIDs (Unique IDs) for the objects. The current policy is that UIDs are deleted on import, if you leave the "Remove the objects unique id on add (and import)" flag in portal_uidannotation checked.

portal_uidhandler

This tool also provides query interface to query and access unique IDs.

reference_catalog

The Reference Catalog is a special type search engine, which maintains the relationship between objects. You can use it to refer and access other related objects from an object.

uid_catalog

The Archetypes UID Catalog maintains Unique IDs of all Archetypes objects.

User Interface

Starting with Plone 2.1, the user interface is much more configurable through the web using the following tools.

front-page

This is the default home page.

kupu_library_tool

This tool configures the Kupu visual editor (default editor for HTML content).

---

portal_css

This tool enables or disables certain style sheets. You can use it to specify the sequence of style sheets of the resulting HTML code. You can also use it to add a custom CSS file to the system as shown in Figure 2.24.

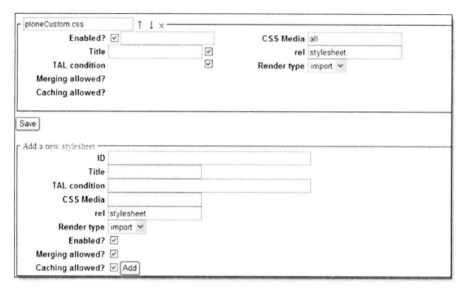

Figure 2.24: Plone portal_css tool

portal_javascripts

This tool enables or disables certain JavaScripts, to specify the sequence of Java-Scripts used in the resulting HTML code.

Smart Folders

Plone 2.1 introduces a new concept called Smart Folders. Smart Folders categorize the content based on certain criteria. Smart Folders are very useful for the types of searches that the News and Events folders rely on - all objects in a very broad category (for example, all recent news, all recent events, and so forth). Plone 2.1 now comes with the following two Smart Folders by default. *Chapter 3* covers Smart Folders in detail.

▶ Events

▶ News

Multi-Language Support

Prior to Plone 2.1, Linguaplone Pack was a plug-in to support multi-languages and translations. Plone 2.1 now includes multi-language support translation services as part of the product.

translation_service

This tool provides access to translation machinery.

Summary

Plone is powerful, flexible, and extensible. It comes with many features, interfaces, screens, tools, and objects, right out of the box. As an application developer, you need to understand these tools to customize your Plone site per your requirements. The rest of the book explains the features, which are useful for you to customize and extend your Plone site and to integrate with the external systems.

Summary

## CHAPTER 3

Getting Started with Plone

If you have never used Plone, this chapter introduces you to some of its basic features, such as creating content, editing content, the underlying fundamentals of the object database and acquisition, and how to use and edit workflow.

Using Plone

Plone is really a Content Management System (CMS). This means that standard Plone allows groups of users to manage digital content in a safe, secure way using a simple interface. This chapter explains this stock interface.

When users work with content, they usually want to perform many common operations. Content operations like create, rename, update, and delete are so common that they have their own acronym: CRUD. Other common operations include managing the state of content and the security associated with the content.

This chapter explains how to work with the default Plone configuration, but your site may be different. The screenshots may differ cosmetically from what you see, but the options available to you should remain the same.

> **Note:** To create any content in Plone, you must log in. While you can remove this restriction, it's generally not a good idea to let strangers create content on your site. You may also want to turn off the ability for users to join your site without your permission.

Inside Plone Objects

Everything in Plone is an *object*. "Object" is a nebulous term, but in this case, it means something inside your Plone site that you can work with and manipulate. For example, in Plone you can store data in folders and pages. Both of these "things" are objects. Everything in Plone is an object because everything in Python is an object, and both Plone and Zope are written in Python. In object-oriented (OO) programming, you deal with objects, not tables. While a relational database spreads related information across many columns of different tables, an object unifies all the information that make up digital content such as a folder, web page, file, or image in one handy bundle.

Plone objects are also Zope objects; the two terms are synonymous. The following list outlines the difference between Python objects, Zope objects, Plone objects, and persistent objects.

▸ Zope uses Python's OO nature to define objects that implement a *web application server framework*. These range from the arcane (SecurityManager) to the familiar (Folder).

▸ The ZODB makes Python objects persistent, saving you from having to create a storage layer for the instances of your objects.

▸ Plone implements a *content management framework* using Zope by taking the following actions:

▸ It introduces a number of conventions regarding templating and mechanisms like actions and file system skins.

▸ It provides rich content objects (such as PloneFolder) that integrate with the UI, workflow, metadata, etc., introduced by Plone.

Plone objects are often subclasses that extend Zope objects. Since Zope is the underlying framework that Plone is based upon, most of the object concepts in Plone come from Zope. However, Plone has many of its own concepts that are not specific to Zope, such as "skins" and HTML form generation, which are discussed in later chapters.

Browsing a Plone Site

Log in to Plone using your site management account as discussed in *Chapter 2*. This will take you to the front page of the Plone site. The name of the template that displays this page (and *every other page* of a Plone site) is **main_template**. *Chapter 4* breaks down this template in detail. If you are logging into an existing Plone site that has already been customized, this screen may look completely different to you. Figure 3.1 shows the standard Plone configuration. To confirm that you are logged in to the site, check your logged in user name in the menu bar.

Figure 3.1: The Plone front page

Accessibility

Click on the **accessibility** link in the top right corner of the page (refer to Figure 3.1) to change the default font size of the web site. You can choose Large, Normal, or Small.

By default, a Plone site conforms to the U.S. Government Section 508 Accessibility Guidelines and W3C-WAI Web Content Accessibility Guidelines.

Site Map

Plone 2.1 ships with a full-featured, flexible site map that provides user- and security-specific site maps of sites without any coding or maintenance. The site map is also color-coded by state, making it easy to do a quick, visual security inspection of your site.

Click on the **site map** link in the top right corner of the page (refer to Figure 3.1) to view the site map of the web site along with the description (you can hold the pointer over an item for a few seconds to get its description).

Full Screen Mode

Click on the **full screen mode** icon (refer to Figure 3.1) to toggle full screen mode. This will help you to view the content area in a wider screen.

Smart Folders

Smart Folders are useful to automatically organize your content. Click on the **Events** smart folder link (refer to Figure 3.1). Plone comes configured with two Smart Folders: Events and News. This chapter explains Smart Folders in detail later.

Display View

Plone allows you to choose the mode in which to display a folder. Click on the **display** link as shown in Figure 3.2.

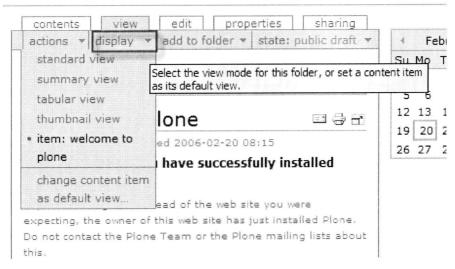

Figure 3.2: Plone display views

Plone supports the following default views:

▸ **Standard view**: displays a list of all content items in the folder with Title, Description, Creator, and Date details

▸ **Summary view**: displays Title and Description of the content

▶ **Tabular view**: displays the content items in a tabular form

▶ **Thumbnail view**: displays images in thumbnail form

▶ **Content Item as default view**: helps you choose one particular content (file or a page) as the default view for this folder

Plone saves the chosen display view for a specific folder until you change the view.

LiveSearch

LiveSearch increases the value of Plone's search engine by simplifying the search process. Results from a search are now instant. As you type letters for a search, possible matches appear below the search box, *without changing the current page*. Handy shortcut keys (such as ALT+4 on Windows Explorer) increase the convenience of LiveSearch, and you don't have to your leave your keyboard to navigate search results.

So, instead of entering a search term, waiting for results, and refining your search, this live feedback on searching makes finding things faster and more effective. Figure 3.3 shows the LiveSearch feature.

Figure 3.3: Plone LiveSearch

Creating Simple Content with Plone

In this chapter, you will learn how to create and manipulate some of the most basic Plone objects. Most Plone objects are *content objects*, which are objects designed to hold web media, files, and other digital content.

Regardless of the look and feel of the site, most Plone sites allow you to create new content by pulling down the **add item** menu as shown in Figure 3.4.

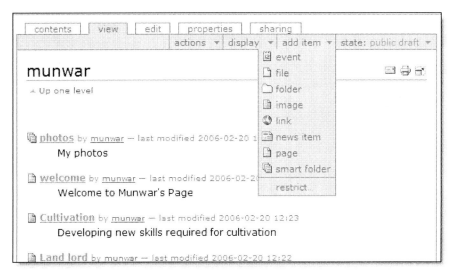

Figure 3.4: The pull-down Add Item menu

This pull-down menu offers a selection of objects that you can add to this Plone folder. A Page object is explained below in detail. All the other objects follow the similar guidelines for adding, creating, viewing, and editing content.

Page

A Page is a multi-purpose object for holding text content that is to be formatted by Plone. It supports a number of text formats, including HTML. You generally use these objects to create a web site for an organization or a business.

Creating and Viewing

To create a page, select **Page** from the **Add Item** menu. This will take you to a new screen where you can edit the initial content of the page as shown in Figure 3.5.

Figure 3.5: Page Content Edit Form

You can edit the page by clicking on the **Edit** tab. If you do not have sufficient privileges to edit this page in Plone, then this tab might not be available. The standard Plone configuration allows you to edit content that you create, so you should be able to edit the page created in the previous example.

▶ **Title**: the title of the page. This appears on most Zope screens to help you identify the object.

▶ **Description**: a short, one-paragraph description of the page

▶ **Body Text**: the body of the page. It can be in plain text, different types of structured text (plain text that conforms to some conventions), or HTML.

▶ **Text Format**: the format of the page. By default, pages can be in HTML, structured text, or restructured text. The last two formats mark up a plain text page with special formatting characters and white space conventions that are then rendered into HTML. Restructured text is a standard component of the Python document utility library and is documented at http://docutils.sourceforge.net/rst.html.

▶ **Upload a File**: upload a document from your computer into this page. The contents of this file become the body of the page. It converts office documents to HTML and catalogs them, as long as a converter is available.

▶ **Related Item(s):** Use the Browse button to locate and insert the content items related to this page. This is usually extremely useful to link Images and Files related to this Page.

▶ **Allow Discussion on this Item**: enable or disable discussion for this page. Choosing *default* will allow you to specify the global discussion policy set for this content type.

Once you finish editing your page, click **Save** to finalize the new page. This will take you directly to the view of the new page. The URL and breadcrumbs have changed to reflect that you are no longer in the root of the site, but are editing a page object.

Notice how Plone has "wrapped" your content in the same template (namely *main_template*) that you saw when you first logged in. This demonstrates Plone's ability to share the look and feel and other site functionality easily.

Editing Properties

Pages have properties that are known as Metadata. Properties are helpful to search this content using the Advanced Search form, to expire the content at a specific time and to make the content effective at a certain time automatically. You can access the properties by clicking the **Properties** tab of the object. This allows you to edit some of the properties of the page object as shown in Figure 3.6.

Figure 3.6: Page Properties Edit Page Form

The properties are described in Table 3.1.

Table 3.1: Page Object Properties

Property	Description
Exclude from Navigation	If selected, the page will not appear in navigation tree
Keywords	Identifies the content by keywords for searching purposes
Contributors	Displays information about individuals who contribute to the content
Creators	Page can have multiple creators; displays information of creators with principal creator first
Effective Date	Specifies the date that the content becomes effective. You can set a time in the future to publish the content on the site automatically. This is useful for time-sensitive content.
Expiration Date	Specifies the date when the content expires
Language	Specifies the content language
Copyright	Displays copyright information for the content

Each content type has different properties, but many of them are common across all content types. Some of them come from the Dublin Core Initiative (http://dublincore.org/), which describes a set of properties common to content across all applications. Plone fully supports Dublin Core.

Event

An Event object contains information about a calendar event. If the site managers permit it, this event can show up on the calendar on the front page, where other users can see it. Events have several self-explanatory properties that specify who, what, where, and when about the event.

File

A File object holds a data file in the Plone site. Plone does not treat the content of this file in any special way; it is just a holding area for "blobs" of data that Plone treats as a "file-like" object. Users can then access this file through the web or through other Plone tools. Files are basic components in any Plone site, because distributing files of information is one of the most common activities for any site. Note that due to the nature of the ZODB, objects are generally read into memory as a whole, unless the implementation takes special precautions. For this reason, storing large (multi-megabyte) files in Plone can hurt performance. There are various products such as Tramline (http://plone.org/products /plonetramline/) that allow such content to be stored on the file system, from where servers like Apache can stream it, without undue pressure on the memory. Work on improving Zope's performance in this regard is ongoing (google for "plone large file support").

Folder

Folders organize Plone objects such as pages, files, images, and many others. Folders are an organizational tool that let you compartmentalize your content and your site's various sections.

Folders are important because they exemplify a common kind of content object in Plone: *containers*. Containers are objects that contain other objects, and they are used throughout Plone and Zope. *Chapter 6* demonstrates how to create your own kind of container objects. *Chapter 7* also highlights containers, when Archetypes are introduced.

You can restrict the types that are addable in a specific folder. Click on the "**restrict...**" link provided in the pull-down **add item** menu as shown in Figure 3.4. The form to restrict the addable types is shown in Figure 3.7.

Figure 3.7: Restrict the types addable in a folder

Image

An Image is a very simple object, like a file, but the data is always in some standard image format like JPG or PNG. Any images that you present on your site will be held in objects of this type. The Image object is clever enough to cache thumbnails.

Plone treats Images as special content and allows various transforms for an image as shown in Figure 3.8.

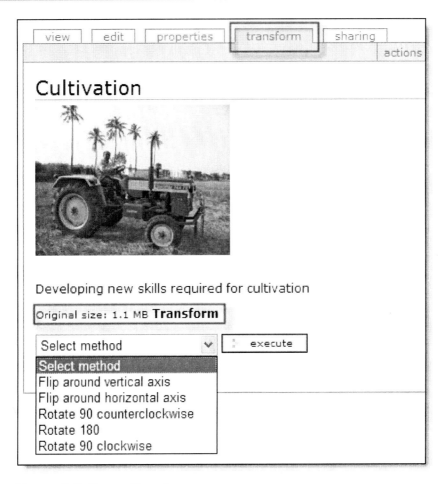

Figure 3.8: Image Transform

Link

A Link object contains a web link to another site and some information about that site. Like all other objects, links have a short name, a title, and a description. They also have a URL property that contains the actual link.

News Item

News Items are objects you use to publish "news" information on the site. News items are typically small articles that spotlight a particular newsworthy event.

Smart Folder objects are less like content objects and more like special search objects that arrange your content in different ways. Smart Folders don't move around or arrange your content; they gather information about content from all over the site, and then present that information. This allows you to construct alternative views to the containment-based one.

Smart Folders allow you to specify criteria according to which objects are selected for display. For example, a criterion such as "older than 3 days" applies across all your content objects to show you any objects that are older than three days. Similarly, you can show all the news items created by the Marketing department in the past week.

Smart Folders can contain **subfolders** and can inherit the criteria of their parent folders. This allows you to create a simple hierarchy of Smart Folders that narrow and refine your search as you move down the hierarchy.

Smart Folders are also RSS-enabled by default, so you can group and syndicate content with just a few clicks.

Creating these Smart Folders is a straightforward task, and the creator can even decide how to list the results visually, all without writing any HTML or a single line of code. In the example given in Figure 3.9, the criteria for the smart folder called "photos" is to display all the "Image" objects created by "munwar."

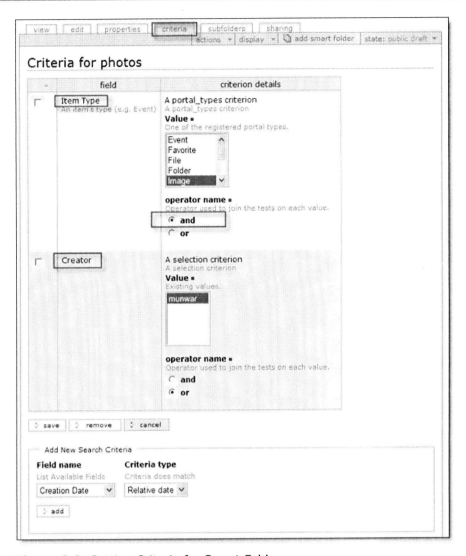

Figure 3.9: Setting Criteria for Smart Folder

Moving through Workflow

Once you create content, one of the most useful things you can do with it is to move it through a workflow that accomplishes an organizational or business goal. The default Plone workflow is shown in Figure 3.10.

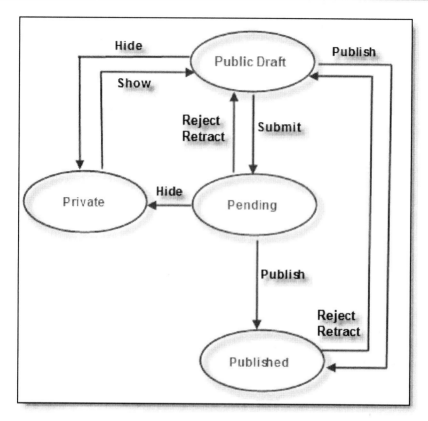

Figure 3.10: Plone Default Workflow

Workflow is a well-defined graph of how content moves through a process. For example, in a newspaper environment, authors write articles, and editors edit and approve those articles for publication. The movement of this content from the author to the editor to publication is workflow.

Workflow generally aids people and groups of people collaborating. Although useful for just one user wanting to take advantage of workflow, it is most often used to coordinate the efforts of teams. For this reason, the following examples are shown from the context of several users.

Plone workflow is content-centric; only content objects move through workflows. Workflows consist of two kinds of objects: *states* and *transitions*. At any one time, a content object is in one of the states in the workflow. The state of a content object is not the content itself; rather, it is a special flag on the content object that tells Plone what state the content is in. Based on this state, Plone can do certain tasks, like put a page that has the "pending" state into a list of content objects that a certain user must review.

A state is stored as an attribute of the object. When the content object is first created, it is in the *initial state* of the workflow. From there, various users of the system can change the state of that content object by *transitioning* from one state to another.

By default, Plone has a simple publication workflow built in. The following example illustrates this feature.

The user **nancy** created a page object called **test**.

Initially, this object is in the **Public Draft** state. She can confirm this when she looks to the right of her toolbar in Plone, shown in Figure 3.11.

Figure 3.11: A page in the public draft state.

The **public draft** state means that others can see the page if they know where to look (for example, if you sent them the link). In order to publish this page, the user must submit it to a site reviewer. To do this, **nancy** clicks on the **Submit** transition shown in Figure 3.11. This will change the state of the page to **Pending**.

Now, when a user **Joe** with the **Reviewer** role logs in to Plone, a box displays on the right, showing pending tasks. Notice that **nancy**'s page displays in this list, as shown in Figure 3.12.

Figure 3.12: Pending content to review

When the Reviewer clicks on that page, he can either **Publish** or **Reject** the page. Regardless of which transition he chooses, the Reviewer can use the "advanced ..." workflow form to enter a comment that becomes part of the workflow history of the page. If the Reviewer publishes it, then the new page shows up on the front page and in site searches.

Editing Workflow Definitions

The preceding workflow is the default one in Plone, but this workflow may not necessarily be what you are looking for. You may either want to customize some of the previous behaviors (like making the initial state "private" instead of "public draft") or define completely new workflows with different states and transitions.

Workflows are defined in the **portal_workflow** tool in the root folder of your Plone site in the ZMI. You can get there by clicking on **Plone Setup** and then on the **Zope Management Interface** link.

Clicking on this tool will take you to the workflow tool's configuration page. This page has several tabs across the top for managing the workflow tools and any workflow definitions that this tool defines. On the first tab is a screen that allows you to map a Plone content type to a workflow definition. Notice that the definitions for most objects shown in Figure 3.13 are **(Default)**.

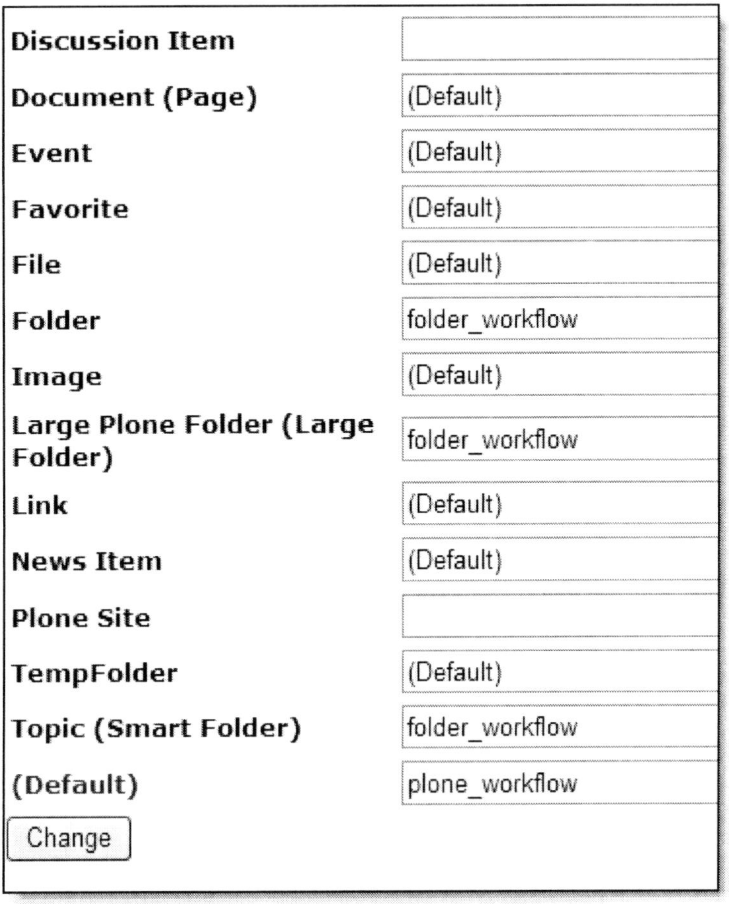

Discussion Item	
Document (Page)	(Default)
Event	(Default)
Favorite	(Default)
File	(Default)
Folder	folder_workflow
Image	(Default)
Large Plone Folder (Large Folder)	folder_workflow
Link	(Default)
News Item	(Default)
Plone Site	
TempFolder	(Default)
Topic (Smart Folder)	folder_workflow
(Default)	plone_workflow
[Change]	

Figure 3.13: Content and their associated workflows

At the very bottom of the list, **Default** maps to the **plone_workflow** definition. This is the workflow with a page object, shown in the example above.

Figure 3.13 also shows the **folder_workflow**. This is a different workflow that is applied to folderish objects in Zope, and defines a workflow that applies to folders.

While it can be convenient to customize a workflow through the Zope Management Interface, it needs to be captured as Python code on the file system if it is to be deployed more than once. A product called DCWorkflowDump can do this for you.

Examining and Editing Workflow

To examine this workflow definition, click on the **Contents** tab. There you will see two workflow definitions: **plone_workflow** and **folder_workflow**. You can also create your own workflow definition here, which is demonstrated in a later example.

Clicking on the **plone_workflow** definition (which is the default for most content, including pages) takes you to a screen with several tabs across the top. These tabs, shown in Figure 3.14, edit the workflow definition.

Start with the **Properties** tab. Workflow has the following properties.

▶ **Title**: the name of the workflow

▶ **'Manager' role bypasses guards**: If checked, the security guards specified will not be applicable to persons with "Manager" role

▶ **Instance creation conditions**: The user creating the instance should have the right to do so by qualifying one of the conditions specified (permission or role or "true" for the given expression)

▶ The next two tabs are **States** and **Transitions**; these are the two most important screens for defining workflows.

States

On the **States** tab, shown in Figure 3.14, you can see all of the states of the **plone_workflow** definition, its transitions, and descriptions of the various elements. The initial workflow state is marked with an asterisk (*). You can change the initial workflow state by checking a workflow state and clicking the **Set Initial State** button.

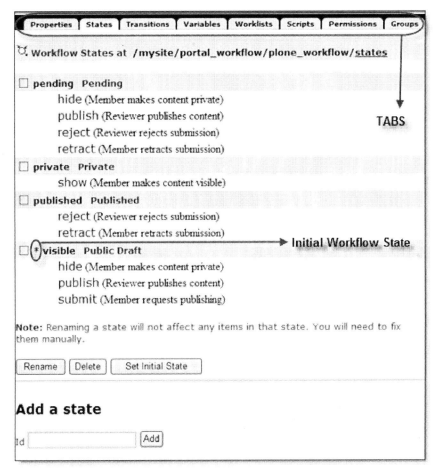

Figure 3.14: Workflow states

The states shown here are the states that apply to all content that move through this workflow. You can edit this workflow here if you want to, but that is generally not recommended because this is the default workflow that comes with Plone. Instead, it is better to add a *new* workflow that copies everything from this workflow that you can then edit.

To do this, go back to the **Contents** tab of the workflow tool and add a new workflow called **plone_archived_workflow** (remember to base it on the default workflow by selecting the **plone_workflow (Default Workflow [Plone])** option button). This will be the new example workflow that you will edit. Click on that new workflow, and click on its **States** tab. It will look exactly like the preceding screen, except it will say **plone_archived_workflow** in the breadcrumbs instead of **plone_workflow**.

To extend this workflow, add a new state called **archived**. This will represent the state of your content when it is published, but no longer active. To create this new state, type "archived" into the **Id** box and click the **Add** button. This is not the same as when the content expires once its expiration time is passed; in this case, it goes back to the visible state.

Now you can see that your workflow has a new state, but in order to get to that state, you must add new transitions.

Transitions

The next tab is **Transitions**. On this tab, you can see all of the transitions of the new plone_archived_workflow definition, its destination states, and its descriptions. On this page, you need to add two new transitions: **archive** and **unarchive**. The **archive** transition will go from the `published` state to the `archived` state. The **unarchive** transition will go from the `archived` state to the `pending` state, where a reviewer can then review it for publication.

After you add the two new transitions, you must click on each of them and edit their properties. Click on **archive** transition and you will see an edit screen as shown in Figure 3.15.

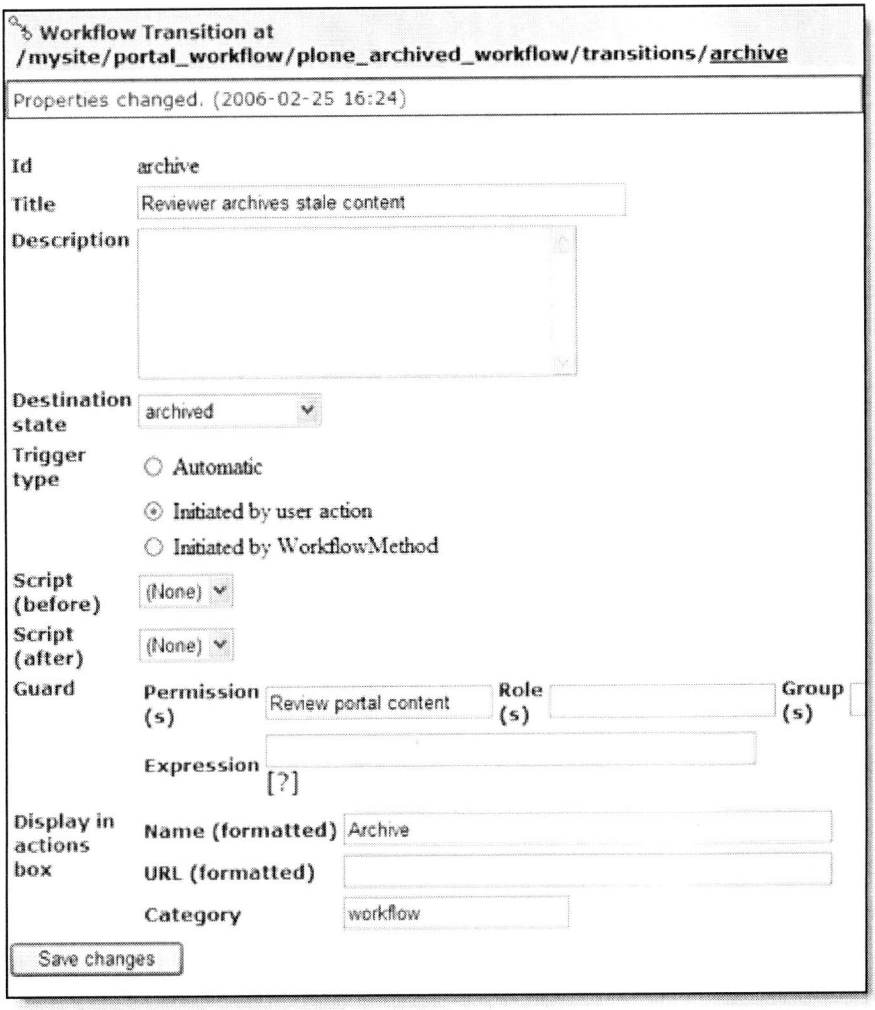

Workflow Transition at
/mysite/portal_workflow/plone_archived_workflow/transitions/archive

Properties changed. (2006-02-25 16:24)

Id	archive
Title	Reviewer archives stale content
Description	
Destination state	archived
Trigger type	○ Automatic
	⊙ Initiated by user action
	○ Initiated by WorkflowMethod
Script (before)	(None) ▾
Script (after)	(None) ▾
Guard	**Permission (s)** Review portal content **Role (s)** **Group (s)**
	Expression [?]
Display in actions box	**Name (formatted)** Archive
	URL (formatted)
	Category workflow

Save changes

Figure 3.15: Workflow Transition Properties

Select the destination state as **archived**. In addition, the **archive** transition should have `Review portal content` in its **Permission** box and `Archive` in its **Name** box. This is so that only users with the **Review portal content** permission can archive content, and the **Archive** action shows up in their menus.

Now, portal reviewers will have a choice besides **retract** when they look at published content. They can also archive that content into the **archived** state.

This example will be expanded upon later to discover content that has become stale and should be archived.

Similarly, click on the **unarchive** transition and select the destination state as **pending.** In addition, the **unarchive** transition should have `Review portal content` in its permission box and `Unarchive` in its **Name** box.

Next step is to link the transitions to states. The **archive** transition will go from the `published` state to the `archived` state. The **unarchived** transition will go from the `archived` state to the `pending` state, where a reviewer can then review it for publication. Click the **States** tab on the top menu. Click the **published** state and choose **archive** as possible transition. Similarly, click the **archived** state and choose **unarchive** as possible transition. Now the states and transitions are defined for plone_archived_workflow.

The last task is to go back to the **portal_workflow** tool and change the default workflow for content to the **plone_archived_workflow** definition. Now the workflow-related actions and screens that your users will have will reflect the new workflow and the new archived state.

Variables

A *variable* is a small bit of data that relates to the content as it moves through the workflow. It is similar to a "property" on the content object, except that it relates to workflow-only information, not content-based information, and its value typically changes from state to state, as the content object is transitioned.

Plone comes with five common variables that hold useful information about the content in the context of the workflow:

▸ **action:** the last transition taken on this object

▸ **actor:** the user who took the last transition

▸ **comments:** any comments provided about the last transition

▸ **review_history:** the history of any previous transitions comments

▸ **time:** the time of the last transition

You can easily create your own variables whose value is the result of a TALES expression. For more information on TALES expressions, see *The Zope Book*. http://www.plope.com/Books/2_7Edition

Worklists

Worklists allow you to define a list of content objects that match a certain work criteria. For example, when a reviewer logs into Plone, the Plone site will show any content objects whose state is **pending**. This worklist will show up on the right of the screen.

Scripts

Scripts are an advanced feature of workflow. They allow you to execute Python code whenever a workflow-related action occurs. You determine what these scripts do. This gives you absolute flexibility when customizing your workflow definition.

For example, suppose that every time content is published on your web site, you want to send e-mail to a group of content collaborators so that everyone knows about the new addition to the site.

To do this, pull down the **Add** menu on the **Scripts** tab, add a new **Script (Python)** object, and name the new object **mail_editor**. Edit this object to contain the code in Listing 3.1:

Listing 3.1

```
msg = """
The content entitled %s has changed. Its URL is %s.
""" % (context.id, context.url)
context.MailHost.simple_send("plone@plonesite.org",
                "editors@plonesite.org",
                "Content has changed.",
                msg)
```

Now click the **Save** tab to save the contents of this script. Go back to the **Transitions** tab and click on the transition **publish**. This transition has a form element named **Script (after)**; pull down this box and select the script object you just created, **mail_editors**.

Folder Workflow

The **folder_workflow** definition for folderish objects is simpler than **plone_workflow** for content. For example, it does not have any states for submitting a folder to be reviewed, since this is a subjective step that depends on the actual human-interpreted content of a content object. Since a folder is merely a collection of content objects that should be reviewed individually, there is no need for this state.

Both authors and reviewers have their own operations when it comes to portal folders. An author can hide or show his folderish object, or a reviewer can "publish" that folderish object, making it public, similarly to how content is published.

Plone Security

Despite best efforts, almost all computer software is vulnerable to attacks and exploits of the most diverse and unexpected kind. Designing software to prevent unauthorized access to your programs and data can be one of the most difficult problems in application design. Application security is much more than just asking for a password. That is simply the beginning.

When people design their own security, they often think that the problem is solved when they finish implementing password protection. Now a much harder problem presents itself: you know who they are, but can you control what they do? In every step of your code, you must verify that what a user is trying to do is permitted.

Plone makes good use of Zope's security model to automate this task. It comes with a built-in security system that works quite well for the standard Plone configuration. It allows managers to create content and users to see and manipulate it in controlled ways. Additionally, it works behind-the-scenes to check security for you. You don't have to worry about constantly checking a user's permission to do things, because Zope checks this permission for you.

However, at some point, you must come up against the concepts in Zope and Plone security if you want to begin developing serious web applications with

Plone. Before you can begin working with it directly, you should know a few basic things about Zope and web security.

When you are writing a web application, you are providing a computer program interface to the Internet. Anyone on the Internet can access it and submit any kind of URL to your server. If your application is not designed with security in mind from the beginning, then the chances are good that you have left yourself open to exploit and attack.

Zope provides a fine-grained security model in order to allow you to control users' abilities. It allows you to protect a class with specific permissions so that all instances of that class will require the user to have those specified permissions to access it. Alternatively, you may declare the class public and only protect individual methods with specific permissions. Finally, you may set the permissions required to access particular *instances* of a class. For example code of this, see *Chapter 5*.

The two basic concepts of security are *authentication* and *authorization*. Authentication is how you ask users to identify themselves. This is usually called *logging in*. This process usually involves typing in a password, but other mechanisms are available.

Now that you know who they are, you can allow them to do things inside your application that unauthenticated users cannot do. However, you don't necessarily want to give authenticated users permission to do *everything*, because that could be dangerous.

You want to be able to control what all users can do inside your system, whether they are authenticated or not. This process is *authorization*. We recommend that you don't try to do this yourself; rather, let Zope's security system do it for you. Zope implements authorization services by using security contexts and wrappers.

High Level Security

Zope's security system is mostly about managing whom you know, and what they are permitted to do. Zope manages all of the underlying details by automatically checking all of your users all of the time against your security settings. The three most important concepts when managing whom you know and what they can do are *users*, *permissions*, and *roles*.

Of course, Zope does not constantly check every single line of code for security -- that would take far too many computer resources, and in most cases, the checks would be superfluous. Zope only checks code that is submitted in a web template or through a web script. Templates and Python code on the file system of your computer runs "unrestricted." This means you should be aware of any third-party products you install, just as you should be aware of installing any kind of program on any kind of computer system. Though file system code can do anything, classes and methods may be protected using security assertions that Zope does check.

Users

Users are objects that represent people working with your web application. This can be anyone: you, your staff, the public at large, or a community of users -- the possibilities are endless.

A user represents someone using the Zope server, a human sitting in front of a web browser, or a web spider such as the googlebot visiting your site. You can categorize users and assign them different roles that determine what permissions the system permits.

Users may be anonymous or authenticated (it's impossible to distinguish between unauthenticated users, so all such users appear as the Anonymous User). Users authenticate themselves by logging in. This distinction is usually one of security. If you don't know your users, they generally don't have permission to do the kinds of things that authenticated users can do.

The scope of this chapter does not cover Zope's underlying security system because it is so flexible. Most Zope users work from the standard security settings and then customize those settings as the needs arise.

Zope's standard security system has three kinds of users: *unauthenticated, authenticated*, and *site managers*. Unauthenticated users have very few permissions, and for the most part, they can only look at objects, not modify them in any way. Authenticated users do not usually have more permissions than unauthenticated users by default, but you can grant them additional permissions as your application needs.

Site managers are kind of like the "gods" of Zope, much like the "Administrator" account on a Windows machine or the "root" user on a Linux box. Site managers have all permissions and can do anything to any object.

You must configure Zope, Plone, and your security requirements into your applications. For example, if you don't want to give any access to unauthenticated users, you can easily do that by reconfiguring Zope's permissions in the ZMI or writing a script that automatically disables unauthenticated access. To do this, just remove the View permission for the Anonymous role.

On the other hand, you may want to authenticate users and offer them more access to your system, but not necessarily elevate them to the site manager level. You can do this easily in the ZMI or with a script to add a new set of permissions to the roles that that apply to that user. You can do this by adding a new role at the bottom of the **Permission** tab and assigning that role whatever permissions you want. Then, assign that role to anyone you want to have those permissions. Note that when configuring Plone, your first stop is the Users and Groups section of the Plone Setup area. A Plone site administrator can usually manage the permissions of site members using only the options available there. You normally won't be adding permissions yourself unless you are developing a new Python product; and in that case, you'll probably do it in the product code instead of through the ZMI..

Members

Zope users are relatively simple objects. They store a user name and password to allow someone to authenticate, and they store the roles that apply to the authenticated user. This is much less than what is required by any community site. (For example, you would need to store at least a full name and an e-mail address.)

Plone addresses this issue by wrapping a simple Zope user in a much richer *Member* object, which associates an extensible set of attributes and metadata with the Zope user. (Zope still provides the authentication and authorization details.) If you are designing any kind of community-based or multi-user system, your application will deal primarily with these kinds of users.

Groups

Groups are a way to bind members together and treat them as one user. Underneath Plone, groups are really users. This allows you to assign roles to groups (roles that all users in the group will share), including local roles. For more details on local roles and the inner workings of Zope's security system, see the security chapter of *The Zope Book* at http://www.plope.com/Books/2_7Edition/Security .stx.

Adding Users, Members, and Groups

If you want to add a new member to your Plone site, go to **Site Setup** and click on the **Users and Group Administration** link. This link will take you to Plone's user management interface, which allows you to add new members and groups to the Plone site.

To add a new user, click the **Add new user** button, which opens the **Registration** screen. Fill out this simple form to add a new user to the site. Add two users to your Plone site.

For every Plone member there exists an underlying Zope user, and for most members of your site, we recommend that you use the Plone membership form because it presents more information about the member than Zope's underlying form. Members also have the roles necessary to work correctly with the Plone system.

To list all the users in your Plone site, click on **Users and Group Administration** link and click the **show all** button. You can control membership such as removing users, by changing their roles as shown in Figure 3.16.

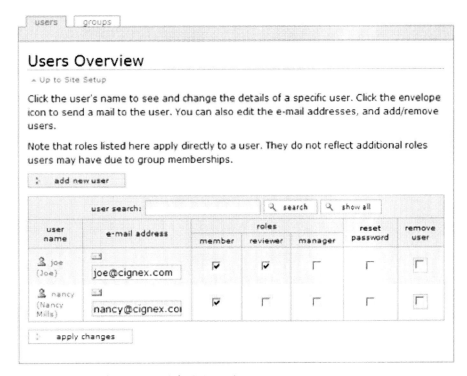

Figure 3.16: Plone User Administration

To manage groups, select the **Groups** tab on the user management screen, as shown in Figure 3.17.

Figure 3.17: The group management screen

You can add groups by clicking the **Add new group** button. This will take you to a form that lets you add a new group to Plone.

Permissions

Permissions are simple strings, such as "Modify Content." A role is associated with a list of permissions, and any protected class, instance, or method in Zope uses the security API discussed in *Chapter 5* to declare the permissions that are required to access them.

When a user with a certain role tries to access some protected method, Zope's security machinery compares the required permission strings with the list of permissions associated with the user's role. For example, to edit a page, a user must have the "Modify Content" permission. If a user does not have that permission, the security system raises an error and aborts the user's attempt to edit the page.

Note: A user may have many roles. In Plone, a user may belong to multiple groups, which, in turn, may have multiple roles.

Roles

Normally, it might seem difficult to manage all of these users and their permissions, but it's not, because Zope makes you collect groups of permissions together using *roles*. A role is a collection of permissions. When your users are authenticated, they are assigned a role with several permissions already defined.

This feature makes managing users and permissions simple. You only need to manage a small set of roles, giving them the necessary permissions that match your application requirements. Then, you manage a set of users, giving them the roles they need to accomplish their particular tasks. Zope's security system takes it from there.

Managing Permissions and Roles with the ZMI

In Zope, permissions are managed in the ZMI. To manage the permissions of any particular object, go the ZMI and access that object's **Security** tab.

Figure 3.18 is only a small portion of the screen, showing only the salient features of managing an object's security. This screen is a grid of Permissions and Roles. To assign permission to a certain role, just select the box where the Permission row and the Role column intersect. In Figure 3.18, you can see that those who have the Manager role will have the permission **Access future portal content**.

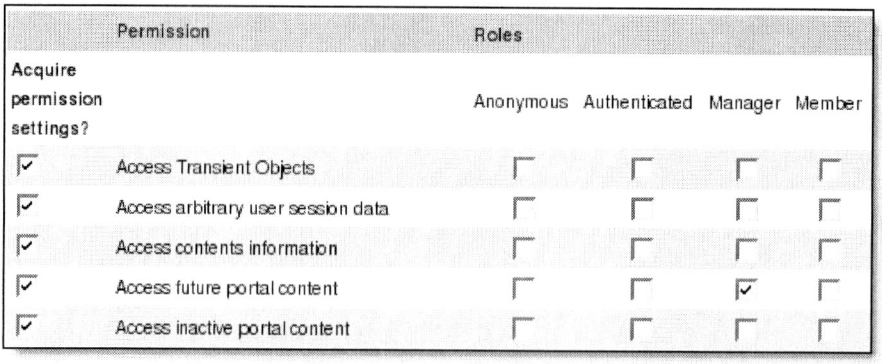

	Permission	Roles			
Acquire permission settings?		Anonymous	Authenticated	Manager	Member
☑	Access Transient Objects	☐	☐	☐	☐
☑	Access arbitrary user session data	☐	☐	☐	☐
☑	Access contents information	☐	☐	☐	☐
☑	Access future portal content	☐	☐	☑	☐
☑	Access inactive portal content	☐	☐	☐	☐

Figure 3.18: Permission management matrix

Note that most of the boxes are unchecked, and the left column of boxes labeled **Acquire settings** is checked. This means that this object does not specify its own security; rather, it *acquires* that security from its parent object. You only need to define this screen once, in the root folder of your Zope system, where many more of the Permission check boxes are selected.

The root security settings are the "default" security policy for the site. If you uncheck the **View** permission for Anonymous users, all of the objects in your Zope site that acquire this permission will now deny access to unauthorized users. This is a flexible and simple way to control your entire site or portions of your site. *Chapter 6* covers much more of this in detail.

HTTP Basic Authentication

HTTP is the most common protocol used on the web, and though you seldom have to concern yourself with it while using Plone, there are some aspects of HTTP security and authentication that you should be aware of.

Basic authentication works by first attempting to access a URL and getting an "Unauthorized" error from the server. This causes the browser to pop up a login box, asking for a user name and password. The initial request is then resubmitted to the server, including the offered credentials. The server either accepts the credentials as valid or returns the same error, causing the browser to pop up the box again, and giving the user another chance to type in the password.

The most important fact to know about HTTP security is that the default authentication system (called "Basic" authentication in HTTP) is very insecure. The user name and password are sent from the client to the server, over the Internet, encoded in a very simple and easy-to-decipher format called "base64," which is no more than a method to encode binary data for representation using only ASCII characters. This format is not meant to be any kind of encryption, and you should never trust it as such.

That being said, almost all web sites use HTTP Basic authentication. This is largely because it is the only authentication scheme supported by all browsers. HTTP Digest authentication (RFC 3310) is more secure, but it still has some issues, and its cross-browser compatibility is lacking. Jan Wolter (http://www .unixpapa.com/auth/basic.html) speculates that the browser writers didn't bother with HTTP Digest authentication because it is a half-measure, and proper security is available by using the HTTPS protocol. If a site is being served over HTTPS, Basic authentication is perfectly secure, as all credentials are transmitted over the encrypted channel.

Installing Products

Products are third-party extensions to Zope and Plone that extend the functionality of the system. Products have many uses and fall into many categories. Most products extend Zope and Plone by offering new content types that implement new, useful behaviors.

Before Plone became very popular, Zope was well-known for its huge spectrum of available third-party products. These products are also useful for Plone, but require much more advanced understanding of the underlying Zope system. For this, we recommend that you read *The Zope Book* and *The Zope Developer's Guide*. These books also cover product installation and development in great detail.

Installing Zope Products

Installing Zope products usually means placing the product in the *Product* directory of your Zope instance. The location of this directory can change, depending on the configuration of the Zope system.

Once a product is installed, you must restart Zope in order to register that product in the Zope system. Once Zope has restarted, you can confirm that the product has been loaded by looking at Zope's Control Panel under the **Products** link.

Installing Plone Products

Installing Plone products is just like installing Zope products, with an extra step, detailed below. You place the new Plone product into the *Products* directory of your Plone instance, but you must also use the Plone **Quick Installer** tool.

The Quick Installer tool registers a product with various Plone tools in order for the product to work properly. For example, many new products must register new Plone content types and skins. These new components must be registered with the **plone_types** and **plone_skins** tools. The Quick Installer accomplishes this.

In later chapters, you'll see how to create your own Quick Installer scripts, but for now you'll just see how to use them from the Plone interface. Go to **Site setup** and click on **Add/Remove Products**. This will bring you to a screen showing available products that have not yet been installed, and existing installed products as shown in Figure 3.19.

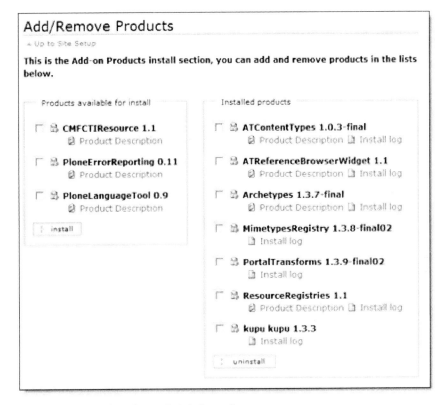

Figure 3.19: The Plone Quick Installer

Installing and uninstalling is simple; just select the product you want to install or uninstall and click the appropriate button. If an error occurs during product installation, then the product will remain uninstalled. An Error Log link will appear next to it, showing you exactly what error caused the installation to fail.

Plone Language Tool

Plone 2.1 includes the Plone Language Tool to provide multi-language support to the Plone content. To install the Plone Language tool, select PloneLanguage-Tool and click on **install** button as shown in Figure 3.19.

Once the tool is successfully installed, you will get a "Language Settings" link on the left side as shown in Figure 3.20.

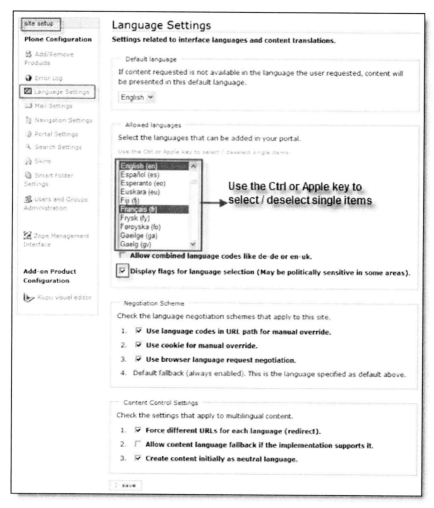

Figure 3.20: Plone Language Settings

To try the multi-language support capabilities of your site, select three languages, **English (en)**, **French (fr)**, **and Arabic (ar)**, and click the **Save** button. Go to the Home page and you will notice language specific flags (little icons). Click the green icon to select The Arabic language. Plone will automatically change the look and feel based on the language tool you choose. For example, in Arabic (where you read/write from right to left), the menu items move to the right side as shown as Figure 3.21.

Figure 3.21: Plone in Arabic

Finding Products

The best place to start when looking for new Plone products is the Plone.org web site (http://plone.org/products). This site catalogs many of the available Plone products and points you towards community discussion boards where you can search for other people's experiences and look for products.

The http://www.contentmanagementsoftware.info site is hosted by the Qintas group and provides up-to-date listings of Zope and Plone products. It's a good place to see what is being currently worked on and what is most active. Another good place to look for Plone products is in the Plone Collective (http://source forge.net/projects/collective). This site contains a code repository that houses not only Plone, but also many third-party products developed by members of the Plone community.

Appendix C has an overview of some of the more popular Zope, CMF, and Plone products. This appendix changes rapidly, so be sure the check it often for new additions.

Summary

This chapter explained much of the high-level object-oriented concepts behind Plone and Zope, including content objects, workflow, security, and product installation. *Chapter 4* delves into how to customize Plone by customizing the underlying skins and types used to display and control a Plone site.

Basic Customizations

Author: Michel Pelletier

Plone contains many features that you can customize to make Plone look and behave the way you want. This chapter explains all of those customizable options and their possible values. It also explains the differences between file system development and Zope through the web development.

Overview

Possibly the most common question from new Plone users is, "How do I change the look and feel of my new site?" Customization in Plone is easy and powerful. At every step in the design, the Plone developers have left some hook or slot where you can change the default action or presentation. This means that if you know what you're looking for, you can quickly make a Plone site do just about anything you want.

The trick is knowing what you are looking for. Because there are so many customizable options, this can become an organizational problem. This chapter will try to make it easier for you to keep track of Plone's many little features that you can customize.

This chapter shows you how to customize the following features using Through the Web (TTW) development:

▸ Skins and Layers

▸ Customize Button

▸ Cascading Style Sheets (CSS)

▸ main_template

▸ Global Definitions

▸ Search

▸ Portlets

At the end, this chapter shows you how to implement customizations using file system development.

Through the Web (TTW) vs. File System Development

Before you invest too much effort into customization, it is important to understand some of the consequences that exist when you customize your Plone site.

Plone starts with the "standard" look and feel that all Plone sites initially share. Obviously, most users need to customize this standard look and feel into something that suits the needs of the site in question. You have two options for customizing a Plone site:

▶ Configure the Plone instance as it exists in the Zope object database directly, using Plone and Zope's Through the Web (TTW) interface.

▶ Configure a Plone site by creating a collection of files on the file system that contain all of your customizations.

Either approach has advantages and disadvantages. Customizing Plone using the TTW interface is quick and easy, and it gives you an incremental and interactive way to understand the various aspects of Plone. Customizing Plone using the file system is more complex, requiring an understanding of Python and a more disciplined approach to site customization.

Zope's security machinery also limits the methods, modules and attributes that TTW scripts and templates may access. When you program Plone through the web, every script and expression you write is controlled by the security system. This constant security checking adds a small, but noticeable, run-time overhead to your TTW code. File system code does not have this problem because it runs unrestricted.

Which style you choose depends on many factors, but the major consensus among Plone developers and users is that file system development is better for long-term, complex projects, and TTW development is better for learning about Plone or for quick, "one-off" sites that do not require a long-term development plan. Even this comparison is not exactly fair, since any Plone site in production requires a little bit of TTW configuration, even if the majority of the functionality is developed on the file system.

For example, many Plone file system products expose property sheets TTW that should be edited as part of implementation. Another way of looking at it is that TTW is better for prototyping and implementation, and file system is suitable for product development.

TTW development may be simpler and more interactive, but it "locks you in" to keeping all of your customizations and changes in the Zope object database (ZODB). Although some experimental software exists that allows you to

---

"mount" your ZODB as a file system, this is not a good solution to the problem, since ZODB was never intended to be used as a file system in this way. A very useful tool called FSDumpTool is available at http://software.cnx.rice.edu/downloads/zope/FSDumpTool/ that allows you to control this situation using bi-directional file system synchronization.

By keeping your changes and customization in a file system product, you have to deal with the added complexity and discipline required, but you benefit from having all of your customizations and changes in one place, not scattered around an object database where they are virtually inaccessible and irreproducible.

Conversely, in the ZODB, you may find your customizations exactly where they are relevant, while on the file system, a whole collection of disparate changes to various property sheets may be collected in one script, which may only execute when the installation script executes. For example, Plone installations will usually want to customize the navigation tree. This is done only at *portal_properties/ navtree_properties/manage_propertiesForm.*

If you want to find out the current configuration of the navigation tree, that is the one place where you can find it and change it. In a file system setup, the navigation tree may have been configured by the installation script, or anywhere else the developer may have put it.

In this chapter, you will learn how to customize Plone using TTW development. This is so that you can quickly grasp the concepts involved and learn to experiment by trying new things and making mistakes. In *Chapter 5*, you will do many of the same things using file system development techniques.

Skins and Layers

Customizing skins and layers is one of the most common tasks in Plone development. Whether customizing Plone TTW or on the file system, understanding how skins and layers interact is key to understanding how almost anything works in Plone.

Skins

A *skin* is a collection of layers that presents content on your site. When your site is presented to users, it is *skinned* using whatever skin either you have chosen for them or they have chosen for themselves. By separating the presentation components into skins, you can make objects look and act in many different ways.

Plone comes with the Default and Tableless skins, and they look identical. The Default Plone skin uses HTML tables to position some of the elements on the main page, while the Tableless skin uses CSS positional information to position everything, removing the need for a table to do it. Both skins are provided because many browsers do not handle the Tableless skin very well due to faulty CSS implementations.

Layers

A *layer* is a collection of presentation objects like templates, images, or scripts. All of the default Plone templates are contained in layers. You can customize these layer elements in two ways:

▸ Use the **Customize** button.

▸ Create your own layer that overrides the existing Plone layer.

The first method is discussed in this chapter, but only for teaching purposes because it is simple and easy. Real skin development should be done on the file system, which is explained later in this chapter.

The Skins Tool

Skins are managed by the **portal_skins** tool. This tool defines all of the existing skins for your site. By default, Plone comes with two skins: Plone Default and Plone Tableless. They differ only in one layer; the Tableless skin includes the **plone_tableless** layer just before the **plone_templates** layer. It overrides two templates from the **plone_templates** layer, and a style sheet from the **plone_styles** layer. At the moment, the Tableless skin exists to some extent as a test for the standards compliance of browsers. It isn't the default, since compliance is still lacking.

Skins are ordered collections of layers. Each layer defines skin elements to present content on your site. For example, the **plone_templates** layer contains all of the templates that display a Plone site other than those that display content objects (which are in the **plone_content** layer), and the **plone_styles** layer contains all of the CSS style definitions for your site

Layers are checked in order from top to bottom, as defined on the property sheet of the **portal_skins** tool. If a layer doesn't feature in a skin, it's invisible, as far as Plone is concerned. Layers at the top of the list inside a skin are searched before those at the bottom. This is important, because overriding a skin element is usually done by creating a new layer above the layer you want to override.

The **skins** tool effectively boils down all of the skins in a Plone site into a flat namespace. The management interface is hierarchical for the sake of organization, but the skins themselves are flattened. This means that when you create new skins, you should *always* prefix the names of those skins with a prefix unique to your product or project. This will be shown in a concrete example in the *File System Development* section.

The Customize Button

All elements within a layer have a **Customize** button. This button is a very important feature of Plone, though often misunderstood.

When you click the **Customize** button on a skin element, Plone makes a copy of the element you are customizing and places it in the **custom** layer inside the skin. The **custom** layer comes before most other layers, so this new copy of the element will override the element inside the other layers. This includes not only file system layers, but any layer after it in the skin's list of layers.

Customization is useful because it allows you to quickly copy a master site template and configure it through the web. It allows rapid prototyping and emergency hotfixing. (It is not intended for deployments.) However, customization is problematic because after you make changes you cannot easily reproduce those changes.

This problem is one of the woes of TTW development, so please only click on the Customize button when learning about Plone, not in a production environment. In a production environment, it might be necessary to customize as a hotfix. In such a case, the content of the custom layer serves as documentation of what the next release should address, and should go away when the update is released. At the 2004 Plone conference in Vienna, one of the Zope founders, Paul Everitt, coined it the "customerize" button, because only the customer should assume the risks of clicking it.

Warning: For the remainder of these examples, you can click on the Customize button to try it out, but remember this warning: only do so to learn Plone or to implement "quick and dirty" sites.

Cascading Style Sheets

Many of Plone's visual elements are defined using Cascading Style Sheets (CSS). CSS is a system for adding style to the structure of your HTML documents. Style elements include fonts, colors, spacing, position, and many other visual attributes.

Plone's CSS is defined in the **plone.css** skin element in *portal_skins/plone_styles/ plone.css*. You should never customize this CSS; rather, you should customize the **ploneCustom.css** skin element. This is so your changes will not be overwritten when Plone is upgraded from one version to the next.

CSS works by associating style attributes with certain tags or identifiers. The identifiers are associated with HTML tags via `class` or `id` attributes. Plone's visual style is defined entirely by these style declarations. When a Plone template is rendered into HTML, its tags are associated with the correct style element, separating the structure of the document from its visual presentation. At this level, it isn't Plone-specific. When the rendered HTML is delivered to the browser along with the CSS style sheets, the browser associates the tags with the CSS style rules, and it handles the visual display and layout accordingly.

You do not need to use Plone style definitions if you do not want to; you are free to completely customize your application as you see fit. However, it helps to follow the Plone standard by using the same CSS parameter names in your style sheets.

For example, all applications have some kind of background color. Normally, the background color is defined by the **base_properties** style sheet's **background-color** property. If you disregard this property in your own style sheet and hard-code a background color, then the background color you define in your style sheet won't reflect the value of the property. If another Plone user tries to set that property, he'll find that it doesn't work because your template disregards it.

The syntax to customize a CSS element is to reference it using the DTML syntax in Listing 4.1 (DTML is not covered in this book, but for an excellent reference see *The Zope Book* at http://www.plope.com/Books/2_7Edition/DTML.stx):

Listing 4.1

```
&dtml-variableName;
```

This kind of DTML variable reference will be rendered into the value of the variable whose name is **variableName**, with the CSS code in Listing 4.2:

Listing 4.2

```
.myBackground {
    color: &dtml-backgroundColor;
}
```

This creates a new CSS element called **myBackground**, whose **color** attribute comes from the standard Plone property **backgroundColor**. This means you can now customize the **myBackground** style element with your own custom attributes, but still inherit the standard color that works with other Plone style elements that may use that property.

Table 4.1 lists the properties available in the **base_properties** sheet:

Table 4.1: base_properties Style Sheet Properties

Property	Description
logoName	file name of the portal logo
fontFamily	font family used for all text, excluding headers
fontBaseSize	base font size from which all text is calculated
fontColor	main font color
backgroundColor	background color
linkColor	color used on normal link
linkActiveColor	color used on active link, while clicking and holding down (:active pseudo-class)
linkVisitedColor	color used on visited link (:visited pseudo-class)
borderWidth	width of most borders in Plone
borderStyle	style of the border lines, normally solid
borderStyleAnnotations	style of border lines on comments, etc.
globalBorderColor	border color used on the main tabs, the portlets, etc.
globalBackgroundColor	background color for the selected tabs, portlet headings, etc.
globalFontColor	color of the font in the tabs and in portlet headings
headingFontFamily	font family for h1/h2/h3/h4/h5/h6 headings
headingFontBaseSize	base size used when calculating the different heading sizes
contentViewBorderColor	border color for content view tabs
contentViewBackgroundColor	background color for content view tabs
contentViewFontColor	font color used in the content view tabs
textTransform	transformation (for example, lowercasing) to apply to text in portlets, tabs, etc.
evenRowBackgroundColor	background color of even rows in listings
oddRowBackgroundColor	background color of odd rows in listings

Table 4.1: base_properties Style Sheet Properties (Continued)

Property	Description
notifyBorderColor	border color of notification elements like the status message, the calendar focus
notifyBackgroundColor	background color of notification elements like the status message, the calendar focus

The plone.css file contains even position information. For example, you can easily swap the positions of the left and right bars by changing the style definitions in the **plone_css** page.

main_template

The **main_template** of your Plone system is in *portal_skins/plone_templates/ main_template*. This template is the "heart" of your Plone site, because it defines the common look and feel that affects all content in your Plone site.

The main_template is a very complex page template. This section will lead you through most of the elements of main_template and how you can customize each one.

Before you begin, you should become familiar with Zope Page Templates -- specifically, the Template Attribute Language (TAL) and the Macro Expansion Template Attribute Language (METAL). They are both documented thoroughly in several locations, including *The Zope Book 2.7 Edition* by Chris McDonough, et al., which you can find at http://www.plope.com/Books/2_7Edition/ZPT.stx.

Plone's main_template heavily uses page template METAL macros. Macros are reusable pieces of HTML that can be expanded into a template. Macros can define "slots" that can be filled in by the template which uses the macro when the macro is expanded.

They are like miniature page templates; they define a dynamic "chunk" of code that you can reuse anywhere in your site. Consider, for example, a menu bar on your site. This menu bar should be used everywhere on the site, but in different places the menu should contain different items. By using a macro, you can reuse the menu over and over and change the menu items by just filling in the appropriate slot.

The main Plone page is divided into three columns. The center column is the place where most user interaction and information is presented, while the left and right columns usually contain *portlets*. Portlets are small, typically box-shaped information areas that are configurable in several different ways.

Portlet placement is defined by variables that are properties on a root Plone object. To see these properties, log into the ZMI, make sure you are in the root of the Plone site object, and click on the **Properties** tab. This will show you several portal-related properties, including `left_slot` and `right_slot`. These two properties define the locations of the portlets that appear on your Plone site by default, as shown in Figure 4.1.

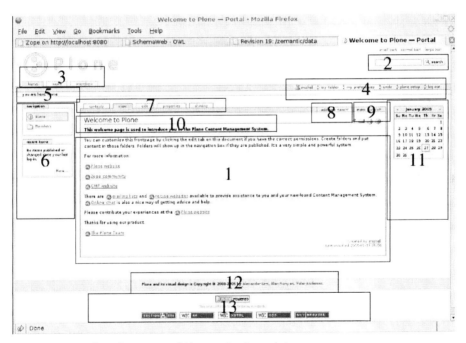

Figure 4.1: The elements of the main_template

On this main screen you can see most of the elements that are defined in main_template.

Note: This is the authenticated user's view, and many of the elements shown aren't presented to anonymous users.

1. **Main slot:** The main slot is the very center of the screen, containing the current content or form in Plone. Typically, this is the part that changes the most. The METAL name for this slot is **main**.

2. **Search form:** This slot is defined by the **search** template. You can type in any kind of free text query into this box and it will do a text search on your Plone content. If you want to do a more advanced search, see the documentation in the *Search* section for the ZCatalog and the **search_form** template.

3. **Portal tabs:** These tabs are links to pages that should be on every page in the portal. Think of them as site-wide "global" tabs.

4. **Personal bar:** This bar contains actions pertaining to the current user. For example, if the user is authenticated, a link to the member area and a link to logout typically display. If the user is not authenticated, then this bar shows only a login link.

5. **Breadcrumbs:** This navigational aide tells users where they are in the Plone site. This portlet describes the path of the current object visually, from root to object, from left to right. This is a common way of representing the file system-like hierarchical structure of Zope and Plone.

6. **Left slot:** This slot typically contains useful portlets. You can customize the portlets that appear in this box by going to the ZMI and clicking on the **Properties** tab of the portal object. There, you can customize the **left_slots** property.

7. **Content tabs:** These tabs offer views of different aspects of the current content. They are the actions on a content type in the **content_tabs** category.

8. **Content drop-down lists:** These lists allow you to add new content to the current object and to change the state of the object.

9. **Document actions:** These actions apply to content. They are typically icons whose actions have the **document_actions** category.

10. **Byline:** This line contains the author and other descriptive information about the current object. This is usually short (no more than one line long) so that it can be presented neatly.

11. **Right slot:** This slot usually contains portlets. Default Plone suppresses the right slot on member pages, so portlets in this slot must not be crucial for members to use the site. It must be acceptable to only see it occasionally (for example, when you return to the homepage). You can customize the portlets in this slot by going to the ZMI **Properties** tab of the portal object and editing the **right_slots** property.

12. **Footer:** The footer of the site. This is typically where you put anything that always appears on your site's footer, like small logos or navigation links. Keep it compact for visual neatness.

13. **Colophon:** The colophon is usually where small print legalisms like copyrights and other information is shown.

The top-level macro in Plone's main_template is called **master**. This macro defines the outermost HTML document that defines the site's common look and feel. For the most part, Plone's main_template consists of calls to macros defined in sub-templates to render each individual section. The header and footer, for example, come from two other templates called `header.pt` and `footer.pt`. They are expanded into the main_template using the METAL `use-macro` instruction. See Listing 4.3.

Listing 4.3

```
<head metal:use-macro="here/header/macros/html_header">
```

The **master** macro of main_template defines the following slots (see Table 4.2):

Table 4.2: Slot Definitions for the **master** Macro of main_template

Slot Name	Definition
doc_type	This slot can be filled with a new HTML **doc_type** definition. You should override this slot only if you want your HTML pages validated against a different version of the HTML standard.
top_slot	This slot offers a place to insert any kind of custom TAL. To avoid generating invalid HTML, you can only insert TAL or METAL statements here that influence rendering by defining global variables and do not generate any HTML.
column_one_slot	This slot defines column one, typically on the left.
portlets_one_slot	This slot is inside the column one slot and defines where portlets for that column should go.
content	This slot defines the content for the page and contains an inner macro named **content**, which defines the following three slots:
header	The header slot for the content
main	The main slot for the content
sub	The sub slot for the content
column_two_slot	This slot defines column two, typically to the right.
portlets_two_slot	This slot defines the portlets for column two.

In addition to defining slots, main_template uses several other macros defined in sub-templates in order to build the entire page. For example, the **portlets_one_slot** defines the left column's portlets, but it is up to the macro **here/portlets_fetcher/macros/left_column** to actually render the content of the portlets. Plone's main_template calls these other macros. See Table 4.3.

Table 4.3: Macros Available in main_template

Macro	Description
here/global_defines/macros/ define	This macro defines all the global names to the TAL and METAL that are called when the page is rendered.
here/header/macros/ html_header	This macro defines the HTML header for the document.
here/global_cache_settings/ macros/cacheheaders	This macro defines any cache headers that the document should issue to a request. Cache headers are interpreted by any proxies such as squid, which the request might traverse on the way to the user's browser.

Table 4.3: Macros Available in main_template (Continued)

Macro	Description
here/global_siteactions/ macros/site_action	This macro defines site-wide actions, shown as tabs across the top of the screen.
here/global_searchbox/ macros/quick_search	This macro defines the quick search box.
here/global_logo/macros/ portal_logo	This macro defines the logo for the site.
here/global_skinswitcher/ macros/skin_tabs	This macro defines tabs for switching skins. A default Plone doesn't have any; the contents of this macro are in a `<span tal:condition="nothing">`....`</span>` section.
here/global_sections/ macros/portal_tabs	This macro defines the tabs across the top that are portal-specific.
here/global_personalbar/ macros/personal_bar	This macro defines any personal links and tabs such as login, logout, etc.
here/global_pathbar/ macros/path_bar	This macro renders the "breadcrumbs" for the UI navigation.
here/portlets_fetcher/ macros/left_column	This macro renders the left column of the page.
here/global_contentviews/ macros/content_views	This macro renders the content views.
here/global_contentviews/ macros/content_actions	This macro renders the content bar.
here/global_statusmessage/ macros/portal_message	This macro renders any portal messages.
here/viewThreadsAtBottom/ macros/discussionView	This macro renders a slot for discussion, if there is any.
here/portlets_fetcher/ macros/right_column	This macro defines the right column.
here/footer/macros/ portal_footer	This macro defines the portal footer.
here/colophon/macros/ colophon	This macro defines the portal colophon.

Global Definitions

Going through Plone templates may be a bit confusing, but the Plone developers have chosen a good design and variable naming scheme to make customization easy once you understand where to look. For example, any time you are working with a Plone template, you have access to a number of pre-defined variables that help you access objects and methods in Plone.

Several of these pre-defined variables access services that were discussed in *Chapter 2*. Each of these services is available to you through the common Plone global definitions. These definitions reside in *portal_templates/global_defines.py*. Table 4.4 contains a list of all of the global definitions and their meanings:

Table 4.4: Common Plone Global Definitions

Definition	Description	TALES Expression	Notes
utool	The Portal url tool.	`nocall:here/` `portal_url;`	This variable returns the portal URL tool, which generates URLs for the Portal. For more information on the `nocall` syntax, see *The Zope Book's* advanced templating chapter.
portal	The top level Plone site object. This will be "called" any time you use it.	`utool/get` `PortalObject;`	By calling the portal object, it will return a rendered version of the portal root. This is usually not very useful.
portal _object	The top level Plone site object, but not called when you use it.	`nocall:portal;`	Unlike the previous variable, it returns just the portal root object instead of rendering the object and returning you HTML. This is usually more useful.
portal_url	The URL to the top level Plone site.	`utool;`	
mtool	The membership tool.	`nocall:portal/` `portal_membership;`	This is useful for calling methods on the membership tool from templates.

gtool	The groups tool.	`nocall:portal/`
		`portal_groups`
		`| nothing;`
			This is useful for calling methods on the groups tool from templates.

Table 4.4: Common Plone Global Definitions (Continued)

Definition	Description	TALES Expression	Notes
gdtool	The group data tool.	`nocall:portal/` `portal_groupdata` `| nothing;`	
atool	The actions tool.	`nocall:portal/` `portal_actions;`	
aitool	The action icons tool.	`nocall:portal/` `portal_actionicons` `| nothing;`	
putils	The Plone utils tool.	`nocall:portal/` `plone_utils;`	
wtool	The workflow tool.	`nocall:portal/` `portal_workflow;`	
ifacetool	The interface tool.	`nocall:portal/` `portal_interface` `| nothing;`	
portal_title	The title of the portal.	`portal_object/` `Title;`	
object_title	The title of the current object being displayed by this skin.	`here/Title;`	
member	The current authenticated member.	`mtool/` `getAuthenticated` `Member;`	
check Permission	An alias for the membership tool **checkPermission** method.	`nocall:mtool/` `checkPermission;`	
members folder	Returns the members folder.	`mtool/getMembers` `Folder;`	
isAnon	Boolean method returns **true** if the user is anonymous, **false** otherwise.	`mtool/` `isAnonymousUser;`	
actions	Returns a list of actions for the current object.	`python: portal` `.portal_actions.` `listFilteredAction` `sFor(here);`	

Table 4.4: Common Plone Global Definitions (Continued)

Definition	Description	TALES Expression	Notes
keyed _actions	Returns a list of key actions for the current object.	`python: portal. keyFilteredActions (actions);`	These are actions that have been filtered to show only those that are relevant to the user's current roles, possibly the current workflow state, and the "action category" of the current content object.
user_ actions	Returns the current user actions.	`actions/user;`	
workflow _actions	Returns the current workflow actions.	`actions/workflow;`	
folder _actions	Returns the current folder actions.	`actions/folder;`	
global_ actions	Returns the current global actions.	`actions/global;`	
portal_tabs	Returns the portal tabs, if they exist; nothing otherwise.	`actions/ portal_tabs |nothing;`	
wf_state	Returns the current workflow state for the current object.	`python:wtool.g etInfoFor(here, 'review_state', None);`	
portal _properties	Returns the portal properties tool.	`portal/portal _properties;`	
site _properties	Returns the site properties property sheet.	`portal_properties/ site_properties;`	
ztu	The ZTUtils module.	`modules/ZTUtils;`	This is useful for page templates that batch search results, which is shown later in this chapter.

Table 4.4: Common Plone Global Definitions (Continued)

Definition	Description	TALES Expression	Notes
actions	Available actions	`options/` `actions|actions;`	This is a shorthand name for actions passed into a request, or the actions available for the current content object, if any.
wf_actions	Available workflow actions	`workflow_actions;`	This is a shorthand name for any workflow_actions associated with the current content object.

isFolder	Tests to confirm the current object is a folder.	`python:here.get`
		`TypeInfo().getId()`
		`insite_properties.`
		`use_folder_tabs;`
			This variable is **true** if the current content object is a folder.

template_ id	Returns the template id	`options/template_`
		`id | template/`
		`getId | nothing;`
			This variable is the id of the current template being used to render the current page.

tabindex	The iterator of all tabs on the screen	`python:Iterator` `(pos=30000);`	By convention, each form control in Plone gets an index number that identifies it. This variable generates tab indexes, determining the order in which form fields are selected when you navigate through a document by pressing **Tab**. Its value is 30000 to place it after Archetypes base_edit (7000), left portlets (20000), and right portlets (20000).
here_url	The URL for the current object.	`here/absolute_url;`	
sl	The left slot.	`slots_mapping/` `left;`	

Table 4.4: Common Plone Global Definitions (Continued)

Definition	Description	TALES Expression	Notes
sr	The right slot.	`slots_mapping/right;`	
default _language	The default language settings, or nothing if no setting.	`site_properties/default_language |nothing;`	
allowed _types	List of currently allowed types in this folder.	`here/getAllowedTypes;`	
is_editable	Returns true if the current object can be edited.	`python:here.show EditableBorder (template_id= template_id, allowed_types= allowed_types, actions=actions );`	
current _page_url	Returns the current page URL, taking into account virtual hosting.	`request/VIRTUAL_URL |string:${request/SERVER_URL}$ {request/PATH_TRANSLATED};`	
lockable	Returns true if the current object can be locked.	`python:hasattr (here, 'wl_isLocked');`	
isLocked	Returns true if the current object is locked.	`python:lockable and here.wl_isLocked();`	

Search

In Zope, objects can be just about anywhere inside the containment hierarchy, and the ability to search for an object quickly is an important part of many Zope and Plone based applications.

The ZCatalog is analogous to a real world index in a book. Often, you know that a certain piece of information is in the book, but you don't know exactly where. Rather than searching for the information from the beginning of the book to the end, it makes much more sense to look the information up in the index.

ZCatalog plays the same role in Zope. The ZCatalog stores information about your objects, and you can search the catalog for objects that match various criteria. You do not need to write scripts to search for your objects; the ZCatalog does all of this searching for you.

When you click the **Search** button, the ZCatalog looks in special structures inside the catalog called *indexes*, looking for objects that match your search criteria. These indexes are created when your site is first created. Any time new content is added, removed, or edited in Plone, the indexes within the catalog are updated to reflect those changes.

When used properly, the ZCatalog can do some amazing things very quickly, like search through many megabytes of text, generate reports on your objects, and display or organize your objects in ways more complex than the containment hierarchy permits.

The catalog indexes information from your object's attributes and methods. The attribute or method to index is determined by the name of the index in the catalog. For example, the index id will index an object's `id` attribute. The attributes and methods indexed are determined by the value of the `Indexed attributes` property of the index. This defaults to the name of the index. If the catalog tries to index an object and finds that the name matches a method, that method is called. For example, the `getSearchableText` index will call the `getSearchableText` method on an object, if it exists.

If a cataloged object does not contain an attribute or method that matches the name of an index within the catalog, that object is simply passed over and will not be indexed. For example, many objects do not have a `getSearchableText` method, so those objects will not appear in any index for that property.

Warning: Watch out for attributes that are acquired. For example, if a container has a `getSearchableText` method but none of its children do, all the children will acquire their container's method and be indexed under the text returned by it. This can cause confusion when someone searches for one object and gets many that have acquired that value.

Catalog Queries

Catalogs are searched with a *query*. A query can be a simple query value using a keyword argument like a dictionary or a string, or a more complex query object. For most simple queries, keyword arguments are fine, but more complex searches may require a dictionary or query object. Different kinds of indexes may interpret the query in their own way. Later in this section you will see an example of each kind of index.

The catalog maintains indexes with names like `id` and `Title`. These indexes store information about objects for that particular attribute. For example, the `id` index stores all of your content's ids, and lets you search for content that has a certain id or range of id values.

Catalogs are queried by calling them with query arguments. For example, from a Python script you could perform all of the following queries on a standard Plone catalog. See Listing 4.4.

Listing 4.4

```
# example Catalog queries
# returns list of everything created by the member "michel"
results = here.portal_catalog(Creator="michel")

# returns everything with the "book" and "sales" subject
# keywords
results = here.portal_catalog(Subject=("book", "sales"))

# everything that contains the word pattern "PloneLive*"
results = here.portal_catalog(searchableText="PloneLive*")
```

Table 4.5 is a list of default ZCatalog indexes for portal_catalog.

Table 4.5: Default ZCatalog indexes for portal_catalog

Name	Index Type	Description
Creator	FieldIndex	The member who created the object
Date	FieldIndex	The date of the object
Description	TextIndex	A description of the object

Table 4.5: Default ZCatalog indexes for portal_catalog

Name	Index Type	Description
SearchableText	ZCTextIndex	The searchable content of the object
Subject	KeywordIndex	The subject keywords of the object
Title	TextIndex	The object's title
Type	FieldIndex	The CMF type of the object
allowedRoles AndUsers	KeywordIndex	Users and Roles allowed to see this object
created	FieldIndex	The date the object was created
effective	FieldIndex	The date the object is effective
expires	FieldIndex	The date the object expires
getId	FieldIndex	The id of the object
id	FieldIndex	Also the id of the object
in_reply_to	FieldIndex	The reference to the original article to which this field is in reply
meta_type	FieldIndex	The meta type of the object
modified	FieldIndex	The time and date of the last modification
path	PathIndex	The physical path to the object
portal_type	FieldIndex	The portal type of the object
review_state	FieldIndex	The workflow state the object is in

Each of the indexes in Table 4.5 can be queried according to its own type. Below is documentation for each index type.

Field Index

A field index is the simplest type of index in the ZCatalog. It maps a value from an attribute or method to a list of objects that match that value. A Field index then queries for objects that match that value. For example, one of the most common field indexes in Plone is the `id` index. It indexes the `id` attribute of Plone objects. If you want to search for all objects with a particular id, you would use the index in Listing 4.5.

Listing 4.5

```
# returns list of everything created by the member "michel"
results = here.portal_catalog(Creator="michel")
```

ZCText Index

A Text index breaks text down into individual words (called *splitting*, which is a language-specific feature), then indexes the words and the objects that contain those words. It also keeps track of some scoring information to show more relevant objects before less relevant ones.

Text indexing is commonly used to search for documents that contain certain words or phrases. Text indexes can also be queries with "and" and "or" to combine or intersect search results from multiple query terms.

Many Zope objects implement the method **searchableText** that returns the "searchable text" of the object. By creating a text index with this name, you can search existing Zope objects. To see an example of this kind of index, go to the **portal_catalog** object, click on the **Index** tab, and click on the **searchable-Text** index as shown in Figure 4.2.

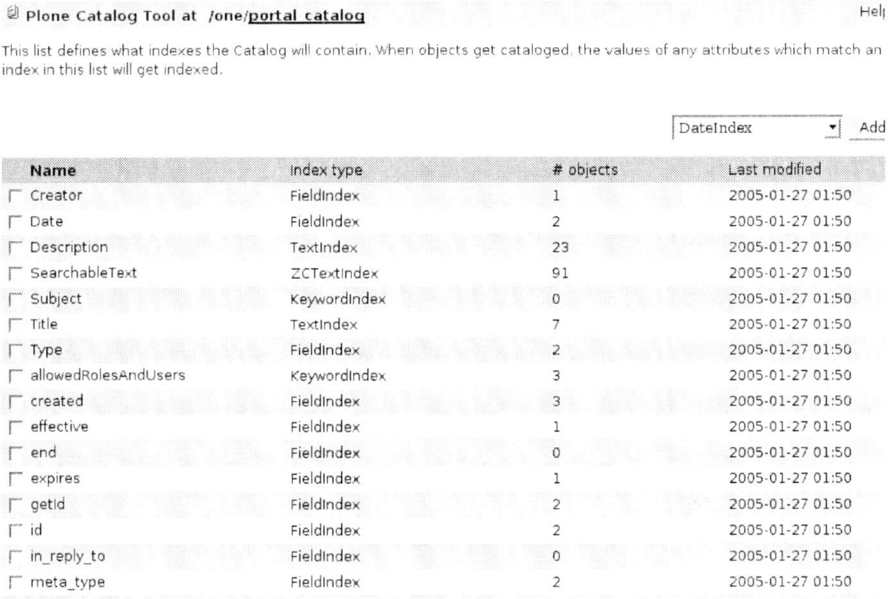

This list defines what indexes the Catalog will contain. When objects get cataloged, the values of any attributes which match an index in this list will get indexed.

DateIndex ▾   Add

Name	Index type	# objects	Last modified
☐ Creator	FieldIndex	1	2005-01-27 01:50
☐ Date	FieldIndex	2	2005-01-27 01:50
☐ Description	TextIndex	23	2005-01-27 01:50
☐ SearchableText	ZCTextIndex	91	2005-01-27 01:50
☐ Subject	KeywordIndex	0	2005-01-27 01:50
☐ Title	TextIndex	7	2005-01-27 01:50
☐ Type	FieldIndex	2	2005-01-27 01:50
☐ allowedRolesAndUsers	KeywordIndex	3	2005-01-27 01:50
☐ created	FieldIndex	3	2005-01-27 01:50
☐ effective	FieldIndex	1	2005-01-27 01:50
☐ end	FieldIndex	0	2005-01-27 01:50
☐ expires	FieldIndex	1	2005-01-27 01:50
☐ getId	FieldIndex	2	2005-01-27 01:50
☐ id	FieldIndex	2	2005-01-27 01:50
☐ in_reply_to	FieldIndex	0	2005-01-27 01:50
☐ meta_type	FieldIndex	2	2005-01-27 01:50

Figure 4.2: ZCTextIndex example

A ZCTextIndexZope allows you to query for a text pattern using the wildcard characters **?** and *****. The question mark operator matches one character, and the asterisk operator matches one or more characters. The query **b?b** would match any three-character word whose first and last characters are "b," and the query **b*b** would match any length word whose first and last characters are "b." See Listing 4.6.

Listing 4.6

```
# returns everything that contains words that begin
# with the pattern "PloneLive*"
results = here.portal_catalog(searchableText="PloneLive*")
```

When performing text searches, keep these points in mind:

▸ The ZCatalog filters out certain extremely common words (called *stopwords*) and any single-letter words.

▸ The ZCatalog catalogs words with numbers in them, but not standalone numbers.

▸ You can control how text is indexed in your object to a certain extent. This is covered in more detail in *Chapter 6*.

▸ Text searching can be very language-specific. If your language is not supported by the ZCatalog (like Japanese or Chinese variants), you should look for another text searching component. Zope Japan Corp. distributes a Japanese text index that works with the ZCatalog.

Keyword Index

Keyword indexes are like field indexes, but instead of indexing only one value to a sequence of matching objects, a keyword index matches a list of values to a sequence of matching objects. This allows you to search for objects that have one or more unique values within this list. See Listing 4.7.

Listing 4.7

```
# returns everything with the "book" and "sales" subject
# keywords
results = here.portal_catalog(Subject=("book", "sales"))
```

Plone's keyword feature allows you to tag objects with certain application-specific keywords.

Simple Searching

Simple searching uses an HTML form to pass query terms to the catalog. Plone provides the simple search portlet described earlier, but for more advanced searching of the catalog you will need to create your own custom form.

You can access many of the advanced search features from Plone's advanced search form. This form is in the **search_form** template. To view the form, simply append **search_form** to your portal's URL as shown in Figure 4.3.

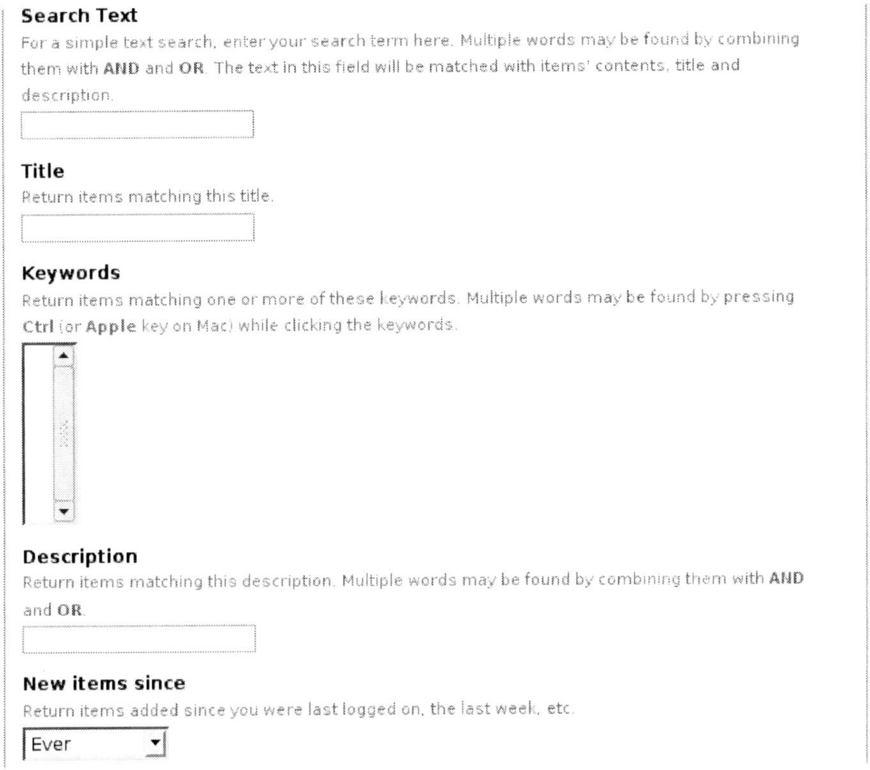

Search Text

For a simple text search, enter your search term here. Multiple words may be found by combining them with **AND** and **OR**. The text in this field will be matched with items' contents, title and description.

Title

Return items matching this title.

Keywords

Return items matching one or more of these keywords. Multiple words may be found by pressing **Ctrl** (or **Apple** key on Mac) while clicking the keywords.

Description

Return items matching this description. Multiple words may be found by combining them with **AND** and **OR**.

New items since

Return items added since you were last logged on, the last week, etc.

Ever

Figure 4.3: The Plone advanced search form

Note: The source code for this form is a good way to learn about complex catalog queries.

Zope can automatically generate a simple HTML form for you that can query Plone's catalog. To create this form, follow these instructions:

1. Go to your Plone's ZMI interface and select **Zope Search Interface** from the pull-down menu. A form displays and asks you what kind of search and result templates you want to generate and which catalog to generate them against.

2. Give the two templates common-sense ids (like **search_form** and **search_results**).

Chapter 4: Basic Customizations

3. Select **portal_catalog** from the list.

4. Be sure to generate Page Templates and not DTML. (The scope of this book does not cover DTML forms.)

5. Click **Add**.

You have now created a new search form and result page. Note that this is Zope only. The search form is simple; it presents you with HTML input boxes for each kind of index in the catalog, as shown in Figure 4.4.

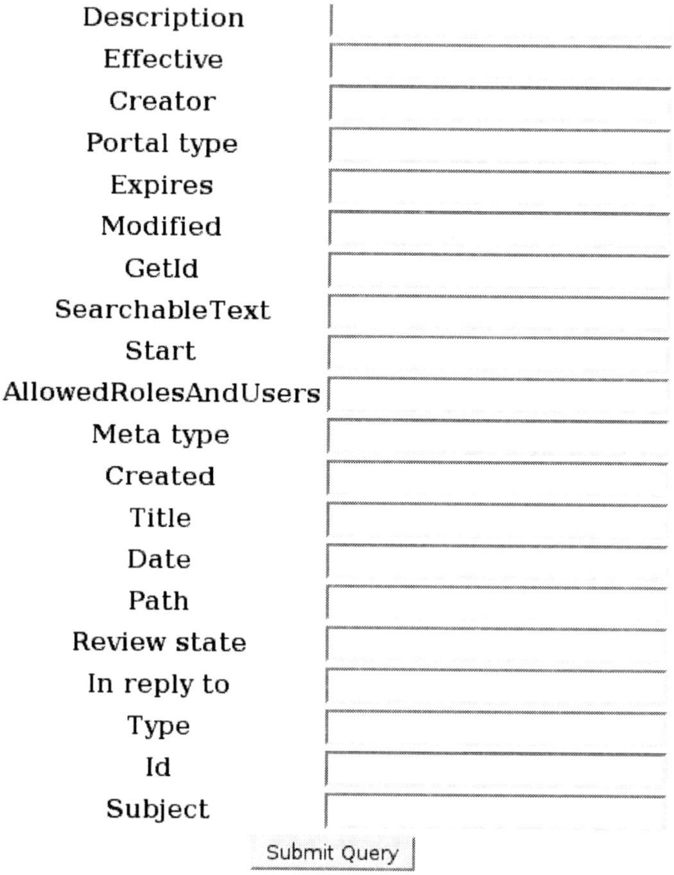

Description	
Effective	
Creator	
Portal type	
Expires	
Modified	
GetId	
SearchableText	
Start	
AllowedRolesAndUsers	
Meta type	
Created	
Title	
Date	
Path	
Review state	
In reply to	
Type	
Id	
Subject	

Submit Query

Figure 4.4: A ZSearch Interface Form

The result form iterates over the results of the query you entered into the search form. See Listing 4.8:

Listing 4.8

```
<body tal:define="results  here/portal_catalog;
    start request/start|python:0;
    batch python:modules['ZTUtils'].Batch(results,
    size=20,
    start=start);
    previous python:batch.previous;
    next python:batch.next">
```

Most of the work of the result form is in the first line of this snippet, **here/ portal_catalog**. This code causes the catalog to be "called" with the current query. Because the query is encapsulated within the **request** object (this template was called by the query form) this one line of code automatically picks up the query from the request and returns any matches to the query into the **results** object.

The variables **start, batch, size, previous** and **next** show only 20 results at a time. For more information on batching, see *The Zope Book, Chapter 8.*

The automatic forms that are generated by the ZSearch Interface tool are a good place to start, but often you need to highly customize them to get a better search page. Plone's **search_form** template is the best place to look for more complex examples of HTML forms that query a catalog.

For example, the HTML code in Listing 4.9 generates a selection box that lets the user pick from a list of unique keywords that are returned by the **uniqueValues()** method on the catalog:

Listing 4.9

```
<div class="field">
    <label for="Subject" i18n:translate="label_keywords">Keywords
    </label>

    <div class="formHelp" i18n:translate="help_search_keywords">
    Return items matching one or more of these keywords.
```

```
        Multiple words may be found
        by pressing <strong>Ctrl</strong> while
        <strong>left clicking</strong> the keywords.
        </div>

        <select name="Subject:list"
            id="Subject"
            size="7"
            multiple="multiple"
            tabindex=""
            tal:attributes="tabindex tabindex/next;"
            tal:define="contentSubjects here/Subject;
                usedSubjects python:here.portal_catalog.uniqueValuesFor
                    ('Subject');"
            >
        <option value="#"
            tal:repeat="subject usedSubjects"
            tal:content="subject"
            tal:attributes="value subject"
            i18n:domain="plone-metadata"
            i18n:translate=""
            >dummy</option>
        </select>
    </div>
```

Notice how the method **uniqueValues()** defines a sequence that is then iterated over using **tal:repeat**. This creates an HTML selection box with all of the unique keywords in the catalog's **Subject** index. If the user selects one of these items in the HTML form, then only items that match that keyword will be returned. Note that in this context, the terms "Keyword" and "Subject" are identical; the latter is used with the catalog because it is the name used in Dublin Core.

Date range searching is another useful advanced technique. For example, you might want to find all of the objects that are newer or older than a certain date, or that fall between a range of dates. This is also simple to do with an HTML form. Listing 4.10 is the code from Plone's **search_form**:

Listing 4.10

```
<div class="field">
    <label for="created" i18n:translate="label_new_items_since">
    New items
        since</label>

    <div class="formHelp"
i18n:translate="help_search_new_items_since">
    Return items added since you were last logged on, the last week,
etc.
    </div>

    <tal:datetime define="today python:DateTime().earliestTime()">
    <select name="created:date"
        id="created"
        tabindex=""
        tal:attributes="tabindex tabindex/next;"
        tal:define="yesterday python:(today-1).Date();
            lastweek python:(today-7).Date();
            lastmonth python:(today-31).Date();
            ever string:1970/02/01 00:00:00 GMT;">
    <option value="#"
        tal:condition="not: isAnon"
        tal:attributes="value python:member.getProperty
    ('last_login_time')"
        i18n:translate="last_login">Last log-in</option>
    <option value="#" tal:attributes="value yesterday"
        i18n:translate="time_yesterday"> Yesterday </option>
    <option value="#" tal:attributes="value lastweek"
        i18n:translate="time_last_week"> Last week </option>
    <option value="#" tal:attributes="value lastmonth"
        i18n:translate="time_last_month"> Last month </option>
    <option value="#" tal:attributes="value ever" selected="selected"
        i18n:translate="time_ever"> Ever </option>
    </select>
    </tal:datetime>

    <input type="hidden" name="created_usage" value="range:min" />
</div>
```

Notice that this HTML box is a bit "fuzzy;" it does not require you to specify
exact dates, but asks you if you want objects created since yesterday, last week,
last month, or ever. These values are calculated in the **tal:define** block on the
<select> tag. Each value is an option on the following select list. Notice the
hidden input field in the last line. This is the special field that tells the catalog that

this is a minimum bounded range search. You can also provide a maximum bound or both to do "older than" searches or range searches within two dates.

Catalog Results

The catalog returns a sequence of results that match your search criteria (or no results at all). These results are called *records*, and each record points to the content object that matches the search criteria. Records are an important optimization, because if the catalog returned the objects themselves, it could be a very costly operation in terms of memory and database access.

The catalog returns records and not the objects themselves because retrieving an object from Zope's object database requires that the object be "awakened" by reading the object from the database file into memory. For one or two objects, this is not an expensive operation, but catalog queries can return many, many objects that match a query. If all of these objects were to be awakened from the database just to present search results to the user, catalog queries would be abnormally slow and consume lots of computer resources.

Because the catalog does not actually awaken the objects that its records point to, the catalog must have some way of keeping track of information in the record that is useful to you. For example, the description is often useful in search results, but without awakening the object, the description is usually inaccessible.

Metadata

Metadata solves this problem by keeping track of useful record information in metadata tables. Metadata tables simply store useful information about cataloged objects to be returned in records without awakening the objects to get that information. Metadata are usually small values, ids, short descriptions, author information, copyright, or other small bits of information that is useful to see in search results.

Warning: Think twice about including information in the catalog metadata. Any attribute which is defined as metadata is stored twice: once on the object to which it belongs, and once in the catalog. If you include metadata indiscriminately, you can double the size of your database.

Note that ZCatalog metadata is not the same as Dublin Core (DC) metadata. The DC standard is a well-known set of object attributes that all Plone objects support. ZCatalog metadata is used mostly for generating reports about search results without having to get that information out of the database from the object itself.

Metadata is managed using the **Metadata** tab on the ZCatalog. This is a simple form that lets you input the names of the metadata columns. Each name should match some attribute or method on your objects. When an object is cataloged, the value of this attribute or method is placed into the metadata table. When the record for that object is returned, the values in the record come from this table.

The Catalog is used in many places in Plone. Most of the portlets are, in fact, just special scripts and templates that get their results from the **portal_catalog**. In particular, topic objects create special "canned queries" of the catalog.

Topics

Plone folders are good for organizing content in one place, but sometimes you may want to organize the objects many different ways. A Plone topic lets you create an object that looks like a folder, but whose contents are really the result of catalog searches. Plone topics are really just "canned queries" to the **portal_catalog**. In other words, a topic is a pre-configured catalog query that builds the results of the topic.

The topic UI allows you to add and edit the criteria that build the topic collection. Additionally, topics can be nested, causing the outer criteria to apply in addition to the inner criteria. This allows you to build complex and powerful hierarchies of your objects that don't necessarily match the hierarchy of your site.

For example, you might want to create a topic that shows everything in your site that has the keyword "Inventory." This is easy to do by creating a topic that queries the **portal_catalog**'s `Subject` index.

1. Create a new topic called `SalesItems`.

2. On the **Add** screen, enter a name, title, and short description.

3. Select the **Inherit criteria** checkbox to acquire criteria from a topic above, or select the **Limit results** checkbox to limit the results to a specified number.

After adding the topic you will be taken to the new topic. Click on the new topic's **Criteria** tab, which is shown in Figure 4.5.

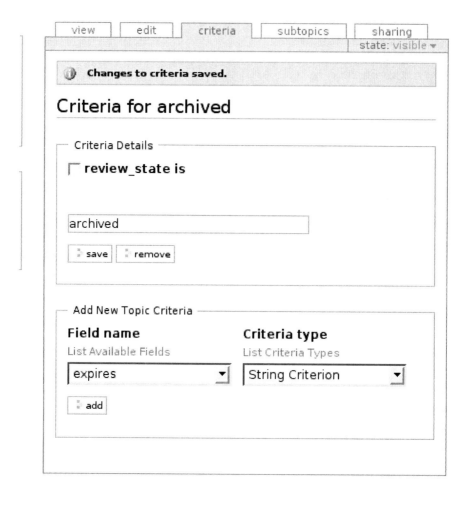

Figure 4.5: Adding criteria to a topic

This tab allows you to specify criteria for the contents of this topic. From the dropdown box, select one of the **portal_catalog**'s indexes, and select a type of match. For example, you can match text, an integer, or date exactly, and you can use "and" and "or" operators. You can only create one criterion per index -- you cannot, for example, create two criteria on the Creator index.

Create a new criterion on the Subject index, specify **exact text match**, and click **Add**. This will add the new criterion. On that page you can now specify the text value **Sales**. Now any item that contains the keyword "Sales" will show up in this topic. Since this may include a large number of items, click on the **Properties** tab of the topic and select the **Limit results** checkbox to specify a reasonable default number of items to show to the user.

The **Inherit criteria** property, when checked, causes the topic to inherit any criteria it may acquire from a topic above it. This is useful for creating hierarchies of topics where each node in the hierarchy's search results is narrowed by the topics above it.

For example, in the SalesItems topic, create an Invoices topic with the same criteria and the keyword "Invoice," but be sure to check the **Inherit criteria** box on the new Invoices topic. Now when you visit the URL **http://site/portal/SalesItems/Invoices**, you will see only those items that have the keywords of "Sales" *and* "Invoice." This is because the Invoices topic inherited the criteria of the SalesItem topic using a trick of acquisition.

Portlets

As you have seen, much of Plone can be customized through main_template, but this is just the overall layout of the page. If you want to customize some of the elements within the main_template you will need to customize some other templates in Plone.

Each portlet in Plone is defined in its own template with the prefix portlet_. There are other templates that are only for backwards compatibility and should not be used.

portlet_calendar.pt

One of the most interesting examples of a Plone portlet is the *calendar* portlet. It is an excellent example of using TAL to generate dynamic HTML tables.

portlet_events.pt

The *events* portlet is a simple portlet that displays a list of upcoming events. It performs a catalog query to get the events in question. Typically, you would customize this portlet either to change the structure of this list or to change the query itself.

portlet_favorites.pt

The *favorites* portlet displays a list of objects inside a member's "Favorites" folder, if one exists. Typically, you would customize this portlet either to change the structure of this list or to change the location of the "favorite" items.

portlet_login.pt

The *login* portlet displays a login box. This box is automatically displayed when an unauthenticated user visits the site (unless you have customized the site to hide the standard login box). You would have little reason to customize this portlet other than to change the structure of the login form.

portlet_navigation.pt

This portlet displays the navigation menu typically on the left of a Plone site. This portlet is parameterized by a number of properties that allow you to change how the navigation content is displayed. These properties are defined on the **navtree_properties** property sheet. See Table 4.6.

Table 4.6: navtree_properties Property Definitions

Property	Description	Default
showMyUserFolderOnly	This option tells Plone to only show the logged in user's member folder. Even if the user navigates to elsewhere on the site, only the home folder displays.	On
showFolderishSiblingsOnly	If selected, only other folders or folder-like objects display in the navigation box. This can be useful if you anticipate that folders will contain a great many objects. If not selected, all content displays.	On

Table 4.6: navtree_properties Property Definitions

Property	Description	Default
roleSeeUnpublishedContent	This option specifies a list of Roles that can see unpublished content in the navigation portlet. By default, the list is Manager, Reviewer and Owner.	
croppingLength	This option defines how long the names of navigation entries can be.	256.
idsNotToList	This option specifies a list of ids that should not be shown. This is useful for "hiding" content that should not show up in the navigation portlet.	None

This is probably some of the most complex TAL code in Plone, and may be replaced soon with something more user-friendly. For now, you should avoid customizing anything in this portlet that is not glaringly obvious to you.

portlet_news.pt

The *news* portlet displays recent news items. This list of items is generated by a catalog query, much like the **portal_events** portlet described above.

portlet_prefs.pt

This portlet displays a list of "configlets" that configure a user's personal preferences.

portlet_recent.pt

This portlet shows any recent content that has been published on the site. This list of recent content comes from a catalog query.

portlet_related.pt

This portlet shows content that is related to the current content being displayed. This list of related content comes from a keyword catalog query.

portlet_review.pt

This portlet displays a list of items that the current user can take action on. For example, if the user has the "Reviewer" role, this portlet will show any documents in a workflow state that are pending review.

File System Development

Even though TTW development can help you learn Plone, you should always develop serious web sites using file system development. This section shows you how to customize your site using file system development tools. Once you are familiar with these tools, you will see why file system development is so important. Most importantly, file system developers can take advantage of source control tools like Concurrent Versions System (CVS) or subversion (SVN) to manage their code as their projects evolve in time.

In addition to source control tools, many file system utilities and development tools are available, like **grep** and **find** and even higher-level tools like Interactive Development Environment (IDE) editors that you can use to develop Plone code. For example, advanced development editors like Emacs, Eclipse and Boa Constructor can manage file system code, and all are quite good at doing Plone file system development because they can understand both HTML and Python.

If you do not have an IDE editor that you commonly use, I recommend IDLE or Eclipse. IDLE is a simple Python editor that comes with Python itself, and Eclipse is a more serious cross-language IDE that has more support for advanced features like source control, and visualization tools for your code.

You can download the examples in this section from the PloneLive subversion repository at http://svn.plonelive.com/. This URL will point you to the various products and examples that you can download for this book. This chapter's examples are in the *PloneLive* directory on that site, and you can check them out from the following subversion URL: http://svn.ploneline.com/PloneLive/Products/PloneLive.

Creating a Product

You could, conceivably, directly edit the templates and files that come with Plone to change the look of the site, but that would be very dangerous, since you should never modify those files unless you are doing development on the Plone software itself. To make changes, ship them in a special package called a "Product" and invoke some configuration code inside that product to make the changes you require to your site (optional).

All of these actions mimic those that you would have done using the TTW interface, but instead of consisting of a series of clicks that change the database, your product will execute a sequence of Python code that makes those same changes.

Creating a Product that makes skin changes and customizations is just one of the things that you can do with file system development. In addition to cosmetic changes, you can define new content types with customized behavior. Various techniques for doing this are shown in *Chapters 5, 6*, and *7*.

Product Layout

Plone products come packaged in a folder named after the product. In the case of site customizations, you want to name this folder after something that represents your site. This example uses the name "PloneLive" to indicate that this product installs the PloneLive site changes into a Plone site.

The PloneLive folder must contain three other things:

▸ **An** *__init__.py* **file:** This file makes the PloneLive folder become a Python "package." This is necessary so that Python knows how to import the files defined in this package. For more information on Python packages, see the Python documentation (http://www.python.org/doc/).

▸ **A** *skins* **folder:** The *skins* folder is not technically required, but all products that have skins or change existing skins has this folder by convention. Here you will place any templates that your product provides or overrides.

▸ **An** *Extensions* **folder:** The *Extensions* folder contains any installation scripts or Zope *External Methods* that are used by the product. External Methods are documented in The Zope Book (http://www.zope.org/).

Skins

The folder that contains your skins must contain a folder for each of the layers within that skin. For the `PloneLive` skin, this will contain the following sub-directories:

▶ **plonelive_templates:** This layer contains all of the templates that PloneLive provides or overrides.

▶ **plonelive_images:** This layer contains images for the PloneLive sites.

▶ **plonelive_scripts:** This layer contains all of the scripts for the PloneLives sites.

Each directory holds one layer that will be registered with the skins tool when the installation script runs.

Initialization: The QuickInstaller

By placing your product package into a Zope's instance home's *Products* directory (which was explained in *Chapter 1*), you have made that product available to Zope and Plone. In order for your changes to take effect on any one Plone site object, you must execute an installation script. This process was described in *Chapter 2*.

Installation scripts are necessary because most products need to register either their types or their skins with the Plone portal. Based on the way the underlying CMF system is designed, these types and skins are registered into the Zope database, so an installation script needs to be called in order for these registrations to take place. Another reason for requiring an installation script to register a Plone product is that a single Zope instance may host multiple Plone sites that won't all share the same set of products.

An installation script is an External Method that initiates the changes you want to make to a Plone site object. This script is analogous to when you went through the object database making your own changes by clicking through the menus. Instead of doing that task every time you want to install a new site, this script automates that task for you.

Unfortunately, there is no easy way to record the changes you make as you click and dump them to a file system product. The FSDump product is available, but it does not handle incremental changes. It only dumps database changes to a file system, so if you want to make a site for production purposes, you should start with a file system-based product.

One problem with file system-based products is that it is more difficult to develop them interactively than it is to develop a TTW site. As you make major changes in the evolution of a file system-based product, you must re-load a product often and make other changes that may break your objects. This is the trade-off with TTW development: file system development has more risks but better long-term rewards.

Distributing Your Product

Once you have developed your product, you can distribute it by zipping up the product's source directory. Be sure to remove any useless files, especially the .pyc files that the Python interpreter creates for each of your .py files. If you give a product with stale .pyc files to users, they may receive spurious errors with incorrect path and traceback information. These files are the compiled versions of their more readable source brethren, and they are only an optimization to prevent the compiler from compiling the same file over and over again, even if it has not changed. There is no need to ship these files; your users do not need them.

Once you have cleaned up your product and tested it, it is best to package it in a *tarball* - a file that has been archived using the **tar** program and zipped up using the **gzip** program. On Windows, you can create these files with the WinZip tool, or alternatively you can package your file as a .zip file using an archiver like pkzip or WinZip. Note that most UNIX users will be able to open a .zip file, so you can use either .tgz or .zip for distributing products.

On UNIX, you can issue the command in Listing 4.11 from your Products directory:

Listing 4.11

```
$> tar -czvf PloneLive-0.1.tgz PloneLive/
```

This command will create a new file named *PloneLive-0.1.tgz*. Of course, you can name it anything you want. Instruct your users to simply unzip that file in the *Products* directory of their Plone instance home and to run the Quick Installer utility to install the product.

Summary

This chapter covered a large area of Plone functionality, much of it Zope-specific, that is commonly used throughout many web applications based on Plone and Zope. These techniques and features will be used throughout this book and in the example applications that can be downloaded from Plone-Live.com. A brief summary of these concepts include:

▸ Skins and Layers

▸ Customizing Standard Plone Skin Features

▸ Customizing Plone Cascading Style Sheets

▸ Cataloging and Searching

▸ Creating a File System Skin Product

Chapter 5 will move to a new and important area of Zope and Plone: Security and the Security API.

Membership and Security

Author: Munwar Shariff

Zope has a powerful security system that prevents users from calling methods or accessing objects for which they do not have permission. Plone uses this security system to provide a flexible and configurable membership system for controlling the content, workflow, search, and security policies. This chapter explains the framework behind this membership and security system.

Introduction to Zope's Security API

Chapters 2 and *3* introduced you to most of the high-level security concepts of Zope and Plone. Serious developers must be familiar with Zope's security API (Application Program Interface). This API is well-designed and very easy to use.

Zope has a powerful security system that prevents users from calling methods or accessing objects for which they do not have permission. Python's highly dynamic nature allows you to wrap objects with a security context, which allows site administrators to specify a fine-grained security policy.

The Zope security framework is based on the principle that users shall take no action without explicit permission from the security framework. All other actions are denied. Users will receive an error if they try to access a Zope object for which they do not have permission.

The security framework decides who can do what in Zope. It bases these decisions upon the security policy for the site. You define the security policy according to your needs. For example, if you only want users with a certain role to view a folder in Zope, then you give only that role the View permission. This was explained in detail in *Chapter 3*.

Security and Acquisition Context

When a user attempts to access an object, Zope first checks that user to see whether he has permission to access the object. Often, a user's permission depends upon on the *context* in which the user attempts to access the object. For example, a user may call a Python script in the context of a certain folder, but may not have permission in all other cases.

The security context that determines a user's permissions is based on the acquisition context. Based on the acquisition context, Zope compares an object against a security policy that is defined by the **Permissions** tab on every folder, as well as all the security declarations in the code, which defines how permissions pertain to methods or classes. Thus, if an object is used in the context of a folder, it acquires that folder's security policy. This can happen more than once if an object is nested inside several folders, and each folder defines its own policy or acquires the policy from the folder containing it.

Low-Level Security, Context, and Wrappers

Zope's security system is based on *security contexts*. A user accesses an object within a certain context. This context depends on how the user accessed the object. This is important in Zope because objects can be stored in one place (objects in the ZODB are always stored as attributes of a parent object that contains them) but used from another place using the mechanism of *acquisition*, which was discussed above.

For example, you have two Document objects in the root of your Plone site called A and B. You would access object A through the web with a URL such as http://localhost:8080/site/A (assuming your Plone id is "site"). In this case, the security context consists of only the Zope root object, the Plone "site" object, and A. If you access object B via the path http://localhost:8080/site/A/B, the security context consists of object B *in the context of* object A.

Security contexts work by creating invisible, nested wrappers around objects. In the above example, object A is wrapped in a security context wrapper. This is the security context when the user accesses A directly. When you access object B via the path "A/B," B is wrapped in a security context, which is also wrapped by the security context of A. This continues up to the Zope root object. This is known as "nesting."

Nested security context is essential, because while B may grant many permissions, A may be very restrictive. In this case, you want to keep A's restrictions in place because they override B's permissiveness. In other words, A is the "parent" of B in the acquisition context.

By wrapping all of your objects, Zope can control access to the objects. Now you know who your users are (because you have authenticated them), and you can control what they are authorized to do. If a user tries to access an object without permission in the acquisition context of the object, the security wrapper raises an error and aborts the unauthorized attempt.

TTW vs. File System Code

Only "through the web" (TTW) code is constrained by the security system. That is, the system differentiates between code that comes from a "trusted" source and code that comes from a "distrusted" source.

In restricted execution mode, you are only allowed to import a small set of well-known Python modules. You cannot import most of the Python library because Zope does not grant access to these modules. This is for good security reasons; since that module code does not exist, the Python library code is not considered "safe."

Therefore, to allow access to other modules in Zope's restricted execution environment, you must declare any modules that you wish to use. By declaring these modules, you are identifying them as safe to use in TTW code. Keep in mind that *you* must make this determination. For example, if you allow your TTW code to execute in the *os* (Operating System) module, you are granting that code the ability to do common **os** functions, like reading and writing files; you probably don't want this kind of security risk.

Tip: To allow access to other modules in Zope, refer to the module_access_examples.py and README.txt files in your ZOPE_HOME/lib/python/Products/PythonScripts folder.

The Security API

The security API has two parts: the *declarative* API and the *authorization* API. The declarative API declares the permissions that protect your objects, and the authorization API checks to see whether a user has permission for a given object.

ClassSecurityInfo

Objects that interact with Zope's security machinery must declare the permissions that protect their methods and attributes. Some common ClassSecurityInfo API methods are listed below:

▶ declarePublic(): This method can be passed any number of strings that are public methods on ClassSecurityInfo. Public methods can be called at any time, and are unconstrained by the security system. Be careful using this method, as it can create holes in your security settings.

▶ declarePrivate(*names): Like declarePublic(), this method can be passed any number of strings that are private methods on ClassSecurityInfo. Private methods cannot be called by restricted code (like a Python script or page template). Private methods can still be called, like any other Python object, in unrestricted code.

▶ declareProtected(permission, *names): This method takes an initial string argument that defines a permission. All following arguments are string names of methods on this object that are protected by the given permission. This is the most commonly used method on the ClassSecurityInfo interface and associates a permission with a method.

SecurityManager

The security manager class provides authorization methods that allow you to check the permissions of a given user with a given security context. Usually, this is used in file system code to check if the current user has permission to take a certain action. Since Zope checks security automatically, these methods are usually necessary only in a handful of circumstances. For example, the Verbose-eSecurity product (see *Chapter 2*) overrides these methods to provide a detailed explanation of security access errors. Two of the most common SecurityManager API methods are listed below:

▶ validate(accessed, container, name, value, context, roles): This is a low-level method that validates access to an object through the security policy by providing a specific context object, such as the 'context' value in a page template.

▶ checkPermission(permission, object): This method checks if the current security context allows the given permission on the object. This is a commonly used method and is the standard way to check permissions from Python code.

RoleManager

Classes that wish to manage roles and permissions subclass the RoleManager class. For example, folders inherit from RoleManager. Anything that has a **Permissions** tab should subclass from RoleManager. Three of the most common RoleManager API methods are listed below:

▶ manage_role(role_to_manage, permissions): This method sets the given permissions on the role. This is equivalent to checking the various permissions for the given role on the security ZMI tab for the given role manager.

▶ manage_permission(permission, roles): This method sets the roles for the given permission. This is equivalent to checking the various roles for the given permissions on the security ZMI tab for the given role manager.

▶ permissionsOfRole(role): This method returns a list of dictionaries that describe all of the permissions with respect to this role. Each list item has an item['name'] that is the name of the permission and item['selected'] that is either 'SELECTED' if the permission is checked or '' if the permissions is not checked.

▶ rolesOfPermission(permission): This method returns a list of dictionaries that describe all of the roles with respect to this permission. Each list item has an item['name'] that is the name of the role and item['selected'] that is either 'SELECTED' if the role is checked or '' if the role is not checked.

Users and User Management

You can use Zope user objects to discover information about the current user, such as the user name and assigned roles. These methods can present feedback information to your users or provide other user management interfaces. Two common API methods are listed below:

▶ getUserName(): This method returns the name of the current user.

▶ hasRole(role): This method returns true if the user has the given role. You should not use this method as a rule, since it "short circuits" the security machinery; it checks only for the presence of a role, and doesn't pay attention to the security settings of specific objects or methods. To check whether your user should be able to access something, do it by permission, with the string AccessControl.getSecurityManager().checkPermission (permission).

In Zope, user objects are stored in user folders. A user folder is any acl_users object (see *Chapter 2*) inside Zope that implements the user folder API. This name is hardcoded into Zope's AccessControl module (do not use any user folder name other than acl_users). Two of the API methods are listed below:

▸ getUserNames(): This method returns a list of all of the user names defined in this folder.

▸ getUserById(id): This method returns a user object that corresponds to the given id.

If you want to store your users in a different kind of user folder, it must generally provide these same methods to work as a user folder. Several other types of user folders use different authentication mechanisms.

CatalogUserFolder

The CatalogUserFolder (CUF) is an example user folder that can add a significant performance improvement to sites with very large memberships. A standard Zope user folder keeps all of its users in a PersistentMapping object. This object is a persistent object (that is, stored in the ZODB) that is a mapping, meaning it works for the most part like a Python dictionary.

The problem with PersistentMapping is that the *whole* object must be loaded into memory from the database, even if you are accessing just one of its items. So, anytime one user is fetched, they are all fetched. This may not be a problem if you have less than one hundred members or so, but gets to be more and more of a performance drag as the mapping gets larger and larger.

For very large collections of users, it is more efficient to keep them in a persistent data structure that does not require the entire membership being loaded in from the database just to get one user. ZODB provides such an object called a BTree.

A BTree is also a mapping, so it works essentially the same as a PersistentMapping, but instead of loading the whole collection when it's accessed, only a small portion of the BTree needs to be loaded. This saves a lot of memory, and the ZODB caching mechanism can be more effectively utilized, caching only active members and not loading the rest.

The CUF also has an internal ZCatalog object that indexes all of the user objects. Currently, it field indexes the id and text indexes the user name of a user object (in the case of plain Zope user objects, these are the same thing). For more information on the ZCatalog, see *The Zope Book, 2.7 edition.*

Installing CUF is easy. Just drop it into your *Products* directory like any other Zope product. This will provide you with a new item in the ZMI add list called Catalog User Folder. You can add a CUF to any folder in your Zope site, and it will act and look exactly like a plain Zope user folder.

The CUF product also comes with a migration External Method that allows you to take a plain Zope user folder and replace it with a CUF by doing a one-time migration. Before running the method, you will have a plain folder; after running the method, you will have a CUF instead that contains the exact user data that the folder it replaced contained. You only need to run this migration once, and your application will continue to run with the CUF.

CUF is licensed under the ZPL 2.1 and developed specifically as example software for this book, and to propose a possible solution to CMF's standard user folder scalability problems without having to move to a much more complicated system like LDAP. CUF is available from the PloneLive.com site or from the CIGNEX public SVN (https://svn.cignex.com/public/).

Plone Membership Framework

Traditional membership systems address two basic criteria: Authentication (who can access) and Authorization (what they can do).

In a typical content management system, *end users* need to have a membership system to access premium content, to set their preferences, and to receive notifications and alerts. Members of the web site can collaborate with other members by submitting forms, sharing documents, and sharing ideas via discussion forums. Members can secure their personal data and documents, and they can selectively share them with other members. Members can control and follow the business process through a workflow. Members can have many such benefits.

In a typical content management system, *content administrators* need to have a membership system to restrict access to certain data (for certain people), to delegate content management responsibilities, and to have ownership of the content. Content administrators can make people responsible for owning the content and keeping it current. Content administrators can define a workflow process to automate the existing business process. Content administrators can have many such benefits, based on the nature of the web site.

The Zope user framework handles only Authentication and Authorization. The Plone membership framework extends this with member metadata, workspaces, and so forth, and provides a set of tools to configure and control the membership. These tools are described briefly in *Chapter 2*. Figure 5.1 explains how various tools communicate with each other to provide a sophisticated Membership framework in Plone.

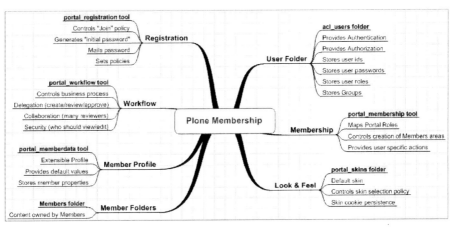

Figure 5.1: Plone Membership Framework

Managing Groups

Zope does not support the notion of "groups," but Plone does. *Groups* are a logical categorization of members who have the same permissions in common. A role is a collection of permissions. You can assign roles to a group. A user assigned to a specific role has different permissions than another user with a different role assignment. Groups provide a common workspace for a group of users in the web site. To grant privileges to the workspace, the site manager puts users into the group with the necessary permissions. By default, Plone does not come with any groups, so you must create them.

For example, in order to manage your Plone site, you may add a group called *SiteManagers*, give it the *Manager* role, and add the managing Plone members to that group.

In order to support groups, Plone uses a special user folder called the Group User Folder (GRUF). GRUF supports the group data that Plone uses to implement its sharing architecture. GRUF looks like a standard acl_users folder, but it contains two *additional* user folders for the users and the groups, respectively. From Zope's perspective, Plone groups are just another user, so you must treat groups as users by assigning roles to them. In fact, in Plone, you can *only* assign roles to groups. To assign a role to a member, you must create a group, assign the role to the group, and put the member in the group.

From the perspective of the GRUF implementation, a group is a special role for a user. Listing 5.1 is the structure of a typical GRUF layout:

Listing 5.1

```
- acl_users (GroupUserFolder)
  |
  |-- Users (GroupUserFolder-related class)
  | |
  | |-- acl_users (UserFolder or derived class)
  |
  |-- Groups (GroupUserFolder-related class)
  | |
  | |-- acl_users (UserFolder or derived class)
```

Within GRUF, you can *look up* users in more than one user source, but they're *stored* in only one user source. A source can be any valid Zope user folder-derived object (for example, LDAPUserFolder, CatalogUserFolder (discussed above), and SimpleUserFolder, in addition to the standard Zope user folder).

To change membership sources, visit your Plone site object in ZMI. From the **Contents** view, click the **acl_users** folder (Group-aware user folder), then click the **Sources** tab. Add users and groups via the Plone interface. This will ensure that member and group workspaces are created, and roles are assigned as appropriate.

Audit Settings

The *Audit* management tab tracks how the site security is applied. This allows you to have a precise abstract of the security settings for a small set of permissions, with the values of Read or Write. This management tab won't change anything in your security settings; it simply displays information.

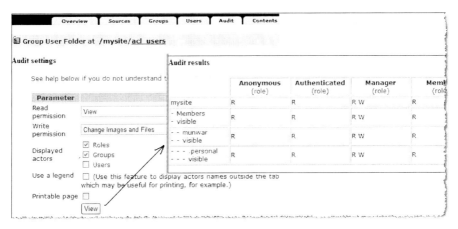

Figure 5.2: Group User Folder's Audit tab

Managing Roles and Permissions

A role is a collection of permissions. Users are assigned roles, and Plone objects (or specific methods or attributes of objects) are protected by permissions. The Zope security system works by checking the permissions (which users have by virtue of their roles) against the permissions that are required to access the object or its methods or attributes.

Zope Roles

In the Zope framework, every user who visits a web object (URL) is assigned one or more roles. This implies that every user will have a minimum of one role assigned (either *Anonymous* or *Authenticated*). The Zope framework supports the following four predefined roles, which you cannot delete:

▸ **Anonymous**: This role is automatically assigned to the user who has not logged into the site. You cannot assign this role to any user manually.

▸ **Authenticated**: This role is automatically assigned to the user who has logged into the site. You cannot assign this role to any user manually.

▸ **Owner**: This user is the creator (owner) of the current object that is being accessed. The object stores the ownership information. This is always a *local role* because it's only relevant in the context of the specific objects that the user has created. If you assign the Owner role to a user, it becomes meaningless because it stops distinguishing between objects that they have created and object created by others.

▸ **Manager**: This user has logged into the site and has administrator access to the site. Users with this role can create, configure, and control the Plone site. This is the most powerful role, and you must be very careful when assigning this role to any user. Generally, site visitors or users of your web application should not have the Manager role. This role is closely tied to the through-the-web administration of Zope. It's less confusing and tidier to create new roles that are a natural fit to your site, rather than trying to bend the built-in Zope roles to the needs of your application.

▸ The Zope framework also supports the following special assigned roles, which are not visible in the security tab of any object.

▸ **Local Role**: Local roles allow you to give particular users extra roles in the context of an object, in addition to the roles they already have. You can access local roles from the Security tab by following the *local roles* link.

▸ **Proxy Role**: Proxy roles allow you to control the access that a script has. Proxy roles replace the roles of the user who is executing the script. This can be used to both expand and limit access to resources. Python scripts in ZMI contain a *Proxy* tab.

▸ **Executable**: Ownership is most important for Zope objects that execute content supplied through the web, such as scripts and SQL methods. The abilities of these executable objects are constrained by the abilities of the object's owner, as well as the user causing the object to execute from a Zope security point of view. In other words, an executable cannot perform operations that its owner could not perform directly.

Plone Roles

In addition to the four predefined roles supported by Zope (Anonymous, Authenticated, Owner, and Manager), Plone provides the following two roles:

▶ **Member**: All users who join the site are assigned the *Member* role. Members can create content in their own folders and set their own preferences. Usually, users with the Member role are content creators.

▶ **Reviewer**: This role allows users to publish and reject content submitted by members. When reviewers log in, they will see a pending message in their personal bar or items awaiting approval or rejection for publication.

Adding New Roles

When you are designing the web application, you will need more roles for security and control purposes. Most administrators create new roles based on organizational requirements and the designations of the people who are going to use the web site. For example, an "HR Manager" role would control the Jobs section of a web site. Similarly, a "PR Manager" role would control the News Items of a web site.

To add a new role, go to the ZMI of your Plone site object, click the *Security* tab, and scroll to the bottom of the screen. A form is provided to add or remove a role.

Instead of creating new roles, you can achieve the security and control by sharing the folder with certain users (*local roles*) and by using *guarded permissions* for workflow. These techniques are explained later in this chapter in *Securing Folders* and *Securing Workflow* sections. Adding too many roles will affect the performance of the web site because the Zope security framework checks for user roles to provide access to an object. Be sure you have a strong design requirement to add new roles.

Permissions

Permissions are simply arbitrary strings. These strings can be associated with objects or specific attributes or methods of objects. You can use any permission to protect anything; there is no necessary connection between a specific permission string and a method or action. When you click on the Security tab of any folder or any object in your Plone site, you will see a long list of permissions. The most important ones are described in Table 5.1.

Table 5.1: Permission Definitions in Plone

Permission Name	Description
Access contents information	This grants the ability to access an object's metadata and content. Users must have the View permission to view the object. If a user has the View permission, but not the *Access contents information* permission, on an object, the user can find that object in search results but cannot access the complete content of the object.
Add portal content	This grants the ability to add instances of the existing portal content types to the site (such as Document, News Item, etc.).
Add portal folders	This grants the ability to add folders to the site.
Add portal member	This grants the ability to join the Plone site and become a Member.
Copy or Move	This grants the ability to cut/copy/paste objects from one folder to another.
Delete objects	This grants the ability to delete an object from a folder.
List folder contents	This grants the ability to list the content of a folder.
List portal members	This grants the ability to list all the members of the site.
Modify portal content	This grants the ability to edit and update portal content information.
Reply to item	This grants the ability to reply to discussable content.
Request review	This grants the ability to the content creators to submit the content for approval.
Review portal content	This grants the ability to the content approvers to review and publish the content.
View	This grants the ability to view the object. This is the most important permission to control.

Note: Refer to *Zope Developer Guide* to learn more about Zope security and permissions (http://zope.org/Documentation/Books/ZDG/current/AppendixA.stx).

Default Plone Security

Table 5.2 contains the default security set by a Plone site upon creation. You can check the security by clicking the *Security* tab in ZMI. Table 5.2 lists important permissions for your reference. Some of them are derived from the parent(s) (one or more Zope folders, up to the Zope root folder), based on the *Acquire Permission Settings* check box. If any of the acquired permissions have been changed in a parent folder, these settings may be different. In Table 5.2, "X" indicates that the role has the listed permission, and an empty column indicates that the role does not have the listed permission. Roles are Anonymous (A), Owner (O), Member (M), Reviewer (R), and Manager (Mgr)

Table 5.2: Default Plone Security

Permission	A	O	M	R	Mgr
Access contents information *(acquired)*	X	X	X	X	X
Add portal content *(acquired)*		X			X
Add portal folders *(acquired)*		X			X
Add portal member *(acquired)*	X	X	X	X	X
Copy or Move *(acquired)*	X	X	X	X	X
Delete objects *(acquired)*		X			X
FTP access *(acquired)*		X			X
List folder contents *(acquired)*		X			X
List portal members *(acquired)*			X		X
List undoable changes *(acquired)*			X		X
Manage properties *(acquired)*		X			X
Modify portal content *(acquired)*					X
Reply to item *(acquired)*			X		X
Request review *(acquired)*		X			X
Review portal content				X	X
Set own password			X	X	X
Set own properties			X	X	X

Table 5.2: Default Plone Security

Undo changes *(acquired)*		X			X
Use external editor			X	X	X
View *(acquired)*	X	X	X	X	X
View management screens *(acquired)*		X			X

From Table 5.2, you can see that Anonymous users can access your site (*Access contents information*), see the content (*View*), join (*Add portal member*), and become a member of your web site. The Reviewer role has additional permissions, such as *Review Portal Content*. The Manager role has all permissions, including a great many not shown above. Most Zope and Plone products define permissions of their own that will extend the list of available permissions.

Note: Roles and permissions are case-sensitive. Be sure to use proper names in your scripts to check roles or permissions programmatically.

Securing the Portal

Permissions and roles structure the interaction of your visitors with the site. Having distinct roles makes it easy for site members to accomplish their tasks efficiently, without having to wade through masses of irrelevant content or options. Additionally, the security configuration must protect the portal from abuse. The battle between hackers and security professionals has moved from the network layer to the web applications themselves. Hackers are using tricky maneuvers like SQL injection, cross site scripting, cookie poisoning, and authentication hijacking to gain access to and control of web servers. If you are in charge of designing or administering a public web site, you must embrace the fact that you cannot trust your users. To be on the safer side, you might extend this concept to an extranet or even an intranet.

By default, Plone is configured to allow the following actions. They all have implications for the site load and for privacy, so you might have to change the configuration as required.

▶ Anonymous users can search for members of your web site.

▶ Anonymous users can search for content on the web site. Using the *advanced search form* (http://your-site-url/search_form), Anonymous users can find out keywords, content types, and authors of your web site.

▶ Without your permission, Anonymous users can join your site, become a *Member* of the site, and create a password.

▶ Once Anonymous users become members of the site, they can create (upload) content in their member areas of the web site.

▶ When new content is added to the site (such as News, Documents, Files, etc.), it is *visible* to everyone without being approved.

▶ When new content is added to the site, it is searchable by anyone.

The subsequent sections explain how you can control the above default settings of your Plone site to make your site more secure.

Disable Join Feature

To create any content in Plone, you must first log in. By default, Plone allows users to *join* your site and create their own user name and password. To stop Anonymous users from joining your site, select the *Authenticated* and *Manager* roles for the *Add portal member* permission and deselect the *Acquire* check box.

By default, the **join** form (located at *portal_skins/plone_forms/join_form*) is visible to Anonymous users, even if you turn off the *Add portal member* permission. However, the Plone framework will not allow users to join the web site. If you want to change the form to provide a message to all the users who want to join your web site, you must customize and edit the join_form.

Control Password Policy

In some situations, you might allow users to *join* your web site, but they must provide a valid e-mail id to ensure that they're authentic users. By default, users can choose their own password when registering to the web site. You can define the password policy in such a way that the Plone framework will create the initial (random) password and e-mail it to the user. If the user provided a valid e-mail id, only that person will receive the initial password.

Figure 5.3 explains how to set the password policy for your web site. Click on the **plone setup** link in the top menu; then click on the **Portal Settings** link. Under **Password policy,** choose the **Generate and e-mail member's initial password** option button.

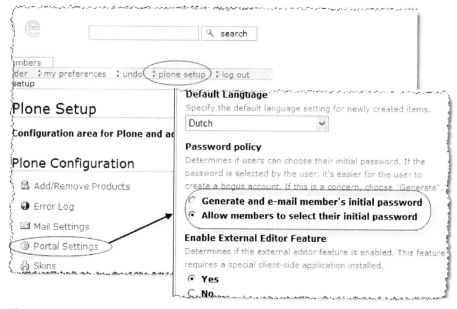

Figure 5.3: Control password policy

After making the changes, the join form looks completely different and doesn't allow users to choose their initial password.

Warning: A vandal could abuse this to bombard others with Plone e-mail and to bloat the Plone server with spurious member objects. The only way to make a Plone site (or any site) secure is to remove the power plug. Everything else is a trade-off between usability and security.

Tip: To change the content of an e-mail message, customize the *registered_notify_template.dtml* template. You can see all the templates used in your web site by going to the *portal_skins/plone_templates* folder of your Plone site from ZMI.

Limit plone_forms

Most of the generic forms used in the web site are in the *portal_skins/plone_forms* folder of your Plone site. To change certain forms, copy them to the *custom* folder and edit them as needed.

Certain sensitive forms are visible to Anonymous users, such as mail_password_form, join_form, member_search_form. To hide sensitive forms from Anonymous users, copy them to the *custom* folder and secure them by granting the View permission only to Authenticated users and the Manager.

Help

The Plone framework provides a placeholder for you to add online help for your web site. You can find out whether you have implemented the skins (added online help) by typing the following URL, as shown in Figure 5.4:

http://<your-portal-url>/help

Be sure to customize this form and provide some valuable information. Secure the form to display sensitive information to members.

Figure 5.4: Plone Help Skin

Securing Folders

The most basic Zope security pattern is to define a global security policy on the root folder and acquire this policy everywhere. Then, as needed, you can adjust the policy deeper in the object hierarchy to augment the global policy. Try to limit the number of places where you override the global policy. If you find that you have to make changes in a number of places, consider consolidating the objects in those separate locations into the same folder so that you can make the security settings in one place.

Folder Permissions

Typically, you would group similar content using a folder. To secure the folder, go to that folder and click on the Security tab in the ZMI. Deny the View and Access contents information permissions to the Anonymous role. That way, users who haven't logged in won't be able to access anything in that folder.

Here is a sample scenario. You have two roles defined in your web site: *JobsCreator* and *JobsAdmin*. You want people with the *JobsCreator* role to create all the documents related to Jobs in your web site. Similarly, you want people with the *JobsAdmin* role to review and approve the documents related to Jobs. One way to implement this requirement is to create a folder called *Jobs* within your web site and secure it by setting the required permissions as shown in Table 5.3.

Table 5.3 lists the important permissions. An "X" indicates that the check box is checked (role has the listed permission), and an empty cell indicates that the check box is not checked (role does not have the listed permission). For all permissions listed below, uncheck the *Acquire Permission Settings* (APS) check box. Roles are JobsCreator (JC), JobsAdmin (JA), Owner (O), Member (M), Reviewer (R), and Manager (Mgr).

Table 5.3: Folder Permissions

Permission	APS	JC	JA	O	M	R	Mgr
Access contents information	X						
Add portal content		X				X	
Add portal folders		X			X		
Delete objects			X		X		
List folder contents	X	X			X		
Modify portal content			X		X		
Request review				X			
Review portal content		X			X		

Manager has full access to your folder. No one except those with the *JobsCreator* role can add content to this folder. *JobsCreator* can modify or delete the content that he created.

With the security settings above, there are two things that *JobsAdmin* can do and *JobsCreator* cannot do: adding folders (*Add portal folders*) and publishing the content (*Review portal content*). The *Review portal content* permission will allow any particular role to approve and publish the content within that folder and sub-folders. This is explained in the *Securing Workflow* section of this chapter.

For a given content object, permissions can change, based on the workflow state of the content and parent folder's permissions (such as *Access Contents Information*, *Modify Portal Content*, or *View*).

Tip: Don't turn off the View permission for the site root. That will prevent Anonymous users from viewing the login page.

Sharing (Local Roles)

The Plone framework allows you to collaborate with other content contributors. You can grant others the ability to add and modify content in a folder that you own or manage by giving them roles specific to the folder and its sub-folders.

To give another content contributor *local roles*, navigate to a folder where they require additional permissions and click on the **Sharing** tab. This takes you to the *folder_localrole_form*, where you can assign additional roles to or remove roles from users. To find a user to whom you will assign additional local roles, enter the user name or e-mail address into the **Search Term** field. Be sure to select the drop-down option that corresponds to the search term you have entered (for example, if you choose to search for a user by e-mail address, select **E-mail Address** from the **Search by** drop-down list).

Click the **Search** button to retrieve a list of users matching your query. Select the check box next to the appropriate users. Select the role you'd like to give them from the **Role to Assign** drop-down list. Click the **Assign local roles to selected users** button to complete the process.

Note: Setting the permissions on a folder or any content object is fragile. If the object's workflow state changes, the permissions will be reset to whatever is configured for the destination workflow state. It's more manageable to handle security in terms of workflow.

Securing Workflow

Even though you secure your portal and folders, the content inside these folders can be accessible to Anonymous users. The best way to secure the content on your web site is by securing your workflow.

In your web site, the content objects of a given content type will be associated with a workflow (explained in detail in *Chapter 3*). The portal_workflow tool handles this association. Workflows are "state machines," each representing the life cycle of a given family of content types, and specifying the "workflow actions" that are possible in any phase of the life cycle. Currently, the main workflow engine used by Plone is *DCWorkflow*. Security is handled by manipulating the permissions on objects as they enter different workflow states.

Set Initial State

When new content is added to the site (such as News Item, Document, File, etc.), it is *visible* to everyone without approval. That means anyone (including Anonymous users) can access your content without logging into your site. This is because the default workflow for Plone is plone_workflow. Its initial workflow state is *visible* (to everyone), as shown in Figure 5.5. An asterisk (*) marks the initial state.

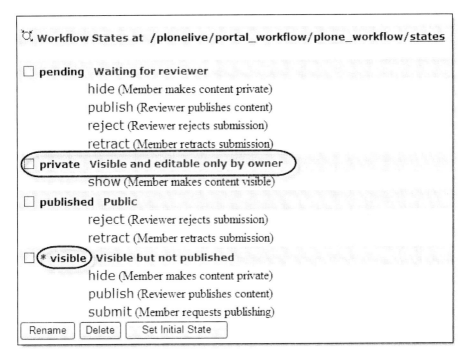

Figure 5.5: Workflow - Set Initial State

To modify workflow settings, go to portal_workflow in ZMI, click on the **Contents** tab, click on the **plone_workflow (Default Workflow [Plone])** link, and click on the **States** tab.

You can set the initial workflow state to *private* by selecting the **private** check box and clicking on the **Set Initial State** button. Now, when the content is created, it will be in the *private* state, and visible only to the owner. The owner can then submit the content for publishing. Once the content is published, it is visible to everyone.

Warning: Be very careful while changing the default settings of your workflow, as it will affect the security of your web site.

Control Permissions

As you are already aware, security is handled by manipulating the permissions on objects as they enter different workflow states. By default, *plone_workflow* changes the following four permissions, as shown in Figure 5.6:

▶ Access contents information

▶ Change portal events

▶ Modify portal content

▶ View

Figure 5.6: Permissions managed by workflow

The permissions listed on the **Permissions** tab will be modified on the object when it enters different workflow states. You can add permissions by using the **Add a managed permission** drop-down list. Similarly, you can remove permissions from the list.

To know the permissions set for the *visible* state, click on the **States** tab, click on the **visible** state, and click on the **Permissions** tab. Figure 5.7 shows the form.

Another way to control security for the *visible* state is to remove the *Access contents information* and *View* permissions for *Anonymous* and add those permissions to *Member*. Now, when the content is created, it will be visible only to members of your web site, not everyone.

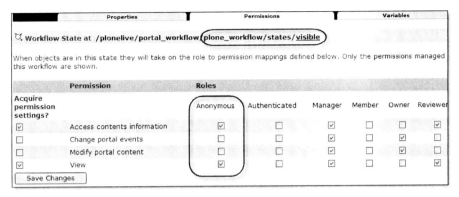

Figure 5.7: Permissions set for Visible state

The new workflow security settings are applicable only to the objects that will go through the workflow transitions in the future. The security will not be changed for the objects that have already gone through the workflow transitions. To make the new workflow security to take global effect immediately, go to the portal_workflow tool, scroll to the bottom of the screen, and click on the **Update security settings** button.

Set Guards

As explained in the previous sections of this chapter, users with the *Review portal content* permission on content can publish the content. This is because the *publish* transition of plone_workflow has a guard with the *Review portal content* permission. Guards determine whether the current user can perform a particular workflow transition on content, based on the combination of permissions, roles, or expressions.

In the previous *Securing Folders* section, an example of the *JobsAdmin* role had the *Review portal content* permission. This is to allow users with the *JobsAdmin* role to review and publish the content in the *Jobs* folder. If you want the users with the *JobsAdmin* role to review and publish the content in the entire web site, you might consider using the *JobsAdmin* role as guard for the publish transition of your workflow.

Securing Search

You need to secure your search along with your content. An attacker would not be able to read your files directly, but the search results contain some metadata about your files -- specifically, the Title and part of the Description. For example, if you had an unsecured file with a list of web passwords, an attacker might be able to read some of those passwords. The following sections describe some tools you can use to secure your search functionality.

portal_catalog

The **portal_catalog** tool (which is based on Zope's ZCatalog) is the search engine of your Plone web site. When compared to other commercial search engines, portal_catalog might not be the fastest, but it comes with the following two important features:

▸ **Real time search**: The moment you add or update the content, the application will update the catalog, and the content is searchable. You don't have to run special tools to index the updated content of your web site.

▸ **Secure search**: Your search engine is aware of your content security. If two users with different roles search for the same word, they could get different search results based on what they are allowed to see.

By default, new content is searchable by Anonymous users (without logging in). To understand the explanation given in this paragraph, see Figure 5.8 and Figure 5.9. When you add content, it is in *visible* state. When the content is in visible state, the plone_workflow sets the View permission on that content to Anonymous, Manager, and Reviewer roles. The portal_catalog stores the roles and users who have View permission on this content in an index called *allowedRolesAndUsers*. It displays this content in the search results only to the users and roles listed in *allowedRolesAndUsers*.

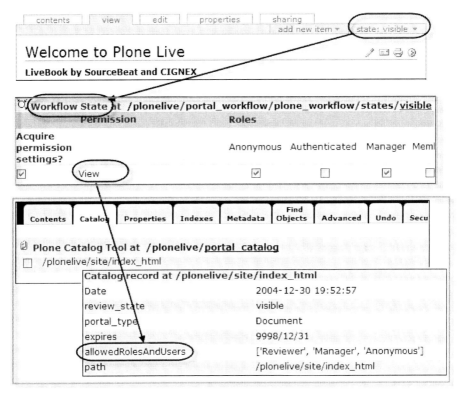

Figure 5.8: Portal_catalog allowedRolesAndUsers

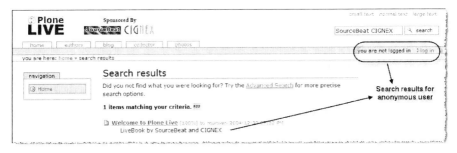

Figure 5.9: Search results for Anonymous user

Be sure the View permission and local roles for your content are set properly to secure your search results.

member_search_form

By default, a Plone web site allows Anonymous users to search for members on the web site. To stop Anonymous users from searching your site's list of members, select the *Authenticated* and *Manager* roles for the *List portal members* permission, and deselect the *Acquire* check box.

Another way to restrict users is to customize *member_search_form* and *member_search_results* (http://<your site url>/member_search_results) forms. Copy the forms from the *portal_skins/plone_forms/* folder to the *custom* folder using the **Customize** button, and secure the form by the granting View permissions to Authenticated users.

search_form

By default, a Plone web site allows Anonymous users to search for content on the web site. To prevent Anonymous users from searching your site, select the *Authenticated* and *Manager* roles for the *Search ZCatalog* permission and deselect the *Acquire* check box.

Even if you secured the search, Anonymous users can discover keywords, content types, and authors of your web site using the *advanced search form* (http://<your-site-url>/search_form). To restrict users, you must customize this form. Copy the form from *portal_skins/plone_forms/search_form* to the *custom* folder, and secure the form by granting the View permissions to Authenticated users.

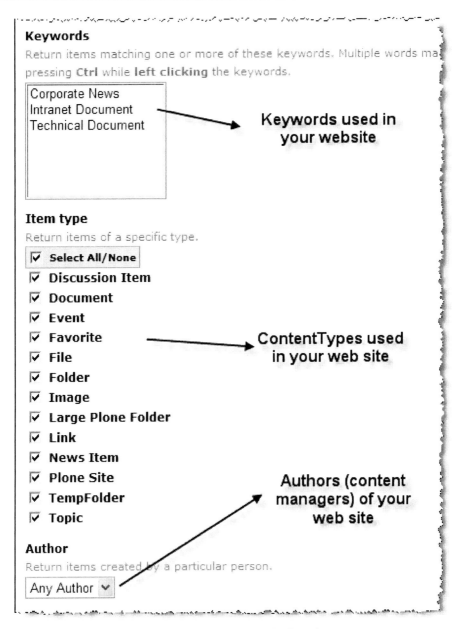

Keywords

Return items matching one or more of these keywords. Multiple words ma
pressing **Ctrl** while **left clicking** the keywords.

Corporate News
Intranet Document
Technical Document

→ **Keywords used in your website**

Item type

Return items of a specific type.

☑ **Select All/None**
☑ **Discussion Item**
☑ **Document**
☑ **Event**
☑ **Favorite**
☑ **File**
☑ **Folder**
☑ **Image**
☑ **Large Plone Folder**
☑ **Link**
☑ **News Item**
☑ **Plone Site**
☑ **TempFolder**
☑ **Topic**

→ **ContentTypes used in your web site**

Authors (content managers) of your web site

Author

Return items created by a particular person.

Any Author ▼

Figure 5.10: Advanced Search Form (search_form)

Managing Member Profiles

The member data tool (portal_memberdata) holds profile and metadata information of Plone members. Plone provides default properties for each member, such as full name and e-mail address. However, you might want to add more properties for each member of your web site.

Members would need additional properties for many reasons. For example, you might want to personalize your web site for each member, based on his or her preferences. Many web sites have information that changes based on, for example, the ZIP code provided. Those web sites try to provide information that is relevant to each user. Hence, you might need more properties for the members of your web site.

Add New Member Properties

Click on **portal_memberdata**; then click on the **Properties** tab. A list of existing (default) member properties displays. Add a property name of "address," with the "string" type, and with no default value.

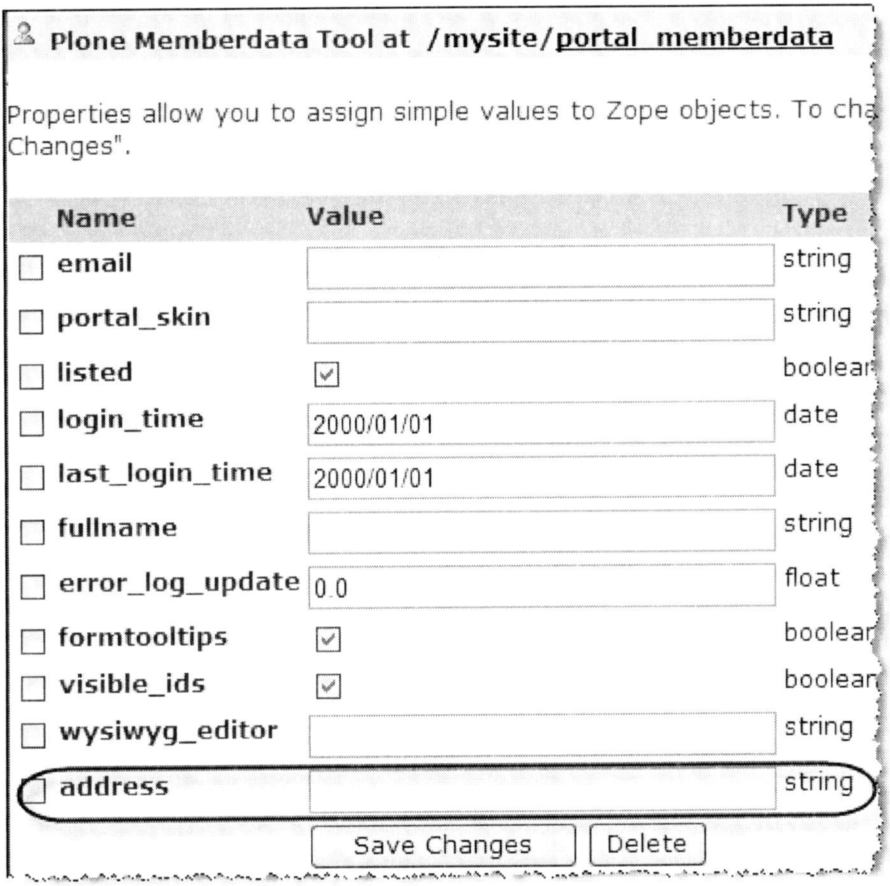

Figure 5.11: Add new property using portal_memberdata tool

Personalize Form

The page template code (skin) for the *Personal preferences* form is located at *portal_skins/plone_prefs/personalize_form*. Customize this form and add the code in Listing 5.2 at the appropriate place in the form. The purpose of this code is to display the address and accept address information from members.

Listing 5.2

```
<div class="field"
     tal:define="error errors/address | nothing;
                 address python:request.get
   ('address', member.getProperty('address', ''));"
     tal:attributes="class python:test(error, 'field error',
'field')">

    <label for="address" i18n:translate="label_address">
   Address</label>

   <div tal:content="error">Validation error output</div>

   <input type="text"
          id="address"
          name="address"
          size="40"
          tabindex=""
          value=""
          tal:attributes="value address;
                          tabindex tabindex/next;"
          />

</div>
```

After adding the above code, click on the **Test** tab to check the layout of the form with the newly added property. Now log in to your web site to see your Personal Preferences, as shown in Figure 5.12.

Figure 5.12: Personal Preferences form with new property

Control Plone Membership

It is possible to remove a user in your Zope installation while objects that were owned by that user remain (for example, someone in your organization leaves, so you remove his account on your Zope server). When you remove a Zope user, objects that were owned by that user still have ownership information that refers to that user. This will not cause an error, but it is important to understand what happens to Zope objects whose owners no longer exist. This is most important for executable objects. Usually, the abilities of executable objects are constrained by the abilities of the object's owner, as well as the user causing the object to execute. If Zope cannot find the user to which the executable's ownership information refers, it will use the special *nobody* or Anonymous user instead. The *nobody* user has minimal privileges, so you should consider this when deciding what to do about a user's owned objects when you delete the user.

CMFMember

Refer to Figure 5.1, "Plone Membership Framework," on page 151, which explains the various tools that hold membership information. If you delete a user

---

from the *acl_users* folder, the member object will not be deleted from the member data tool (portal_memberdata), and the content owned by that member will not be transferred to some other member. This makes the site inconsistent and insecure. The CMFMember product solves such classic problems with Plone membership.

When compared to the default Plone Membership, the CMFMember product will provide these additional and very important benefits:

▶ Member objects are searchable.

▶ Deleting a user deletes the Member object and transfers the ownership to the person who is deleting that user.

▶ The user id (login name) can be changed. (Starting from Zope 2.7.1 onwards, the userid and username are different.)

▶ The user account can be disabled (without deleting the member). The "forgot password" feature will be disabled for those members.

▶ Members can join, but they will not be active until approved.

▶ Privileges (Roles) can be given to a member based on workflow.

▶ The Manager can edit the member profile.

▶ A schema defines the join form and member attributes.

You can download CMFMember from the sourceforge.net web site: http://sourceforge.net/project/showfiles.php?group_id=55262&package_id=118065

Figure 5.13: CMFMember product

Completely read the documentation before trying out this product. Before installing the CMFMember product, you must install the *Archetypes*, *PloneErrorReporting*, and *PortalTransforms* products. This product modifies existing Plone membership tools, creates a new tool called cmfmember_control, and creates a new catalog called member_catalog. The CMFMember product also provides very useful migration utilities to convert the existing member details to CMFMember.

Summary

The Plone membership framework is very secure, flexible, scalable, and customizable. You can decide site policy up front whether to allow users to *join* your site, and whether to allow members to create their own member area. You can secure your content by securing folders or by securing workflow. You can secure the scripts provided in skins by customizing them.

Summary

Creating Portal Types

Author: Michel Pelletier

Eventually, you are going to need functionality that Plone's default types don't provide. For this, you will create your own types that work according to your specifications. This chapter explains how to create new types in Python that work with Plone.

Overview

So far, you made most of your changes directly in Plone or by using a skin-based product. For simple content that uses Plone's stock types, this is fine, but to design a "real" Plone application with more advanced features, you must work with more advanced tools.

Since Plone (and its CMF), Zope, and Python are so object-oriented, implementing new features means creating new kinds of objects, typically using the Python "class" syntax. If you are unfamiliar with Python class semantics, refer to the excellent Python Documentation at http://python.org/doc/.

Archetypes is a new framework in Plone 2.1. It was originally included in Plone 2.0.4, but it wasn't until Plone 2.1 that most of its features were leveraged in Plone. It provides a newer way of developing file system types. However, this chapter covers the older way of doing it, using the CMF-based types. It's worthwhile having an understanding of it, since everything you manually do here also needs to be taken care of by Archetypes. If you don't know what happens "under the hood," Archetypes will be even more mysterious than it needs to be. Additionally, this method is still popular and many Products are coded in this way.

Also, developing Archetypes-based objects really only makes sense for content objects. These objects are good at holding and referencing content, but for simpler framework-level components, you don't need Archetypes. If you want to ship a new kind of Plone tool, for example, you probably don't need to make it an Archetype. The purpose of most tools is to present a Python API to your site. For this, you need only use a simple CMF class. This also makes your tool useful for other CMF-based portal systems other than Plone.

If you are starting a new project and have no need to be backwards-compatible with older versions of Plone, you may proceed to *Chapter 7* and develop your product using Archetypes and Archetype Content Types.

Understanding Types

The term "type" is heavily abused when the worlds of Python, Zope, and Plone collide. In each domain, the words have distinct, but related, meanings.

A Python type, for the purposes of this book, is a class. A class is an object that defines how other objects behave; they are like "blueprints" for the objects that they describe, called "instances." Python types form the underlying object framework for all objects in Python, Zope, and CMF/Plone. For more a more detailed discussion on Python, classes, and types, see the *Python Language Reference Manual* (http://docs.python.org/ref/ref.html).

In Zope, types (more specifically, "meta types," often seen in the source code as an attribute called "meta_type") are the various kinds of objects that Zope knows how to manage in its ZMI. For example, meta types appear in the Add pull-down list in folders, and list and manage the content of folders. Meta types are also human-readable strings that describe the type of an object to the user.

CMF/Plone types are Zope meta types with some additional properties; they are associated with the Types tool, which specifically manages those types, and they have standardized metadata. Additionally, different CMF/Plone types may be based on the same underlying Zope type, having the same meta type but different CMF/Plone types. (The Zope meta type is stored in an attribute called *meta_type*, while the Plone type is stored in *portal_type*.)

To confuse things further, Plone 2 has a new type system called Archetypes, which is discussed in *Chapters 7* and *8*. Archetypes is optional in Plone versions prior to 2.1, but starting with Plone 2.1 it is part of the standard installation. Archetypes makes things easier for most purposes, and for now, it is the final word on Plone "types."

Because CMF/Plone is written using Zope in the Python language, you can see how these definitions collide. Knowing what you mean when speaking about an object's "type" requires experience in the context of the usage. The above descriptions ought to provide some context to understand these distinctions.

Creating New Types

New types are necessary in a variety of situations. While the objects that come with Plone are good for general purpose web applications, at some point you will likely need to customize a type to do what you require of it. To accomplish this goal, you will have to create a new type.

You can customize types using one of two methods:

▶ Use the TTW interface

▶ Use a Python product

If you intend to do any serious programming at all, don't even consider the TTW method. It will be explained here so that you can see how the technique works, but generally, starting with the TTW interface will eventually lock you into a solution that is harder to maintain than a Python product. There is one technique, called *repurposing*, that can be easily explained using the TTW interface.

Once you are developing Python products, you have a large degree of freedom. For example, the Zope security system is not implicitly enforced for Python code on the file system. You can make security assertions in your code and do security checks explicitly. The assertions that you make will be enforced when the code is called through the web. However, once the security assertions have been satisfied, you have total control over Zope and all its objects. With that control you can do damage, or allow some other malicious user to do damage, if you don't know what you're doing.

In order to avoid these problems, it is important to follow these guidelines:

▶ Reuse existing framework components when possible, rather than writing your own.

▶ Test new programs thoroughly before releasing them.

▶ Be sure that you always validate input from a distrusted user.

▶ Understand the purpose of objects, their methods, and what will happen when you call them.

▶ Always remember that there is an Undo function in Zope.

Repurposing

The simplest way to create a new type is to repurpose an existing one. A repurposed type is simply an existing type with a new name and possibly some different skins and actions. The underlying Python type of the object does not change, but some of the properties (such as *portal_type*), actions, and skins of the new type may be different.

You can repurpose types easily using the TTW interface. Go to the **portal_types** tool (discussed in *Chapter 2*), where you will see all of the existing types. Select **Factory Type Information** from the Add menu, and click the **Add** button. In the next screen, enter an id for your new type and select a type upon which to base your new type from the **Use default type information** pull-down list.

Step back for a minute and think about why you would need to do this. For example, in your application, you may have a need for a *News* type – say, a Press-Release – which is similar to the default one, but with different actions and skins. You still want it to be a news type, but you don't want it to look or respond to actions like the default site type, and you don't want to change the default site type just to fit this one requirement, because you may need the default behavior somewhere else.

Using this mechanism, you can copy an old type to a new type and configure that new type's skins and actions. Unfortunately, using this method, you cannot configure much more than the skins and actions. To see this in practice, create a new type with an id of *PloneLiveEvent* and a base type of *Event* by going to the portal_types tool and selecting **Factory-based Type Information** from the Add pull-down list.

Now select the new PloneLiveEvent portal type from the Types tool. From here, you can change some of the properties on the new event type, and you can change the default actions or add new actions, but you can't add any new properties. Underneath, it is still an Event object.

The repurposing mechanism is useful as a more general concept because you can also repurpose types using file system-based development. In large applications that have many similar kinds of objects, repurposing may be right for you. Additionally, the Archetypes framework makes repurposing obsolete to a certain

---

degree, so be sure you want to commit to this style of design if you are creating a new type.

Repurposing is similar to subclassing, but its intent is different. Subclassing is a mechanism for taking one type and deriving a completely different type from it. While it may appear that repurposing also does this on the surface (in the Types tool interface), underneath, a repurposed type is no different from a Python type in the original object. Remember that the term "type" can be confusing in this way; by repurposing a *portal* type, you are creating a new portal type, but the underlying *Python* type is the same. It's the Plone equivalent of a goat in sheep's clothing.

Repurposing a content type only changes the way the type appears to Plone, not the way it appears to Python. Subclassing a content type would change the way it appears to Python, which is a more fundamental change.

For more background on object-oriented programming, many books and web sites are available that can give you a quick introduction. For Python programming, the best place to start is the Python web page at http://python.org/. It contains a collection of links, books, and information on Python and object oriented technique in general.

CMF File System Types

Today, Plone uses several different ways of defining new types from file system-based code. The most recent type system is Archetypes, but this is very new. Most existing Plone products use the "old" type system that comes from CMF, but several of the most significant new products use Archetypes (for example, PloneArticle, PloneHelpCenter, and PloneSoftwareCenter).

The CMF is the "core" of the Plone product. The CMF used to provide all of the services that Plone depended on. However, as new services were added to Plone, the two have begun to diverge in some features and merge in others. The most recent divergence is the type systems that come with Plone.

These types provide the foundation for most Plone sites. The types in the Types tool with the prefix of "CMF" are provided for backward and cross-compatibility with CMF.

CMF products are just like the products discussed in *Chapter 5*. They are Python packages with a special function in their *__init__.py* files that registers them with Zope. The only difference is that in addition to the initialization code and skins, CMF products provide new portal types and register them with Zope so that they can be added through the web.

Python Command Line Development

Zope applications are usually web-based, which can make it difficult to track down bugs or weird behavior, since you must use a web browser in order to trigger errors and test development. To help developers interactively execute code and look for bugs, Zope comes with a Python command line interface that you can use to test your application instead of a web browser.

The command line debugger lets you use the standard Python interactive interpreter prompt to inspect and manipulate your Zope objects. Anyone coming from Python development will be instantly comfortable in this environment, as this interactive method is the way almost all people learn how to write Python code.

The best command line tool to use while debugging Zope is the `zopectl` script that comes with Zope in the *bin* directory of the instance home. This script is a command line launcher and debugger for Zope, and we highly recommend using it.

The zopectl program can start, stop, restart, and debug any Zope site. If you are unfamiliar with command line tools, this might seem awkward at first, but ultimately it is much more productive. To see how this works, follow these steps:

1. Shut down your Zope system and go to your site's instance home (for more information about instance homes, see *Chapter 1*).

2. Run the zopectl command as shown in Listing 6.1. (Note that zopectl does not work on Windows):

Listing 6.1

```
bin/zopectl
 bin/zopectl
program: /home/michel/CIGNEX/sites/three/bin/runzope
daemon manager not running
zopectl> start
. daemon process started, pid=7900
zopectl>
```

This command starts zopectl, and the **start** command starts your Zope server in the background.

3. You can continue to issue commands to zopectl, as shown in Listing 6.2:

Listing 6.2

```
zopectl> stop
. daemon process stopped
zopectl> debug
Starting debugger (the name "app" is bound to the top-level Zope
object)
>>> app.objectIds()
['acl_users', 'Control_Panel', 'temp_folder', 'session_data_manager',
    'browser_id_manager', 'error_log', 'index_html',
    'standard_error_message', 'standard_html_footer',
    'standard_html_header', 'standard_template.pt', 'fiz',
    'one', 'Catalog', 'Boby', 'Zing', 'bin', 'jazz']
>>>      # press Ctrl-D to drop out of the debugger
zopectl> start
. daemon process started, pid=7986
zopectl>
```

Notice that the **stop** command stopped the server and the **debug** command started the debugger. This takes you to a Python prompt, where you can interactively work with any of your Zope objects. If you start your Zope server, you can exit zopectl at any time, and your server will continue to run. In fact, you don't need to run the zopectl interactive shell at all; you can issue commands directly to the program as arguments, such as the ones in Listing 6.3:

Listing 6.3

```
$> bin/zopectl start
$> bin/zopectl restart
```

For a complete list of commands, type "help" at the zopectl shell prompt.

Debugging is a particularly useful way to use zopectl. Notice that the Python expression `app.objectIds()` returned a list of all the object ids in the root folder of the Zope site. You can exit the debugger by typing Ctrl-D, and restart the Zope server with `start`. While debugging, you can change the ZODB by creating new instances of persistent objects such as Documents, or by calling methods that change the attributes of any of the existing objects. However, your debugging session takes place as a single Zope transaction. This means that unless you explicitly *commit* the changes you have made, they will vanish when your debugging session ends. If you do commit the changes, other users will see them (if you're running in a ZEO setup), and you will be working in a new transaction.

Note that while you're in a debug session, your site is not available to users using a web browser, so you should not use this technique on a production site. If you want to continue servicing web requests while debugging, you need to run Zope using ZEO. This allows you to occupy one ZEO client with the debugging session, while another client serves web requests. To make it more pleasant to use the debugger, consider using ipython as your shell:

▶ http://zopewiki.org/DebuggingZopeWithPythonDebugger2

▶ http://www.zope.org/Members/klm/ZopeDebugging/ConversingWithZope

▶ http://www.zope.org/Members/michel/HowTos/TheDebuggerIsYourFriend

Jim Fulton, the CTO of Zope Corporation, wrote some tips at http://www.zope.org/Members/mcdonc/HowTos/UsingTheZopeDebugger.

To debug and explore you no longer need to toggle between your code editor to your web browser. Many IDE programs allow you to work with your programs and a command shell in the same window. This is particularly useful when you can keep the debug session and your code in the same tool and screen.

Serious developers use these kinds of tools to create Plone applications. In conjunction with file mining tools such as `grep`, and code version control tools like CVS and Subversion, advanced development techniques can greatly simplify your life as a developer.

CMF Types

CMF types are arranged in the hierarchy shown in Figure 6.1 in the following section. Each of these classes has its own interfaces and implementations. This section contains an overview of the most important CMF types and references for more information.

The CMF is based on two classes that define the behavior of most of its types: PortalContent and PortalFolder. PortalContent defines item objects that can be contained in folders, and PortalFolder defines folder-like objects. These two classes form the top of their respective inheritance hierarchies.

PortalContent

PortalContent objects are objects that are not folders or otherwise contain other objects in a folder-like way. This does not mean PortalContent objects can't have sub-attributes; it just means that the Plone user interface doesn't treat them as folders.

As shown in Figure 6.1, there are six core PortalContent types. PortalContent is not a type that you can add directly to a Plone instance; it is only an abstract type. You must subclass it for it to be useful.

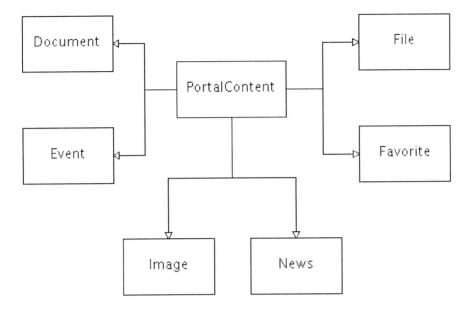

Figure 6.1: High-level view of CMF Types

PortalContent is actually composed of three other classes combined into one. These classes have the following interfaces:

▶ DynamicType

▶ CMFCatalogAware

▶ SimpleItem

Each of these types is described below. Note that this is a high-level overview to give you an idea of how different CMF, Plone, and Zope objects interact.

DynamicType

The Dynamic Type class defines behavior for objects that work in the CMF framework by allowing them to have a "dynamic type," which is the interface used to interact with an object's portal type.

▶ `getPortalTypeName()`: Returns the type name of the object. It returns "None" if objects are uninitialized.

- **getTypeInfo()**: Returns the type information for this object. It returns "None" if the object is uninitialized.

- **getIcon(relative_to_portal=0)**: Returns a path to the icon for this type. It is an optional argument to return the icon path relative to the portal URL.

CMFCatalogAware

The PortalContent class includes the CMFCatalogAware class in order to support portal content interacting with the portal catalog. These indexing methods of CMFCatalogAware are useful to override if you want to modify the way your content is cataloged. Note that if you subclass and override any of these methods, the underlying CMFCatalogAware method must also be called. If you don't know what that means, then you shouldn't be overriding these methods. This is because Plone depends on the catalog for many of its functions, and if objects are not properly cataloged, you may expect things to break.

- **indexObject()**: Indexes the object in the portal catalog. Permission: ModifyPortalContent

- **unindexObject()**: Removes the object from the portal catalog. Permission: ModifyPortalContent

- **reindexObject(idxs=[])**: Reindexes the object in the portal catalog. If the *idxs* parameter is present, only listed indexes are reindexed. The metadata is always updated. It also updates the modification date of the object, unless specific indexes were requested. Permission: ModifyPortalContent

- **reindexObjectSecurity()**: Reindexes security-related indexes on the object (and its descendants). Permission: ModifyPortalContent

- **notifyWorkflowCreated()**: Notifies the workflow that *self* (a new instance) was just created. Permission: Private: Unrestricted Python Only

- **opaqueItems()**: Returns opaque items. (Opaque items are sub-elements that are contained by anything other than an ObjectManager. Currently, this is hard-coded to the talkback item that contains the threaded discussion of an object.) Permission: AccessContentsInformation

- **opaqueIds()**: Returns opaque ids. (Opaque ids are sub-elements that are contained by anything other than an ObjectManager.) Permission: AccessContentsInformation

▶ `opaqueValues()`:Returns opaque values. (Opaque values are sub-elements that are contained by something that is not an ObjectManager.) Permission: AccessContentsInformation

▶ `manage_afterAdd(item, container)`: Acts as a hook which is called when the object is created or moved. CMFCatalogAware uses it to add newly created objects to the catalog.

▶ `manage_afterClone( item)`: Acts as a hook which is called when the object is cloned. CMFCatalogAware uses it to notify the workflow tool of the new object.

▶ `manage_beforeDelete( item, container)`: Removes self from the catalog. (It calls a hook when the object is deleted or moved.)

SimpleItem

The base class SimpleItem comes from the core classes of Zope. It has existed since the inception of Zope, and it has grown and changed over the years. In other words, it is not a very "simple" item anymore. To highlight every method and attribute of this class is unnecessary, so only the more modern and useful members of this class are described here:

▶ `getId()`: Returns the id of the object. Don't be tempted to get the id in any other way (such as accessing the id attribute directly); always use this method.

▶ `title_or_id()`: Returns the title or the id.

▶ `title_and_id()`: Returns the title and the id.

▶ `absolute_url()`: Returns the absolute URL of the item.

▶ `absolute_url_path()`: Returns only the path portion of the absolute URL to the item.

▶ `getPhysicalPath()`: Returns the path (an immutable sequence of strings) to the item.

▶ `unrestrictedTraverse(path)`: Traverses down a path as a web request would, and returns the object it finds.

PortalFolder

PortalFolder forms the folder building blocks for Plone. This class defines all of the folder-like behavior for CMF and Plone. The major functionality derives from Zope's own Folder class. The exact class hierarchy of Zope, CMF, and Plone is a bit confusing to take in all at once, but Zope folders are really just another mix-in super-class. See Figure 6.2.

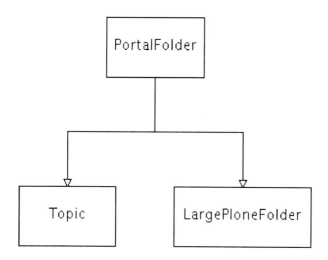

Figure 6.2: Hierarchy of Portal Folders

Folder objects are special because they implement methods that Zope, CMF, and Plone can use to work with the contents that they contain by design. You can be very flexible with PloneFolder objects, because they do not constrain you too much on how you can implement your collection.

For example, the Topic type is a folder object that shows the result set of a set of Catalog queries (see *Chapter 3* for more on Topics). A Topic contains only Criteria objects; it just *appears* to hold objects that are from somewhere else, collected in one place inside the Topic.

Like the PortalContent class, the PortalFolder class is a mix of many Python super-classes. PortalFolder objects are identical to PortalContent objects; they implement the same methods, so folder objects work like all other objects, except that they have more features: they can contain other objects.

The major difference between PortalContent and PortalFolder objects is that PortalFolder objects implement the ObjectManager interface. This is an old Zope interface that, like SimpleItem, has grown in complexity over time. Following are the most important methods from the ObjectManager interface:

- **objectIds(type=None)**: Returns a list of the ids of the contained objects. Optionally, you can pass an argument specifying what object meta_type(s) to restrict the results to. This argument can be a string specifying one meta_type, or it can be a list of strings to specify many. Permission: Access contents information

- **objectValues(type=None)**: Returns a sequence of contained objects. Like objectItems and objectIds, it accepts one argument -- either a string or a list to restrict the results to objects of a given meta_type or set of meta_types. Permission: Access contents information

- **objectItems(type=None)**: Returns a sequence of tuples, each element of which is a sub-tuple with two elements: the object's id and its value. Like objectValues and objectIds, it accepts one argument -- either a string or a list to restrict the results to objects of a given meta_type or set of meta_types. Each tuple's first element is the id of an object contained in the Object Manager, and the second element is the object itself. Permission: Access contents information

- **__getitem__(id)**: Returns a child object with a given child id. If there is no child with the given id, a KeyError is raised. This method, which is also used when an object is subscripted, makes it easy to refer to children that have ids containing "." characters, such as file extensions (*folder.__getitem__('file.ext')* and *folder['file.ext']* are equivalent). Permission: Access contents information

Note: This function doesn't use acquisition to find children. It only returns direct children of the Object Manager. By contrast, using dot notation, or **getattr**, will locate children (and other attributes) via acquisition, if necessary.

The following two methods are not in the object manager interface, but they are very useful when using PortalFolders:

- **batchedFolderContents()**: Returns the contents of the folder in batches, so that it is easy to display the content of the folder one screen-full at a time.

Chapter 6: Creating Portal Types

It is useful for custom displays of Plone folders. Permission: Access contents information.

▶ `getAllowedTypes()`: Displays the list of sub-types that this container allows itself to contain. It is useful for showing menus of available types to the user to add to a folder. Permission: Access contents information

When to use PortalContent or PortalFolder is, of course, entirely up to you. The next two sections explain how to extend both kinds of types into a simple product that contains both PortalFolder and PortalContent classes.

The Book Type Example

The Book type defines a new folder-like type that represents a printed book. Books are typically organized into a collection of chapters and have properties like "author" and "publication date." Since books *contain* chapters, an example Plone book type would do well to subclass from PortalFolder.

This type is defined in the example product *CMFPloneLive/Book.py*. Listing 6.4 is a listing of that Python module, broken down into small chunks so that it is easier to digest. For a complete listing of the code, see the CMFPloneLive product.

Listing 6.4

```
#
# Import CMF classes and properties
#
from Globals import InitializeClass
from Products.CMFCore.CMFCorePermissions import View,
ManageProperties, \
  ListFolderContents

from Products.CMFDefault.SkinnedFolder import SkinnedFolder
from AccessControl import ClassSecurityInfo
```

The above imports bring in the necessary classes for this new product. The next example will use each of these objects. Below is the Factory Type Information (FTI) tuple, which is an important, but complex, object. It may be hard to understand at first, but it is an important part of CMF types.

The FTI describes how CMF/Plone's Types tool should register the new type. It contains important information such as the product, constructor, actions, and permissions with which the new type is associated. The FTI object is really just a tuple containing a dictionary that maps keys (like meta_type) to values that may themselves be complex (for example, the following **actions** key). See Listing 6.5.

Listing 6.5

```
# the factory type information defines
# CMF metadata for your type.

factory_type_information = (
  { 'id'                 : 'CMFBook'
  , 'meta_type'          : 'CMF Book'
  , 'description'        : """\
Books contain chapters.
"""
  , 'icon'               : 'folder_icon.gif'
  , 'product'            : 'CMFPloneLive'
  , 'factory'            : 'addBook'
  , 'filter_content_types' : 0
  , 'immediate_view'     : 'folder_edit_form'
  , 'actions'            : ( { 'id'        : 'view'
                            , 'name'       : 'View'
                            , 'action': 'string:${object_url}/folder_view'
                            , 'permissions'  : (View,)
                            , 'category'     : 'folder'
                            }
                          , { 'id'          : 'edit'
                            , 'name'        : 'Edit'
                            , 'action': 'string:${object_url}
/folder_edit_form'
                            , 'permissions'  : (ManageProperties,)
                            , 'category'     : 'folder'
                            }
                          , { 'id'          : 'foldercontents'
                            , 'name'        : 'Folder contents'
                            , 'action': 'string:${object_url}
/folder_contents'
                            , 'permissions'  : (ListFolderContents,)
                            , 'category'     : 'folder'
                            }
```

Chapter 6: Creating Portal Types   PAGE **195**

```
                           )
  }
,
)
```

Listing 6.6 is the constructor object for the book type. This is a standard function in Plone, and almost all constructors virtually do the same thing: add the
new type to a container. In certain cases, you may need to do special initialization
in this function, such as populating a new folderish object with some default
content.

Listing 6.6

```
def addBook( self, id, title='', description='', REQUEST=None ):
    """
    Add a new CMF Book instance to the container "self"
    """
    sf = Book( id, title )
    sf.description = description
    self._setObject( id, sf )
    sf = self._getOb( id ) # This acquisition-wraps the new instance.
    if REQUEST is not None:
        REQUEST['RESPONSE'].redirect
    ( sf.absolute_url() + '/manage_main' )
```

Listing 6.7 is the class itself:

Listing 6.7

```
class Book(SkinnedFolder):
    """ A placeholder class for Books. """

    meta_type = 'CMF Book'

    security = ClassSecurityInfo()
```

Listing 6.8 is the class initialization:

Listing 6.8

```
InitializeClass(Book)
```

Most of the preceding code is just boilerplate code to get your new type to work with the Zope, CMF, and Plone frameworks. Once you get past this first hurdle, you can customize your type to do anything you want.

Viewing Books

Now that you have created a Book type, you need an HTML interface to show the book. The full ZPT code for displaying books is very long and complex because it is information-rich HTML and does *batching*, showing only one screen-full of folder contents at a time. Listing 6.9 contains a few relevant sections from the *folder_contents.zpt* file:

Listing 6.9

```
<div metal:fill-slot="main"
  tal:define="standalone python:1;
              myfolder python: here_url==mtool.getHomeUrl();
              contentTypes python: here.getAllowedTypes();
              contentTypeIds python:[t.getId() for t in contentTypes];
              num_types python: len(contentTypes)">

  <form name="folderContentsForm"
    method="post"
    action="folder_object"
    tal:attributes="action here_url"
    tal:define="batch python:
    here.batchedFolderContents(suppressHiddenFiles=1);">
```

This chunk of code defines the variables you need to render the Book. The most important variable, batch, is the contents of the folder wrapped in a special object that returns the contents in batches, so that they can display one screen-full at a time. See the *PortalFolder* section for more information about **batched-FolderContents()**.

The Chapter Type

The Chapter type is a document-like type, contained inside the Book type. It represents a chapter of a book and holds the book data. It subclasses the Plone Document class, which is a subclass of PortalContent.

You can create chapters inside any kind of PloneFolder object, but when you create them inside Book objects, they get special treatment because they "link-in" to the greater book structure as defined by the book class.

For example, a stand-alone chapter object will have no ability to navigate to the "next" and "previous" chapters, because it is not contained in a book class. By putting that same chapter object into a book object that has several chapters already in it, the chapter-by-chapter navigation features will work.

The following code is broken down into small chunks so that it is easier to digest. For a complete listing of the code, see the CMFPloneLive product. First is Listing 6.10.

Listing 6.10

```
from Products.CMFDefault.Document import Document
from AccessControl import ClassSecurityInfo
```

These are standard imports. You need **Document** because Chapter will subclass it below. The ClassSecurityInfo object is necessary to make security declarations on the class. As shown above, all Plone CMF types must have a Factory Type Information object that describes the content type and how to create instances of it. See Listing 6.11.

Listing 6.11

```
factory_type_information = (
  { 'id'                : 'CMFChapter'
  , 'meta_type'         : 'CMF Chapter'
  , 'description'       : """\
Chapters contain book chapters that can be formatted
    using 'Structured Text.'
They may also contain HTML, or "plain" text.
"""
  , 'icon'              : 'document_icon.gif'
  , 'product'           : 'CMFPloneLive'
  , 'factory'           : 'addChapter'
  , 'immediate_view'    : 'metadata_edit_form'
  , 'actions'           : ( { 'id'              : 'view'
                            , 'name'            : 'View'
```

```
                              , 'action': 'string:${object_url}/
document_view'
                              , 'permissions'    : (View,)
                              }
                           , { 'id'              : 'edit'
                              , 'name'           : 'Edit'
                              , 'action': 'string:${object_url}/
document_edit_form'
                              , 'permissions'    : (ModifyPortalContent,)
                              }
                           , { 'id'              : 'metadata'
                              , 'name'           : 'Metadata'
                              , 'action': 'string:${object_url}/
metadata_edit_form'
                              , 'permissions'    : (ModifyPortalContent,)
                              }
                           )

   }

  ,
  )
```

Listing 6.12 is the constructor for Chapter objects. It is very simple, and like the one for Book objects, it creates a new book object and assigns it to a container using the **_setOb** method.

Listing 6.12

```
def addChapter(self, id, title='', description='', text_format='',
               text=''):
    """ Add a Chapter """
    o = Chapter(id, title, description, text_format, text)
    self._setObject(id,o)
```

Now is the important part: subclassing. Below, the Python class **Chapter** subclasses the **Document** class. Only two class attributes are created (for now) that define the object's meta type and security information. See Listing 6.13.

Listing 6.13

```
class Chapter(Document):
```

```
meta_type = 'CMF Chapter'

security = ClassSecurityInfo()
security.declareObjectProtected('View')
```

Listing 6.14 is the class initialization:

Listing 6.14

```
InitializeClass(Chapter)
```

Remember, much of this code (like InitializeClass) is just boilerplate code you need to make a new type in Plone. Once you have cleared this initial hurdle, you can design your new class to do anything you want.

Viewing Chapters

Now that you have a Chapter type, you need to present your chapter objects to the user. Do this by using the skinning techniques shown in *Chapter 5*.
Listing 6.15 is a simple page template that displays a chapter object:

Listing 6.15

```
<html xmlns="http://www.w3.org/1999/xhtml" xml:lang="en"
    lang="en"
    metal:use-macro="here/main_template/macros/master"
    i18n:domain="plone">
<body>

<metal:main fill-slot="main">
    <tal:main-macro metal:define-macro="main"
        define="len_text python:len(here.text);">
      <h1 tal:content="here/title_or_id"
class="documentFirstHeading">
        Title or id
      </h1>

      <div metal:use-macro=
    "here/document_actions/macros/document_actions">
          Chapter actions (print, sendto etc)
      </div>

      <div class="documentDescription"
```

```
          tal:content="here/Description">
          description
     </div>

     <p tal:condition="python: not len_text and is_editable"
        i18n:translate="no_body_text"
        class="discreet">
          This chapter does not have any body text,
click the edit tab to change it.
     </p>

     <div class="stx"
          tal:condition="len_text"
          tal:attributes=
"class python:test(here.Format() in ('text/structured',
                                      'text/x-rst', ),
'stx', 'plain')">
          <div tal:replace=
"structure python:here.CookedBody(stx_level=2)" />
     </div>

     <div metal:use-macro="here/document_byline/macros/byline">
        Get the byline - contains details about author
and modification date.
     </div>
   </tal:main-macro>
</metal:main>

</body>
</html>
```

The preceding page template, when applied to a chapter object, displays that chapter in HTML to the end user. You can customize this template to make it look any way you want, and using the techniques discussed in *Chapter 5*, you can override various aspects of Plone's template features.

Product Initialization

Every product must have an *__init__.py* file that contains an **initialize** function to register that product with Zope, CMF, and Plone. *Chapter 5* used this init file to register a skins directory. This section has a similar *__init__.py* file that expands on *Chapter 5*'s concepts.

Additionally, the CMFPloneLive product has a *config.py* module. This module defines some useful constants for the Product that are also used in the installation script, shown in Listing 6.16:

Listing 6.16

```
import Book
import Chapter

bases = ( Book.Book,
          Chapter.Chapter,
          )

factory_type_information = Book.factory_type_information + \
    Chapter.factory_type_information

constructors = ( Book.addBook,
                 Chapter.addChapter,
                 )
```

The preceding code is used for the init file and the installation script. The code in Listing 6.17 is some standard import code that brings the various classes and other objects needed to initialize your type into the scope of this module:

Listing 6.17

```
import sys
from Products.CMFCore import DirectoryView
from Products.CMFCore.CMFCorePermissions import AddPortalContent
from Products.CMFCore.utils import initializeBasesPhase1
from Products.CMFCore.utils import initializeBasesPhase2
from Products.CMFCore.utils import ContentInit
from config import *
```

These next three lines are possibly the most arcane incantations in all of CMF/Plone. They are necessary for a variety of reasons, but mainly to help Plone find the correct skins inside your product when it is registered, and to help Zope correctly recognize your content classes when they are registered. These lines are needed for CMF-based products only; *Chapter 7: Archetypes* does not use them. They are essentially implementation details that you have to specify in order to get your product to work. See Listing 6.18.

Listing 6.18

```
GLOBALS = globals() # All the names defined at the time of import.
    uses this to find  the filesystem path of the product
this_module = sys.modules[ __name__ ]
z_bases = initializeBasesPhase1( bases, this_module )
    # Stuff that happens during import
```

The method call in Listing 6.19 registers your skins directory with the Plone skins tool. *Chapter 5* used this same technique to add skins to Plone:

Listing 6.19

```
DirectoryView.registerDirectory('skins', GLOBALS)

def initialize(context):
    initializeBasesPhase2( z_bases, context )
    # Stuff that only happens upon installation within a Plone site.
```

Listing 6.20 is an important part of Plone registration. The ContentInit class initializes your content objects all in one call. You have to pass in the base classes, permission, constructors, and factory information into this class.

Listing 6.20

```
ContentInit( 'CMFPloneLive'
            , content_types=bases
            , permission=AddPortalContent
            , extra_constructors=constructors
            , fti=factory_type_information
            ).initialize( context )
```

The code in Listing 6.20 uses the factory object `ContentInit` to initialize the two content objects. The module imports "*" from the `config` module, which allows you to refer to the bases, constructors, and `factory_type_information` variables directly.

The QuickInstall Script

In order to install your types and skins into a particular Plone site, you need to install that product using Plone's "QuickInstaller" application. This was shown

---

Chapter 6: Creating Portal Types   PAGE **203**

in *Chapter 2* and *Chapter 5*. The Install.py script shown in *Chapter 5* just added skins to the skins tool. This Install.py script also registers the new types with the Types tool. See Listing 6.21.

Listing 6.21

```
from Products.Archetypes.Extensions.utils import install_subskin
from Products.CMFCore.TypesTool import ContentFactoryMetadata
from Products.CMFCore.utils import getToolByName

from Products.CMFPloneLive import GLOBALS
from Products.CMFPloneLive.config import fti
from cStringIO import StringIO
import string

def install(self):
    out = StringIO()
    typestool = getToolByName(self, 'portal_types')

    for t in fti:
        if t['id'] not in typestool.objectIds():
            typestool.manage_addTypeInformation
(add_meta_type=t['meta_type'], id=t['id'])
            out.write('Registered with the types tool\n')
        else:
            out.write('Object "%s" already existed in the types
tool\n' % (
                t['id']))

    install_subskin(self, out, GLOBALS)

    return out.getvalue()
```

The installation script returns the log that indicates the success or failure of any installation steps along the way. If your installation script raises an exception during its execution, it will append the exception information to the product installation error log in the Plone control panel. Remember to make it possible to *uninstall* your Product, so if your installation method changes the Plone configuration, you are prepared to revert it when you uninstall.

Product Distribution

As in *Chapter 5*, distributing your product entails cleaning up any unnecessary debris (such as swapfiles, backup files, and CVS directories) and creating a "tarball" (that is, a packaged and gzipped file containing your product's Python package).

You will probably need to start using more advanced file system-based development tools to continue on your learning path to being a Plone development expert. If you are not familiar with them, I strongly suggest that you introduce yourself to the kinds of tools that serious programmers use to collaborate on open source projects.

Here are two tips for those of you using Notepad.

▶ Use a more powerful IDE (such as IDLE or Eclipse), or a programming editor (such as Emacs or vim). For more information on these resources, see the Editors section of the Python Documentation at http://www.python .org/doc/.

▶ Become much more flexible with the Subversion revision control system. You can do this by checking out this book's example code using Subversion. *Chapter 1* explains this procedure.

Speeding Up Development Time

Zope contains a little trick to speed up your development time while you are using Products. If your product contains a file called *refresh.txt*, then your product will have an extra tab in the Control Panel called "Refresh." There you can choose to enable product refreshing.

Product refreshing means that you do not have to restart Zope to load changes to your product. You can simply refresh the product without starting Zope. You can also set your product to refresh itself automatically if it changes. This makes development very quick.

The downside to product refresh is for products that use an advanced technique of initializing global data in their modules when they load. These products cannot be refreshed because they will fail or behave strangely when they try to reinitialize that global data. Other problems may occur with refresh as well.

In general, the ability to quickly refresh a product doesn't save you much time in the end, because the ability to load a product that quickly without testing the new feature inevitably will invite bugs in your product that you will have to waste time fixing down the road. It is always better to have a testing framework like Selenium, discussed in *Chapter 10*, then to rely on something like refresh to save time.

Creating a Tool

As was mentioned in the beginning of this chapter, CMF type knowledge is useful for making new Plone tools. For more information about tools and an overview of Plone's existing tools, see *Chapter 2*.

Plone tools are simple objects that sit in the root of your Plone site. By convention, you should only add tools to the root of a Plone site. You can break this rule if you want to -- Plone won't stop you -- but you should stick with that convention if you want to call your object a "tool."

Tools are generally very simple objects that are used only through the ZMI, and programmatically from Python code or templates. While some tools are Plone-specific, such as archetypes_tool and reference_catalog, most of the tools come from CMF, such as portal_skins and portal_membership. In some cases, Plone has taken an existing CMF tool, subclassed it, and changed it slightly to suit Plone's purposes.

Often, you might need to create a new tool. For example, I recently created a CMF product called CMFRelationTool (http://www.plonelive.com/blog/cmfrelationtool). It added rdflib support to CMF 1.5. This tool works with Plone 2.1 running CMF 1.5 and Zope 2.8 and is part of the Zemantic initiative to add RDF support to Zope and Plone (http://www.zemantic.org/).

The CMFRelationTool is very simple. It adds a new tool to a Plone site that provides a simple API for managing an rdflib Graph object. More information on rdflib and its API is available on the rdflib home page (http://rdflib.net/). See Listing 6.22.

Listing 6.22

```
"""
A CMF tool for managing RDF relations.
"""

from Globals import DTMLFile, InitializeClass
from OFS.SimpleItem import SimpleItem
from AccessControl.SecurityInfo import ClassSecurityInfo
from BTrees.OOBTree import OOBTree

from rdflib import Graph as rdflibGraph
from rdflib.backends import ZODB as ZODBBackend

from config import *

class RelationTool(SimpleItem):
    """ A CMF tool to manage RDF relations."""

    meta_type = portal_type = 'Relation Tool'
    id = TOOL_NAME

    allowed_content_types = ('Graph',)
    filter_content_types = 1

    security = ClassSecurityInfo()

    def __init__(self):
        self._graphs = OOBTree()

    def getGraph(self, name):
        return rdflibGraph(self._graphs[name])

    def addGraph(self, name):
        if self._graphs.has_key(name):
            raise KeyError, ('the graph %s already exists.' %
                             name)
        self._graphs[name] = ZODBBackend.ZODB()

InitializeClass(RelationTool)
```

This code defines the class for the new tool. The tool maintains a Zope
OOBTree object that holds all of the "graphs" inside this tool. An OOBTree is a
very useful persistent object for when you need to hold many objects inside the
same container. The Large Plone Folder object is based on this data structure.

Here you can see that using the structure is very simple; it works just like a Python dictionary.

As with all Zope objects, you need to add some boilerplate code to add the object to a Plone site. Note that this object's "form" method, manage_addRelationToolForm, simply does a redirect; it does not present a form to the user at all. Tools always have the same id, and there can be only one of any kind of tool, so no information needs to be collected from the user. See Listing 6.23.

Listing 6.23

```
def manage_addRelationTool(self, RESPONSE=None):
    """Add a new SchemaEditorTool """

    tool = RelationTool()
    self._setObject(TOOL_NAME, tool)
#


    if RESPONSE:
        RESPONSE.redirect(self.absolute_url() +
                          '/manage_main')

def manage_addRelationToolForm(self, RESPONSE=None):
    """ objects must have docstrings to be published. """
    if RESPONSE:
        RESPONSE.redirect(self.absolute_url() +
                          '/manage_addRelationTool')
```

Notice that this tool does not provide a way for you to specify its id. That's because there can be only one tool per Plone site and its name is always the value config.TOOL_NAME. Listing 6.24 is the config.py module for the product:

Listing 6.24

```
SKINS_DIR = 'skins'
GLOBALS = globals()
PROJECT_NAME = PKG_NAME = 'RelationTool'
TOOL_NAME = 'relation_tool'
```

It simply defines the usual constants for a CMF product. Note that the tool name is 'relation_tool'. A product needs an initialization function to install it into Zope. See Listing 6.25.

Listing 6.25

```
from Products.CMFCore.DirectoryView import registerDirectory
from config import *

registerDirectory(SKINS_DIR, GLOBALS)

from Extensions.Install import install

def initialize(context):
    import RelationTool
    context.registerClass(
        RelationTool.RelationTool,
        permission='Add Relation Tool',
        constructors=(RelationTool.manage_addRelationToolForm,
        RelationTool.manage_addRelationTool),)
```

Notice that this initialization function is different from the one shown for the Book examples above: it does not register a content class, but instead registers a class with registerClass(). Finally, to install the tool into a Plone site, you need to write a quickinstaller script in Extensions/Install.py that creates a new relation_tool in the site's root. See Listing 6.26.

Listing 6.26

```
from cStringIO import StringIO
from Products.RelationTool.config import GLOBALS, PROJECT_NAME

def install(self):
    out = StringIO()
    rt = self.manage_addProduct['RelationTool']
    rt.manage_addRelationTool()
    print >> out, "Successfully installed %s." % PROJECT_NAME
    return out.getvalue()
```

For more information on this code, see the PloneLive.com posting on this product at http://www.plonelive.com/blog/cmfrelationtool.

Summary

This chapter is the first step to "jump the gap" from developing Plone products using the ZMI to developing products in Python code. You learned about Python products that define new portal types, and how to register the classes, skins, and other parts of the product with Plone. *Chapter 7* continues this theme of product development using the newest type system to come with Plone 2.1: Archetypes.

## CHAPTER 7

Archetypes

Author: Michel Pelletier

New in Plone 2.1, Archetypes is a type system to replace the CMF type system described in Chapter 5. This new, schema-driven type system was initially a third-party product, but became so popular that the Plone developers decided to adopt it as the new type system for Plone 2.1.

Introducing Archetypes

Archetypes is a suite of tools that simplifies developing Plone types and provides additional functionality. It simplifies type development by abstracting out complexities such as Factory Type Information and class hierarchies. It also automates many of the most common tasks for creating a new object.

Archetypes provides automatic edit and view form generation for types, freeing the type developer from creating complex HTML pages to present objects. For a deployed application that requires a custom form layout, Archetypes lets you create new HTML widgets that display form elements specific to your application.

This automated, customizable, schema-driven form generation is one of the key features of Archetypes, and is based on four concepts:

▶ Schemas define the data model for an object that Archetypes will use to automatically generate view and edit forms. A schema is an ordered sequence of *fields*. The Schema API allows you to manage a schema's fields dynamically.

▶ Fields define the individual data elements of a Schema. There are many kinds of fields, usually one for each common type of data such as string, integer, text, etc. You can use fields to hold references to other Plone objects. You can also create custom fields to hold data specific to your application.

▶ Widgets define how to render fields into a presentation format, such as XML or HTML. There are many kinds of widgets, usually at least one for each field type. For example, using the IntegerWidget with the IntegerField is the default association, although you can customize widgets and fields.

▶ Validators verify that data provided for a field matches certain criteria. For example, you might want to ensure that when code attempts to change an IntegerField that the data it is trying to set it to is actually an integer. Other criteria include that data is in a certain format (like a URL or email address) or that it matches a certain pattern. The criteria are completely flexible, and most of the default fields come with sensible default validators.

These four concepts form the basis for the four most important features of Archetypes:

▸ Automatic form generation. Previously, it was necessary to create HTML templates to display and edit CMF types, but archetypes can generate their own view and edit interfaces. By defining a schema consisting of a set of fields that are each associated with widgets and validators, the Archetypes framework has everything it needs to create attractive HTML forms and views automatically for you.

▸ Rich library of stock form fields, widgets, and validators. Archetypes has a rich variety of fields, widgets, and validators that let you mix-and-match and customize a schema. All of the HTML form elements have a corresponding standard widget and field. One of the great advantages of Archetypes is that you may switch to more sophisticated or specialized widgets as they become available, without having to change any of your code. They abstract the presentation of fields cleanly.

▸ Ability to provide custom fields, widgets, and validators. Archetypes provides a rich API that is so easy to use that you will rarely need to customize your own fields or widgets. Customizing validators, on the other hand, is a common requirement in most applications.

▸ Automating transformations of content. Content is often represented in multiple formats. The same document may be presented in HTML, Word, OpenOffice, plain text, PDF, and more. Because Archetypes does not require you to use just HTML widgets to render content, you can customize it to render content in many document formats. A very important application of this concept is that of *marshalling*. A field may have various marshallers that transform its contents to formats that specific clients can understand. WebDAV is an important class of such clients. These come into play when you save documents to a Plone site that was mounted as a web drive.

One of the best features about Archetypes is how well-documented for programmers it is. (HOWTOs for beginners are a bit less extensive.) Each kind of schema, field, widget, and validator is fully documented in the `interfaces` package in the Archetypes *Product* directory. These interfaces are an excellent resource for learning how to use the various components of an Archetypes-based system.

In this chapter, you will explore all of these concepts to bring the power of Archetypes to your Plone types.

ATPloneLive Sample

To follow along with the examples in this chapter, download the example Arche-types PloneLive product. Like *Chapter 4*'s example product, it adds two new types to Plone – the Book and Chapter types – but it uses Archetypes instead of CMF.

Download the example ATPloneLive product from the PloneLive.com web site. Install it like any other Plone product, but note that this product will only work on Plone 2.1 or later, or a Plone 2.0.5 that has at least Archetypes 1.3 installed. Archetypes are based on the same Zope product concepts that were discussed in *Chapters 4* and *6*. Like any other Zope product, an Archetypes product consists of a Python package that contains the type definition, initialization, and installa-tion code.

The Type

As in *Chapter 6*, this chapter illustrates how to create Book and Chapter types, but it uses Archetypes instead of CMF types as the basis for these new types. Here is some example code that creates two new types using Archetypes.

First, every Archetypes-based product should have a **config** module that defines some useful constants for your product. See Listing 7.1.

Listing 7.1

```
from Products.CMFCore.CMFCorePermissions import AddPortalContent
from Products.Archetypes.public import DisplayList

ADD_CONTENT_PERMISSION = AddPortalContent
PROJECTNAME = "ATPloneLive"
SKINS_DIR = 'skins'

GLOBALS = globals()
```

This simple snippet of code shows various constants used in the rest of this chapter. The permission, project name, and skin location are the most common constants for an Archetypes-based product. The **globals** constant later registers the new product with the Archetypes framework.

Second, define the new types. See Listing 7.2.

Listing 7.2

```
from Products.Archetypes.public import BaseSchema, Schema
from Products.Archetypes.public import StringField, TextField
from Products.Archetypes.public import SelectionWidget,
    TextAreaWidget
from Products.Archetypes.public import RichWidget
from Products.Archetypes.public import BaseContent, registerType
from Products.Archetypes.Marshall import PrimaryFieldMarshaller
from Products.CMFCore import CMFCorePermissions
from config import PROJECTNAME
```

The above import statements include all of the necessary objects from various libraries that this example uses. In particular, note how the **PROJECTNAME** object is included from the **config** module. See Listing 7.3.

Listing 7.3

```
schema = BaseSchema +  Schema((
```

The above code is, easily, the heart of an Archetypes-based product and is the most important code in this chapter to understand. This code creates an object called **schema**, which is composed of a **BaseSchema** and an additional application specific schema. The base schema of an Archetype is an **id** and **title** field that complies with Zope's need for all types to define at least these two attributes. The next three fields in Listing 7.4 define the data elements specific to a Chapter type, a field to specify the authors of the chapter, and an abstract that gives a high-level summary of the chapter's contents:

Listing 7.4

```
    StringField('author',
required=1,
widget=TextAreaWidget(),
),
```

This field represents the simplest of all Archetype's fields and widgets: the StringField and the TextAreaWidget. This code creates a new StringField whose

---

first argument is its id, which is `'author'`. It also has two keyword arguments: `required` and `widget`. The first specifies whether the field is required, and the second specifies which widget renders this field. See Listing 7.5.

Listing 7.5

```
TextField('abstract',
  searchable=1,
  primary=1,
  default_output_type='text/html',
  allowable_content_types=('text/plain',
   'text/structured',
   'text/restructured',
   'text/html',
   'application/msword'),
  widget=RichWidget(label='Body'),
  ),
```

This code shows a more complex Archetypes widget whose id is `'abstract'`. Notice that this widget has a **searchable** keyword argument that indicates that Plone should catalog it under the SearchableText index. This index is used for full-text searches, but it is not required because there is no **required** argument. The **primary, default_output_type**, and **allowable_content_types** arguments specify what kinds of content this field can contain, what the default content is, and that this field is the primary field for this object. See Listing 7.6.

Listing 7.6

```
  ),
  marshall=PrimaryFieldMarshaller(),
  )
```

This last schema attribute, **marshaller**, defines the object that will marshal content to and from the object. A marshaller is a tool that transforms the content for the document, whether it came from a web form, a word document, an FTP file, or more. The PrimaryFieldMarshaller is the most common marshaller; it places most posted content in the primary field. See Listing 7.7.

Listing 7.7

```
class Chapter(BaseContent):
    """This is a sample chapter. It has an overridden view for show,
    but this is purely optional
    """

    schema = schema # Defined above

    actions = ({
'id': 'view',
'name': 'View',
'action': 'string:${object_url}/chapter_view',
'permissions': (CMFCorePermissions.View,)
},)
```

Here you have your actual Python class. All of the magic is in the schema, but
you can customize this class with your own methods. See Listing 7.8.

Listing 7.8

```
registerType(Chapter, PROJECTNAME)
```

Last, the type is registered. The **registerType** function does this to make it
available to the Archetype system. You can now use it inside Plone like any other
content object.

In addition to a Chapter archetype, you need a Book archetype that will contain
the chapters. See Listing 7.9.

Listing 7.9

```
from Products.Archetypes.public import BaseSchema, Schema
from Products.Archetypes.public import StringField, TextField
from Products.Archetypes.public import SelectionWidget,
    TextAreaWidget
from Products.Archetypes.public import RichWidget
from Products.Archetypes.public import BaseFolder, registerType
from Products.Archetypes.Marshall import PrimaryFieldMarshaller
from Products.CMFCore import CMFCorePermissions
from config import PROJECTNAME

schema = BaseSchema +  Schema((
```

```
        StringField('authors',searchable=1,
                    widget=TextAreaWidget(),),
        StringField('blurb',searchable=1,
                    widget=TextAreaWidget(),),
        TextField('abstract',
          searchable=1,
          required=1,
          primary=1,
          default_output_type='text/html',
          allowable_content_types=('text/plain',
            'text/structured',
            'text/restructured',
            'text/html',
            'application/msword'),
          widget=RichWidget(label='Body'),
          ),
        ),
          marshall=PrimaryFieldMarshaller(),
          )

class Book(BaseFolder):
    """This is a sample book, it has an overridden view
    for show, but this is purely optional
    """

    schema = schema

    actions = ({
        'id': 'view',
        'name': 'View',
        'action': 'string:${object_url}/book_view',
        'permissions': (CMFCorePermissions.View,)
        },)

registerType(Book, PROJECTNAME)
```

This code is nearly identical to the Chapter code above. The magic of Archetypes lies in the way the framework does almost everything for you; you only have to define the schema. In this way, Archetypes is like a schema definition language from which you can derive complex behaviors.

Initialization

Now that you have created the Book and Chapter archetypes, it is time to create the Product initialization file that registers the new product with Zope. This file is the *__init__.py* file explained in *Chapters 3* and *5*. All of these concepts were introduced in *Chapter 6*; in particular, note that Archetypes does not require the **_zbases_initialize_phase1** and **phase2** functions. See Listing 7.10.

Listing 7.10

```
from Products.Archetypes import public
from Products.CMFCore import utils
from Products.CMFCore.DirectoryView import registerDirectory

from config import SKINS_DIR, GLOBALS, PROJECTNAME
from config import ADD_CONTENT_PERMISSION

registerDirectory(SKINS_DIR, GLOBALS)

def initialize(context):

    import ATBook, ATChapter

    content_types, constructors, ftis = public.process_types(
        public.listTypes(PROJECTNAME),
        PROJECTNAME)

    utils.ContentInit(
        PROJECTNAME + ' Content',
        content_types     = content_types,
        permission = ADD_CONTENT_PERMISSION,
        extra_constructors = constructors,
        fti= ftis,
    ).initialize(context)
```

The ContentInit class is the same one used in *Chapter 6*, but the **process_types** function has made registering types much easier.

The Installation Script

Once again, your product needs a Plone installation script in order to register the new skins and content objects with Plone. This is very similar to the installation script shown in *Chapter 5*. See Listing 7.11.

Listing 7.11

```
from Products.Archetypes.public import listTypes
from Products.Archetypes.Extensions import utils
from Products.ArchExample.config import PROJECTNAME, GLOBALS

from StringIO import StringIO

def install(self):
    out = StringIO()

    utils.installTypes(self, out, listTypes(PROJECTNAME),
                        PROJECTNAME)

    utils.install_subskin(self, out, GLOBALS)

    out.write("Successfully installed %s." % PROJECTNAME)
    return out.getvalue()
```

Notice the how the `listTypes` Archetypes function makes this a much simpler script than in *Chapter 4*. You don't need to hard-wire each type because Archetypes knows how to register them, and you don't need to register with the Types tool because Archetypes already knows which types are registered to your project. This example defines `out` as a StringIO instance so that you can write snippets of feedback during the installation process. For example, your product checks for the presence of other products in order to use them instead of relying on a fallback, and you include feedback to reflect this. In the present case, returning a simple string would have sufficed, but using a StringIO provides greater flexibility for the future.

Fields

A field is a data element of a schema that holds a certain kind of data. Fields are more than just placeholders for data; you can also associate them with a *widget* that displays them and a *validator* that validates the data that they contain.

Widgets (discussed in more detail in the next section) are responsible for presenting a user interface that represents a field and, in most circumstances, allows the user to edit the field intelligently.

A validator verifies that any information that a widget or other component attempts to assign to a field is in the right format. For example, in the case of an IntegerField, the built-in integer widget will display an HTML textbox that allows you to edit the integer field. The built-in validator makes sure that the data actually entered into the field is an integer and not some other kind of non-integer character.

Validators are particularly powerful because they can control what happens if the data is invalid. In most cases, the default behavior is to redirect the user back to the form and highlight the erroneous input. However, you can control this behavior by creating custom validators.

All field objects have the arguments displayed in Table 7.1:

Table 7.1: Default Arguments for Field Objects

Field Object	Description	Default Expression
required	This argument specifies whether the field should be required when editing the schema.	False
default	This argument specifies a default value for the field.	None
vocabulary	For selection widgets, this argument defines the vocabulary of the widget, or a list of possible selection terms. Vocabularies offer a powerful way of making dynamic selection widgets.	()
enforce Vocabulary	Set this argument to "true" to enforce the vocabulary and to disallow the user from selecting or entering an invalid term that is not in the vocabulary.	False
multiValued	This argument specifies whether the field can hold single or multiple values.	False
searchable	This argument specifies whether the object should be cataloged as full-text searchable.	False
isMetadata	This argument specifies whether the content object for this field is metadata or is a part of the object's data.	False

Table 7.1: Default Arguments for Field Objects

Field Object	Description	Default Expression
accessor	This argument allows you to specify the accessor function, which gets called when this field is accessed. Archetypes generates accessors for all your fields by default, named get\<Fieldname\> and set\<Fieldname\>, where "Fieldname" is the capitalized version of your field's id. If you want to override this generated accessor, simply define a method with the same name in your Archetype class definition. You only need to use this argument when you want the accessor to be a differently named method.	None
mutator	This field allows you to specify a mutator method (corresponding to the "set..." method) that gets called when the field is changed.	None
mode	This argument defines the mode of the field. R stands for "read" and W stands for write; "rw" means that the object can be read (accessed) and written to (mutated).	'rw'
read_permission	This argument specifies the permission required to read the field.	CMFCorePermis sions.View
write_permission	This argument specifies the permission required to write the field.	CMFCorePermis sions.Modify PortalContent
storage	This argument specifies the storage for the field. It allows you to plug different storage back-ends into your fields so that you can keep your Archetype field data in a relational database.	AttributeStorage ()
force	This argument currently is not in use, though it may be used in the future. See http://plone.org/ documentation/archetypes/ arch_field_quickref_1_3_1	''
type	This argument specifies a type name for the field.	None
widget	This argument specifies the widget for the field.	StringWidget
validators	This argument specifies a sequence of validators for the field.	()

Table 7.1: Default Arguments for Field Objects

Field Object	Description	Default Expression
index	"KeywordIndex", or "<index_type>:schema". This argument is independent of the searchable argument, which specifies whether this class participates in full-text searches. See *Archetypes/docs/quickref.rst* for a more in-depth description.	None
index_method	This argument has two hard-coded strings: '_at_accessor' and '_at_edit_accessor'. With '_at_accessor', the field's accessor retrieves the value for all fields that are indexed. With '_at_edit_accessor', the it uses the edit_accessor method if defined for the field (see *Archetypes/docs/quickref.rst* for a description).	'_at_accessor'
schemata	This argument groups fields. The Archetypes default edit templates use these groups to present field groups as separate tabs.	'default'
language Independent	This argument determines whether a field is translatable. This allows frameworks like LinguaPlone to plug different translations of content into a common site framework. Set it to "true" for values that should never be translated (like proper nouns).	False

Standard Archetype Fields

You can create each Archetype field in a schema by calling the field's type, as you would construct an object from any Python type. All fields accept the default arguments shown above, and some have their own arguments that apply to their specific features. Below is a list of all the stock Archetype fields and their arguments, if any.

StringField

The StringField is the simplest of all Archetypes fields. Shown in the examples above, the string field holds a string of data. String fields are good for simple text attributes like names and addresses. They do not have any special arguments.

TextField

A TextField is like a string field, but is intended to hold a whole body of text, not just a small string. Text fields are ideal for longer text attributes, like descriptions and document content.

In addition to the arguments described in Table 7.1, they have the arguments in Table 7.2:

Table 7.2: TextField Arguments

Field Object	Description	Default Expression
`default_content_type`	This argument is the default content type of the text.	'text/plain'
`default_output_type`	This argument is the default output type of the text.	'text/plain'
`allowable_content_types`	This argument is a sequence of formats that this type is allowed to accept.	('text/plain',)
`primary`	This argument states that this field is the primary field for the schema and that any uploaded data should go into this field.	False

BooleanField

A BooleanField contains either a true or a false value.

ComputedField

A ComputedField returns a computation that is the result of evaluating a Python expression. As such, this is a read-only field. This field takes the expression as an argument named `expression`.

DateTimeField

The DateTimeField contains a date/time object that specifies a point in time.

FileField

The FileField contains a file and has the following additional arguments in Table 7.3:

Table 7.3: FileField Arguments

Field Object	Description	Default Expression
content_class	This argument is the class for handling the content of this file object. It is useful for repurposing this field to handle specific file types.	File
default_content_type	This argument is the default content type of the file data.	'application/octet'

FloatField

The FloatField contains a Python floating point value. This is used to hold numbers that represent decimal values, like 3.14 (Π).

ImageField

The ImageField is like a FileField, but contains image data and has a thumbnail feature. It has the additional arguments in Table 7.4:

Table 7.4: ImageField Arguments

Field Object	Description	Default Expression
original_size	This argument is the original size of the image. This field auto-detects the size if it is not specified.	None
max_size	This argument is the maximum size of the image.	None
sizes	This argument is a mapping of names to image sizes. It is useful for specifying a sequence of sizes the user can choose from.	{'thumb':(80,80)}

Table 7.4: ImageField Arguments

Field Object	Description	Default Expression
swallowResizeExceptions	If true, any exceptions raised in the resizing of an image will be silently ignored and a broken image will be shown.	False
default_content_type	This argument is the default content type of the image. It auto-detects the type in most cases.	'image/png'
allowable_content_types	This argument is a sequence of types that this widget will accept. Customized fields could accept more formats.	('image/gif','image/jpeg','image/png')

IntegerField

An IntegerField contains an integer.

LinesField

A LinesField contains a sequence of text lines.

ReferenceField

A ReferenceField contains a reference to another Archetypes object (the referent) and specifies the relationship between the referent and the referrer. It contains the additional arguments in Table 7.5:

Table 7.5: ReferenceField Arguments

Field Object	Description	Default Expression
relationship	This required field defines the relationship between the referrer and the referent. This is allows you to define complex relationship graphs using Archetypes.	None
allowed_types	This argument is a tuple of portal types that can be the referent; empty means allow all.	()

Table 7.5: ReferenceField Arguments

Field Object	Description	Default Expression
allowed_types_method	This hook decides whether a type is allowed. The default value for allowed type is normally 'allowed_types', but if you set this argument to the name of a method, you can dynamically control the allowed types of the referent.	None
vocabulary_display _path_bound	This argument is the upper bound of vocabulary entries.	5
vocabulary_custom _label	This argument is the label to use for the vocabulary. If given, this will override display_path_bound.	None
referenceClass	This argument defines the class used to instantiate a reference of this type.	Reference
index_method	Normally, the default 'index_method' is the standard '_at_accessor' method. This argument allows you to set the name of a method to call instead of the normal accessor to get the value of the field for catalog indexing purposes.	'_at_edit_ accessor'

Widgets

A *widget* is an Archetype component that presents a field to the user. By separating widgets from fields, you can plug in customized widgets to make your fields behave in ways you want (instead of the default behavior). You can also use widgets to display fields in presentation languages other than HTML.

Widget Types

Archetypes comes with the following widget types. If those types require special constructor arguments, they are described here.

TypesWidget

The TypesWidget displays a certain type and contains some default behavior for very similar widgets. Most of the Archetypes widgets are just simple subclasses of the TypesWidget.

IntegerWidget

The IntegerWidget displays and edits Python integers.

ReferenceWidget

The ReferenceWidget displays and edits a reference to another object. This can be either a list of checkboxes or a pull-down list, depending on the number of possible referents.

ComputedWidget

A ComputedWidget holds a Python expression that is evaluated when the widget is displayed.

TextAreaWidget

A TextAreaWidget displays and edits a text area in HTML. The numbers of rows and columns can be specified as arguments, as shown in Table 7.6.

Table 7.6: TextAreaWidget Arguments

Argument	Description	Default Expression
rows	This argument is the default number of text rows to be displayed.	5
cols	This argument is the default number of text columns to be displayed.	40
append_only	This argument means do not replace the existing text with new data; only append it.	False
divider	This argument is the divider to use between appended entries. Use with append_only.	"\n\n=================\n\n"

LinesWidget

A LinesWidget displays and edits a list of strings. For example, a TextField is rendered and edited using a TextWidget, a TextAreaWidget, or a LinesWidget, among others.

BooleanWidget

A BooleanWidget displays and edits a Boolean value. In HTML, this is represented by a check box.

CalendarWidget

A CalendarWidget displays and edits calendars and allows you to pick dates from that calendar. See Table 7.7.

Table 7.7: CalendarWidget Arguments

Argument	Description	Default Expression
format	This argument is the default time format. (See http://docs.python.org/lib/module-time.html.)	'' (A standard time.strftime string.)

The following arguments in Table 7.8 are not yet supported by the Plone templates.

Table 7.8: Arguments Not Yet Supported by the Plone Templates

Argument	Description	Default Expression
show_hm	Not yet supported by the Plone templates.	True
show_ymd	Not yet supported by the Plone templates.	True
starting_year	Not yet supported by the Plone templates.	1999
ending_year	Not yet supported by the Plone templates.	None
future_years	Not yet supported by the Plone templates.	5

Table 7.8: Arguments Not Yet Supported by the Plone Templates

Argument	Description	Default Expression
helper_js	This argument defines the path to the skin element that provides the JavaScript code for the calendar widget. This is useful when you want to customize the JavaScript behavior.	('jscalendar/ calendar_stripped.js', 'jscalendar/calendar-en.js')
helper_css	This argument defines the path to the skin element that provides the style sheet info for the calendar widget. This is useful when you want to customize the styles for the calendar.	('jscalendar/calendar-system.css',)

SelectionWidget

A SelectionWidget displays a list of selectable options that users can choose to fill a field. The user can choose only one option in a selection widget, as opposed to a multi-selection widget (below), which allows you to choose multiple values. See Table 7.9.

Table 7.9: SelectionWidget Arguments

Argument	Description	Default Expression
format	The possible values include flex, select, or radio. It displays either a selection box, a radio button, or "flex," which guesses the right widget to use based on the selection size.	"flex"

MultiSelectionWidget

A MultiSelectionWidget displays a list of selectable options that a user can choose to fill a field. The user can choose multiple options. See Table 7.10.

Table 7.10: MultiSelectionWidget Arguments

Argument	Description	Default Expression
format	The possible values include flex, select, or radio. It displays either a selection box, a radio button, or "flex," which guesses the right widget to use based on the selection size.	"flex"
size	This argument is the default size of the selection widget.	5

KeywordWidget

A KeywordWidget displays and edits keywords on an object.

FileWidget

A FileWidget displays and edits a file field. In HTML, this usually manifests as a box next to a Browse button that allows the user to choose a file to upload into that field.

RichWidget

A RichWidget can edit text in rich formats, not just plain text. See Table 7.11.

Table 7.11: RichWidget Arguments

Argument	Description	Default Expression
rows	This argument is the default number of rich text rows to display.	5
cols	This argument is the default number of rich text columns to display.	40
allow_file_upload	This argument controls allowed file uploads.	True

IdWidget

An IdWidget displays and edits Zope ids. See Table 7.12.

Table 7.12: IdWidget Arguments

Argument	Description	Default Expression
display_autogenerated	This argument show IDs in edit boxes when they are auto-generated.	True
is_autogenerated	This script determines whether an ID is auto-generated.	'isIDAutoGenerated'

ImageWidget

An ImageWidget is like a FileWidget, but it is designed to hold only image data. See Table 7.13.

Table 7.13: ImageWidget Arguments

Argument	Description	Default Expression
display_threshold	This argument only displays if the size of the image is less than or equal to the threshold; otherwise, it shows a link.	102400

LabelWidget

The LabelWidget is a read-only widget that displays a label on the screen. Users cannot edit the label.

PasswordWidget

The PasswordWidget displays and edits passwords. It's like the TextWidget, but it does not echo the characters back to the user to keep the password private. See Table 7.14.

Table 7.14: PasswordWidget Arguments

Argument	Description	Default Expression
modes	This argument determines when the password field is rendered. Since the password never displays, it doesn't make sense to include it when the field is being viewed.	('edit',)
populate	This argument determines whether this field should be populated with the password (hidden behind * characters) in edit and view modes.	False
postback	If true, you won't have to re-enter your passwords if you made a mistake somewhere else on the form. It's less secure, as it involves repeated unencrypted transmission of the password between the browser and the server.	False
size	This argument is the default size of the field.	20
maxlength	This argument is the maximum length of a password.	'255'

EpozWidget

The EpozWidget is like a TextAreaWidget, but designed to use the Epoz visual text editor. For more information on Epoz, see http://epoz.sourceforge.net/. Note that Epoz will soon be replaced by Kupu.

References

References are a powerful feature of the Archetype system. Based on the underlying ZCatalog, Archetypes tracks and classifies relationships between objects. References are bi-directional; each Archetypes object offers an API to find the objects it refers to and the objects that refer to it.

Archetypes supports the methods in Table 7.15 to manage their references:

Table 7.15: Archetypes Reference Methods

Method	Description
`getRefs(relationship=None)`	This method returns a list of all the referenced objects for this object.
`getBRefs(relationship=None)`	This method returns a list of all the objects that reference this object.
`UID()`	This method returns the Unique ID for this object.
`reference_url()`	This method returns a link to this object.
`hasRelationshipTo (target, relationship=None)`	This method tests if a relationship exists between this object and the target. If the relationship is "None," then *any* relationship between the two objects will be returned.
`addReference(target, relationship=None, **kwargs)`	This method adds a reference from this object to a target. Kwargs are metadata for the relationship.
`deleteReference(target, relationship=None)`	This method deletes a reference from this object to a target.
`deleteReferences (relationship=None)`	This method deletes all references from this object.
`getRelationships()`	This method lists all the relationship types for which this object has references.

Using these methods and the underlying reference catalog, Plone developers can create powerful systems. For example, the LinguaPlone tool that internationalizes Plone content uses the reference catalog to store translations of Plone content. LinguaPlone does this by making references between the "canonical" content (the original language version) and its translations. One canonical copy can have many translations, each with its own reference to the canonical version. Based on this, LinguaPlone has some very smart features; for example, if the canonical version of a piece of content changes, then all of the translations can be automatically moved into a workflow so they can be retranslated.

Using references is also a good way to offer new features to existing objects without changing those objects. Instead of changing an object by adding an attribute or a method to extend it, you can use references to associate new behavior and data with an object. In this way, you can "glue" the parts of your site together logically without changing any underlying Python code on those objects.

This allows you to create applications whose business logic is completely separate (other than the references) from the content object themselves. This is how LinguaPlone can internationalize any kind of Archetypes-aware content object, even if they were never designed with that feature in mind.

Archetypes Tools

Because it has so many features, Archetypes has inspired a whole suite of tools and types based on it. Because Archetypes is a framework, it encourages developers to extend the framework with features that other Plone developers can use in their web applications. These framework-level components take the basic concepts of Archetypes and extend them to solve particular problems.

ArchGenXML

The ArchGenXML tool can be very useful for content developers working with Archetypes. ArchGenXML lets you use visual software design tools based on the UML language to create archetypes automatically in your Plone site.

ArchGenXML is a tool that converts the standard XMI (the standard XML representation of UML) format into a generated Python product. XMI is the format used by many UML editors and other code design editors. Developers use it to store class, method, and attribute information. UML editors use this information to present the information as UML diagrams. ArchGenXML uses it to generate Python code that is based on Archetypes.

ArchGenXML has many advantages. Typically, the most useful way to use ArchGenXML is to build quick, complex prototypes of your application by designing them visually using a UML editor first, and then generating your code from that initial sketch design.

There are some issues that you must consider whenever you make use of code generation from an XMI document. Once you generate the code, you cannot modify it; you must modify the model it comes from and then regenerate it.

Otherwise, you will have to maintain a separate list of changes that you have made to the file since you generated it. This can be frustrating, especially with inflexible code generation tools.

The ArchGenXML framework tries to solve the above problems by checking to see if you have modified the code yourself and leaving that code alone if you have. Note that this only partly solves the problem. If you have made serious changes to the code, then changing the model can lead to problems if you don't know what you're doing.

ATContentTypes

Archetypes provides a wonderful framework for developing types, but it does not come with any types itself. Its purpose is to create new types. Early in the development of Archetypes, the developers began working on an example hierarchy of Archetypes that mimics the CMF-style types, but that are based on the Archetypes framework instead.

This new set of types based on Archetypes is called the AT Content Types, or ATCT for short. ATCT is a set of types that look and act almost exactly like the CMF types from which they are inspired, but instead of complex, hand-generated forms and views, these types leverage the Archetypes system to generate forms and views automatically.

ATCT plays several roles:

▶ It evolves Plone to newer technology, removing the older CMF types that are not schema-driven or very flexible.

▶ It acts as a clear example of implementing Archetypes-based components. Anyone mystified by a particular feature of Archetypes can always turn to ATCT for an example.

▶ It provides base classes upon which you can build your own objects to extend their behavior.

You can download ATCT from The Collective (http://svn.plone.org/collective) for versions of Plone previous to 2.1. ATCT comes with Plone 2.1 by default; by the time you are reading this, you should have ATCT built into your Plone site already. If you are trying to migrate an existing site to ATCT, see below for information on Plone migration.

ATCT Hierarchy

ATCT has a very straightforward inheritance hierarchy. To work as Plone content objects, all ATCT objects subclass from PortalContent (as explained in *Chapter 6*). The Archetypes framework hides most of these details of the CMF, but all Archetypes types are really subclasses of these standard Plone classes.

However, with ATCT, you only need to deal with the same portal types that come with CMF, but in Archetypes form. Since you have less worry about the underlying machinery, you only need to focus on your schemas and their fields and widgets.

ATCT is meant to be backwards compatible with Plone's older CMF types as much as possible. If you do not desire this behavior, you should work with Archetypes to develop your own hierarchy of types – not based on ATCTs, but possibly inspired by them. You have the freedom to choose either path: if you want the easiest and most backwards-compatible transition to Archetypes, use ATCT; if you want to design your own types from the ground up, just use the Archetypes framework to create your own type hierarchy.

Migration

As with any new technology, migration can be an issue. Specifically, migrating from an older CMF-based version of Plone to a newer, post-2.1 Archetypes-based Plone is covered in *Chapter 8*. This section discusses the issues of migrating your Archetypes over time as the object evolves.

Migration is necessary if you have any existing objects that use CMF types that you want to use for the new ATCT types. The migration scripts query your system for every object and evolve those objects from an old CMF type to its corresponding new archetype. This is not a simple process, as the migration script must try to gracefully deal with any possible strange or customized objects that may exist in all of the various systems out there.

Because of this, there is no guarantee for anyone that migration is going to work. Of course, before undertaking any kind of upgrade or migration of an important site, you should back up all of your site's code and data. You could not only lose your data, but you could also lose any means of reproducing what could have been a fixable error.

Migration in Plone is handled by the poral_migration tool in the root of a Plone site. This tool has a Migrate tab that allows you to update your site to the most recently installed version of the software. This screen will also tell you whether your site is up to date. To migrate an existing site, choose the version of Plone that your site used previously and click the **Migrate** button. Migration can take a long time, so be patient, and be ready to take down any error information in case you need to report a bug or resolve a problem.

Summary

This chapter shows you the future of Plone development – the Archetypes framework. Archetypes ships with Plone 2.0.5 and up, and Plone 2.1 will also include the Archetype Content Types (ATCT) package. Using the above techniques, you'll be able to develop higher quality products that contain less boilerplate code and can be used in cooperation with other archetypes with little or no modification. *Chapter 8* covers the more advanced features that will be found in Plone 2.1.

Advanced Plone Features and Products

Author: Michel Pelletier

This chapter covers how to migrate from previous versions of Plone to 2.1. This chapter also covers some of the newer and more advanced features in Plone, including the Archetypes Schema Editor (ATSE), TextIndexNG, and the Selenium function test framework.

Overview

A typical Plone system is a lot of software: Plone, CMF, Zope, third-party products, and possibly other software like relational databases and other Internet-centric applications. All these parts work in concert to produce a usable, flexible, powerful web site.

The previous chapters focused on specific features to accomplish common tasks, customizing templates, developing new types, and so forth, but this chapter highlights a broader set of Plone features that a production system will need. It also covers some useful third-party products in the second half of the chapter.

Migration

As your software and environment evolves, it can become necessary for your object types to change with it. For example, a document repository web site reflects the limited number of features offered by the 1.0 version of your software, but now the 2.0 version offers many more features. To use the new features, the old document objects must evolve to support the newer features.

There are several ways to evolve your software as time goes by. This process of evolving objects is *migration*, a subject with various aspects. For example, you must migrate your own types of objects if you plan on maintaining your software, adding new features over time, and releasing that software to the public. Additionally, the parts your software depends on, like Plone, Archetypes, CMF, and Zope, are also changing over time, so you must consider those migration issues as well.

This section covers both migrating your own types and migrating the underlying framework. Most of the time, you will only need to consider migrating your own types. The only time you need to consider migration the underlying framework is when you change the versions of the underlying software on which your system depends.

As of this writing, Plone is still in version 2.0.5, but the version 2.1 release is imminent. If your existing software runs on 2.0.5, but you intend to migrate it to 2.1, then this section is for you. If you are considering creating new software, you might want to work migrating to 2.1 into your plans now instead of later.

Migrating Base Software

Any Plone system is based on four major underlying software components: Plone, CMF, Zope, and Python. Plone depends on CMF, and CMF depends on Zope (therefore, Plone depends on Zope; you'll soon see why this is important) and Zope depends on Python. Table 8.1 lists the stable and development versions of these three frameworks as of this writing:

Table 8.1: Current Versions of Plone, CMF, Zope, and Python

Framework	Stable	Development
Plone	2.0.5	2.1 beta
CMF	1.4	1.5
Zope	2.7.6	2.8 beta
Python	2.4	2.5

As a rule, you should develop and release your own software against the stable releases for the sake of your users. If you are writing your own custom or in-house software, you can use the more recent development versions; however, you must understand the risks involved in using software that has not gone through a full release cycle.

Additionally, sometimes you cannot use the most recent version of a particular product. For example, the most recent version of Python is 2.4, but Zope 2.7.6 only supports Python 2.3. When one software component depends on another, it typically depends on slightly older versions of software. As a rule, if you use versions of software that are not officially supported by the platform you want to use, you are "on your own"; don't stray from the specific version requirements unless you are prepared to accept the risks and mitigate your own problems that may arise.

You will encounter several issues when considering whether to migrate to a newer version of software:

▸ Backwards compatibility

▸ Bug fixes "breaking" your workarounds

▸ Dependencies of your frameworks

The driving force behind open source software is continuous development and improvement. Once you have begun developing your software, it is inevitable that one of the three base frameworks will release a newer version. Both Plone and Zope work on regular release cycles, so you can expect to make a decision at least once or twice a year: should you require your users use an older version of the software, or should you migrate?

If you don't have many resources and you don't need any of the new features in the newer versions of the software, then by all means use the older software. Zope, CMF, and Plone keep and support (to a limited extent) their older versions exactly for this reason. However, if you need new features, or you are forced to upgrade for some other reason (like a critical bug fix) then you must migrate your software to the new versions of the underlying framework.

Migration is hard to get right 100% of the time. For example, if you developed a workaround for a bug in some of the software you use, and that bug gets fixed in the new version, you may face the possibility of the fix breaking your workaround.

In other words, migration issues *always* include an element of the unknown and the possibility of failure. In general, almost all frameworks try to maintain the concept of backwards compatibility, but this is rarely perfect, and it doesn't apply to bugs that get fixed (it's meaningless to be backwards compatible with a bug!).

The last issue to consider is which of the frameworks to migrate and when to migrate them. To understand this issue, you must track the *dependencies* of your software. Not only must you know which version of Plone your software depends on, but what version of CMF and Zope that your version of Plone depends on. For example, you cannot migrate to Zope 2.8 without first considering if Plone has also migrated to this new version.

Migrating Plone

Plone comes with a built-in migration tool called portal_migration that converts a site running an older version of Plone to the newer version. This process goes through and actually changes your object database, so you must back up your data if you intend to preserve it.

To migrate a Plone site to a newer version, go to ZMI for your site's root folder and click on the **portal_migration** tool. This tool will tell you which versions of which software your Plone depends upon. Now click the **Migration** tab to migrate your site from an older version to a newer version.

Typically, you will see the message "Your Plone instance is up to date" on this screen. You will only see a different message if you have installed a newer version of the Plone software. Since you have not yet started migrating your site, this is normal. To begin migrating, shut down your Zope system (back up your data!) and upgrade to the newest Plone version. This involves removing the old Plone products from your instance home and replacing them with the new Plone version.

Once you have installed the new version of the software, restart your Zope system, go to the portal_migration tool, and the click the Migration tab. Now you can migrate your Plone from the previous version to the new version. Note that this process may take a long time for large sites, so be patient, and monitor your system's progress. If, for some reason, the browser doesn't return a page to you and you've waited a long time, try opening a new browser and returning to the Migration tab to see if the process is complete.

Migrating Your Types

If your changes to an object are minor and only require adding an attribute or two to the object, you can add those attributes to the object's Python class with no problems. Instances that do not have that attribute will acquire it from the class the next time someone accesses them. This is a common ZODB programmer trick for quickly hacking in new attributes to objects. (This trick does not work for changing or removing existing attributes, only for adding them.) For example, consider the simple class in version 1.0 (see Listing 8.1):

Listing 8.1

```
class Document(atapi.BaseContent):

    archetype_name = portal_type = meta_type = "Document"
    security = ClassSecurityInfo()
```

Imagine that you need to add a special attribute called _magic to this class for some internal purpose.

Now the 2.0 version of this software expects all of your instances to have a _magic attribute, but the instances that you created with 1.0 do not have it. You can easily provide this by creating a class attribute. When the 2.0 code looks for the attribute on a 1.0 object, the class attribute will provide a default value instead of raising an error. Listing 8.2 is a 2.0 version of the class:

Listing 8.2

```
class Document(atapi.BaseContent):

    archetype_name = portal_type = meta_type = "Document"
    security = ClassSecurityInfo()
    schema = scema
    _magic = None

    def magicHat(self):
        if self._magic is None:
            self._magic = Hat()
        return self._magic
```

Now when this new class encounters old instances of itself during the execution of magicHat(), the old instances will not have a _magic attribute, but since the class does, it will return the class attribute. The default value for this attribute is None, indicating to the magicHat() method that the *instance attribute* should be assigned a Hat object.

This assignment will only happen the very first time magicHat() is called on an old object. From there, the old instances will have a _magic attribute, indistinguishable from new instances. One downside of this approach is that you must usually check whether an attribute is None or some other reasonable default value to know whether it requires assignment. (This is not always the case; for simple attributes like strings and numbers, a default value works well.)

Be aware that this approach calls the __setstate__ method any time the database loads an object. If you write the method to be "expensive" (consuming lots of processor, memory, or other resources), your application will not scale. A __setstate__ method should always be "lightweight" and never consume lots of execution time or block Zope in any way.

Migrating with the __setstate__ Method

When making a more complex change, the ZODB provides a special hook to control the evolution of your objects. When the object database activates an object, it calls a hook method, __setstate__, on that object to reconstitute the object in memory. This method has the opportunity to evolve the object.

However, using __setstate__ has caveats. As objects evolve, the class must keep track of any previous versions of the class it might run into. This means that the __setstate__ method accumulates a lot of backwards compatible debris over time and may become fragile (it may become unable to convert previous versions to the newest version in rare circumstances).

For example, in the 2.0 version of your object, you removed an attribute that existed in the 1.0 version. For small attribute values, it is safe simply to leave the old attribute behind, but in many cases, this is not possible because the old attribute will waste space or not scale well in the new version. It shouldn't continue to exist in the 1.0 software. To remove it from your old objects, use a __setstate__ method (see Listing 8.3):

Listing 8.3

```
class Document(atapi.BaseContent):

    archetype_name = portal_type = meta_type = "Document"
    security = ClassSecurityInfo()

    def __setstate__(self):
        Persistent.__setstate__(self)
        if hasattr(self, 'old_attr'):
            del self.old_attr
```

This example has a Document type that defines a __setstate__ method. This method is called when the database loads an object, so if it loads an old object (one that *has* the old_attr attribute), the method will remove that attribute. From that point forward, you have migrated the old version to the new version by removing the attribute with the Python built-in command del.

Volatile Attributes

The other use of `__setstate__` is to initialize volatile attributes. In ZODB, it is possible to have attributes that are not stored in the database when the object is serialized. These volatile attributes must begin with the string `_v_`. This indicates to ZODB not to store that attribute.

This is very useful for when your objects need to have attributes or help objects that are not serializable. For example, thread locks and file objects cannot be serialized, so you must re-initialize them every time your object is deserialized from the database (activated). This is most commonly done inside `__setstate__`. Consider the code in Listing 8.4:

Listing 8.4

```
class Document(atapi.BaseContent):

    archetype_name = portal_type = meta_type = "Document"
    security = ClassSecurityInfo()

    _v_hat_lock = None

    def __setstate__(self):
        Persistent.__setstate__(self)
        self._v_hat_lock = Lock()
```

Now every time you save your object, the `_v_hat_lock` attribute is ignored, but when your object is restored, it is re-initialized to contain a fresh lock object.

Warning: It's important to keep in mind that `_v_` attributes may disappear at sub-transaction boundaries. Therefore, your application should always be prepared to re-initialize such attributes upon access.

For more information, go to http://www.upfrontsystems.co.za/Members/jean/zope-notes/dangerous_v_.

Migration Scripts

When using the same base class, you can use __setstate__ to evolve your persistent instances. If you must change the base class of your instances, then you are looking at a more complex problem.

In rare circumstances, migrating instances requires more work because you must change the base classes of existing instances, or because you must change a Plone site in some other way when your new software expects something that your old software does not provide. You would normally do this as a batch process because converting existing objects on-the-fly is not feasible. In such cases, you must write a script that searches through your entire Zope hierarchy looking for instances of the old class in order to convert them.

To migrate a product in this way you must write a *migration script*. Your software's users run this script to migrate from an older to a newer version of your code. Migration scripts can often be a pain to manage, because you typically need a number of scripts to handle all of the combinations of upgrades that your users may encounter. For example, if you have a version 1.0 and 2.0 of your software and you want to provide migration scripts to 3.0, you must provide two scripts and instructions to your users on which scripts to run and how to run them.

Another possibility is that you can reuse ideas from the existing Plone migrations package in *Products/CMFPlone/migrations*. This package is essentially a simple framework for managing the various migration scripts that can evolve any version of Plone from 1.0 to 2.1.

What your migration script does depends on how you want to migrate your software. Inside a migration script, you have total freedom to take a site using your old software and do whatever you want to make it new software. For example, consider that your new software requires an additional index in the portal catalog that does not exist in instances of your old software. You would add an *under_construction* index to the catalog so you can search for your types that have this field set. Listing 8.5 is a simple example migration script that adds an index to the portal catalog:

Listing 8.5

```
def migrate2to3(self):
    cat = self.portal_catalog
    if cat._catalog.has_key('under_construction'):
        cat.addIndex('under_construction', 'FieldIndex')
    else:
        return 'Migration was already run.'
```

To run the script, you must install it as an External Method in your Plone site (see *The Zope Book* at http://www.plope.com/Books/2_7Edition/BasicObject.stx#1-4) and then execute the script. In this case, the script will run and add the index to the catalog. Note how the code first checks the catalog to see if the index already exists. If so, it prints a message indicating this, so if your users accidentally run the script twice they will get a sensible result instead of an error.

Deprecated Features

Occasionally, when you install a newer version of your underlying Python system or if you install older products on your current system, you will see Python raise a "Deprecation Warning," telling you that your code is using a feature of Python that is scheduled for removal in a future major release.

You should deal with deprecation issues immediately, because sometimes they are not just warnings about features that will become obsolete; they may be deprecated for a serious reason, such as an inherent security flaw or data safety issue. Additionally, if you leave deprecations for later, they accumulate and become unmanageable in bulk. Most deprecation warnings tell you what you should be doing instead, and the Python library documentation always describes the new features that supersede deprecated features.

Deprecation warnings are also a sign that you are using obsolete or non-maintained software. You will always have to deal with this risk. If the feature is obsolete, you should switch to the new feature that replaces it (recommended) or switch back to an older version of Python (not recommended). If the software you're using is non-maintained, you might need to adopt the code and bring it in line with the most recent Python features yourself. You must weigh these issues any time you try to use other people's code.

You can also issue deprecation warnings for your own code. If you distribute a product that other people use and you want to encourage those users to upgrade to your software's new features, you can implement your own development plan and keep both the old and the new features, but issue deprecation warnings for the old ones.

Your users' software will still run, but they will be reminded whenever they run it that they should upgrade to the new features. As your software continues to evolve, you can then remove the old features after you have given your users time to upgrade.

You can issue warnings by importing the standard **warning** module and calling the **warn** function with a message and the "warning" category. Standard warning categories are built-in Python exceptions, so you don't need to import them. For example, to issue a deprecation warning, use the code in Listing 8.6:

Listing 8.6

```
def somethingOld():
    import warnings
    warnings.warn('The somethingOld function is deprecated.'
                  ' Please use somethingNew instead.',
                  DeprecationWarning)
```

You can issue warnings other than deprecation warnings; for more information on Python's warning framework, see http://docs.python.org/lib/module-warnings.html.

Archetype Schema Editor

Archetype schemas are generally specified on a class in Python code, but Archetypes provides a framework for dynamically creating and modifying schemas. In other words, you can not only specify a schema in Python code inside your product, you can create and modify schemas on-the-fly. This provides features that you cannot have using only file system-based schemas. For example, you cannot modify a file system-based schema without access to the file system code itself.

Using dynamic schemas, you can create and build schemas on-the-fly without giving any of your users access to the Python code of your system. This feature has led to the development of a through-the-web schema editor that allows users to manage schemas using an HTML interface. While there have been various version of this editor, the current state of this work is the ATSchemaEditorNG (known as the ATSE, which is available at http://zopyx.com/OpenSource/ATSchemaEditorNG/).

This product allows you to use a web interface to manage schemas that Archetypes objects use. You can add fields, change field widgets, change validators, and make other edits to a schema using your browser. You can manage these schemas in one central location, such as a folder, a portal tool, or via acquisition.

Before you decide to use the schema editor, you should understand some important differences between using the ATSE and editing your schemas in Python code inside your products.

When you use schemas from Python code, you edit them by editing Python. This means that you must have access to the code as a developer in order to edit a schema. Obviously, you cannot let your normal users edit these schemas as they may seriously break the Python code. If you want your users to edit schemas without editing Python code, you need to use the ATSE.

The ATSE works by managing schemas using a through-the-web tool called the *schema provider*. The schema provider does not manage schemas in Python code on the file system; instead, it allows you and other users to manage them using a web-based HTML interface that lets you add, remove, and edit fields in a schema.

There is a fundamental difference between editing schemas in Python and editing them through the web.

The major difference is that when you edit schemas through the web, you are now storing those schemas in the object database; they are no longer in the file system. This presents the same problems that earlier chapters mentioned: changes are now encoded into the object database and cannot easily be reproduced by simply installing a product. If you want to reproduce the changes made to one schema using the ATSE inside another Plone site then you must either replicate the clicks needed to edit the schema through the web or automate the editing process using a script.

In general, it is best to avoid these problems altogether and design your applications so that schemas written by the developers are kept in Python code (where they can be easily reproduced and managed using standard developer tools), and schemas managed by your users are kept in the ATSE.

For example, the CMFMember product uses the ATSE to allow you to edit the schema of your site members. This kind of schema is tied directly to your membership applications, and every site will have different, application-specific fields to add to the schema. In this case, it is not important that the schema is not on the file system and is not easily reproducible, since it is very specific to an individual application, not to the CMFMember product or Plone in general.

There are two parts to using the schema editor. The first is determining where you want to manage your schemas: by containment (objects get their schema provider from their parent folder), via a portal tool (typically called schema_editor_tool), or via acquisition (not recommended). Acquisition has the advantage of allowing you to make deep folder hierarchies, but it adds a lot of complexity if another schema provider were to be accidentally imposed in the acquisition context. The portal tool method is the most explicit and unambiguous of the three.

The second part of using the schema editor is designing your content class to subclass from a special mix-in class provided by the ATSchemaEditorNG package. This class links the object to its schema, which is managed by the schema provider. For the editor to edit a schema, your class's schema must be registered with the schema provider so that it can be edited using the schema editor. This is shown in the "Integrating ATSE" section.

Integrating ATSE

ATSchemaEditorNG is very flexible, so how to register your schema is up to you. You can create one type that registers the schema when the type is installed into Plone, or you can dynamically create schemas on-the-fly and register many of them, all without having to write many Python classes for each schema. This chapter demonstrates the static method.

When you install a product into Plone, its installation script is called, and that script installs the skins and types for the product. If you want your product's types to be manageable by the schema editor, you must register its schemas with the schema editor during the installation script. This is a simple one-line call, but the schema editor tool is not installed by default by the ATSchemaEditorNG product. You must also install this tool yourself. Listing 8.7 is the code for your product's *Install.py* module to register both the tool installation and the schema:

Listing 8.7

```
SchemaEditorTool.manage_addSchemaEditorTool(self)
self.schema_editor_tool.atse_registerSchema('Book',
                                           Book.schema)
```

This code registers the Book schema from the ATPloneLive product in *Chapter 7* into the schema editor tool. Now, when you go to your Plone management screen you will see a new tool called schema_editor_tool. This tool does not have a management interface in the ZMI; you must instead go to the editor URL using your browser, by going to the relative URL *site/schema_editor_tool/ atse_editor*. This will bring you to the schema editor.

From this editor you can add fields, edit their widgets, and adjust their properties. Changes to the schema do not apply to the instances directly – you must update them to reflect any changes made to the schema. This feature means that you can edit a schema and then undo any change you made without having to worry about undoing all those changes to the instances also, as long as the changes haven't been *applied* yet. You can update a schema's instances by clicking on the **update schema** link in the lower left panel of the schema editor.

The ATSchemaEditorNG package is still a young product, but don't let this stop you from using some of its more central features like schema management and schema editing. Future versions promise more features, like managing different parts of a schema through the web or in a Python file, and better UI features.

Selenium Function Tests

If you are a programmer, you may already be familiar with functional testing and unit testing. While *unit tests* test each basic building block of a program (for example, the expected return values of each method), *functional tests* test big bundles of methods at once from the perspective that an end user might encounter. While the rendering of a page might entail hundreds of security checks, validations and object lookups, a functional test would only look to see whether the final page conforms to expectations.

The Plone product Selenium (http://jrandolph.com/selenium-plone/) is a particularly good functional testing tool for Plone sites. Selenium features a "browser bot," a JavaScript program that runs inside your web browser. This bot tests your site feature-by-feature, *using the browser itself*. Selenium can open pages, type information into forms, select values, and click check boxes. Using Selenium, you can script what your users will do and see, and control your browser as though it were a marionette to fully test every feature of your site, right in front of your eyes.

To use Selenium, simply install the Selenium Plone product as you would any other product. Now you can begin to use and understand Selenium immediately by running its built-in Selenium tests. For an example of this, install the Selenium product and go to *site/TestRunner.html*. This will bring you to the Selenium test runner, which will load into your browser a contrived Application Under Test (AUT). The AUT is contrived for the sake of example, but in the normal course of using Selenium, your web application itself would be the AUT. See Figure 8.1.

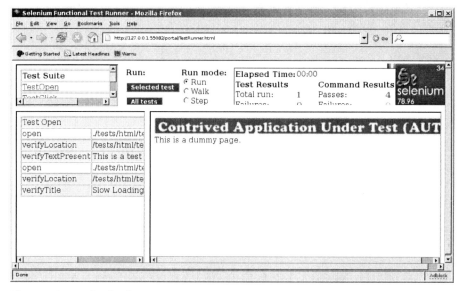

Figure 8.1: The built-in Selenium function tests

This screen is the "test runner." It is composed of three frames. The top frame is the Control frame, containing all of the controls to select and run tests. The left frame is the Test frame, containing the currently selected or running test. The right frame is the AUT frame, containing the application under test. For a quick introduction to how powerful Selenium is, click the **Run All Tests** button. You can also choose what speed you want Selenium to run at, whether Run, Walk, or Step.

The Test frame shows how simple Selenium is. A test is a sequence of commands. Each command tells the browser what to do and what it should expect from the AUT. Each of these commands is documented in Selenium, but looking at the tests can give you a good idea of how to use each command.

Selenium also provides a "driven" mode, where you write a test not as an HTML table of commands, but as a Python script that "drives" the Selenium browser. Using the Selenium product, this is surprisingly easy to do. First, you must install the ZopeTestCase product.

Note: The ZopeTestCase product comes with Zope 2.8, but as of this writing, Zope 2.7.5 is the current stable Zope release and you must download it separately.

Once you have installed ZopeTestCase (refer to the README.txt file that explains its installation), you must install some boilerplate test framework code in your product. By convention, this code, along with the tests themselves, should go in a directory in your product called *ftests*. This package contains a new class that subclasses the ZopeTestCase class and provides Selenium integration. Listing 8.8 is an example of such a class:

Listing 8.8

```
import os, sys, re, xmlrpclib, time

if __name__ == '__main__':
    execfile(os.path.join(sys.path[0], 'framework.py'))

os.environ['EVENT_LOG_FILE'] = os.path.join(os.getcwd(), 'zLOG.log')
os.environ['EVENT_LOG_SEVERITY'] = '-300'



from Testing.ZopeTestCase import FunctionalTestCase
from Products.CMFPlone.tests import PloneTestCase

from urllib import urlencode
from urlparse import urlparse
import webbrowser

ZopeTestCase.installProduct('Selenium')
ZopeTestCase.utils.startZServer(4)

default_user = PloneTestCase.default_user
_d = {'__ac_name': default_user,
      '__ac_password': 'secret'}

import xmlrpclib

class BookFTestCase(FunctionalTestCase, PloneTestCase):

    def afterSetUp(self):
        self.portal_url = self.portal.absolute_url()
        self.folder_url = self.folder.absolute_url()
```

```
        self.qi.installProduct('Selenium')
        # install other products u depend on here
        self._refreshSkinData()
        driver_url = "%s/selenium_driver" % self.portal_url
        self.selenium = xmlrpclib.ServerProxy(driver_url)
        runner_url = "%s/SeleneseRunner.html" % driver_url
        get_transaction().commit(1) # creates app._p_jar
        self.launchBrowser(runner_url)
        time.sleep(15)


    def launchBrowser(self, url):
        webbrowser.open(url, new=0)
```

This class is the basis for all Selenium tests; a ZopeTestCase functional test class merges with a PloneTestCase class with a built-in Selenium browser connection (the `self.selenium` attribute). While that may sound complicated, using it is simple. Listing 8.9 is an example:

Listing 8.9

```
import os, sys
if __name__ == '__main__':
    execfile(os.path.join(sys.path[0], 'framework.py'))


import BanyanFTestCase

member_name = 'member'
member_pass = '123'
member_role = 'Member'


class BookTests(BanyanFTestCase.BanyanFTestCase):

    def testBookLogin(self):
        uf = self.folder.acl_users
        uf.userFolderAddUser(conf_name,conf_pass,
                             [conf_role],[])
        self.selenium.open('/portal/site/login_form')
        self.selenium.type('__ac_name', manager_name)
        self.selenium.type('__ac_password', manager_pass)
        self.selenium.clickAndWait('submit')
        self.selenium.testComplete()
```

This code shows a simple test that logs into a Plone site as a manager. To run this test, you must first set two environment variables that define where are the software and instance homes of the Plone site you want to test. (See *Chapter 1* for more information on software and instance homes.) For Linux or UNIX, use the command in Listing 8.10:

Listing 8.10

```
shell% export SOFTWARE_HOME=/path/to/zope/lib/python
shell% export INSTANCE_HOME=/path/to/instance/home
```

Now that these two variables are set, the test framework has everything it needs to run your new test. All you have to do is run the test module with the Python interpreter (see Listing 8.11):

Listing 8.11

```
shell% python Products/ATBook/ftests/testBook.py
```

This starts the test case that loads Zope, starts it on a private address on your computer (on your localhost interface, 127.0.0.1, and a random port), starts your browser automatically, and points the browser to the Selenium test runner interface. Instead of running the Selenium self-tests like before, this will run *your* test in the Selenium test runner. Now you can write Selenium tests in Python. This has a number of advantages when using Selenium with Plone, especially when you need a way to share tests in a way that other Python developers understand.

LinguaPlone

LinguaPlone is a tool for internationalizing content on your Plone objects. LinguaPlone, or LP, works with Archetypes objects only. You cannot use LP with the older CMF types, as they do not support references.

LP works by storing translations of your content into different languages. This is a different task than translating the UI of your web application. That is the role of the PlacelessTranslationService (PTS), which is discussed in *Chapter 2*. Rather, LP translates the *content* of your object. This is an important distinction.

LP allows you to define one translation of your content as the *canonical* translation. That is the main language in which the document was written. It is the original document, whereas the others are translations. By deeming one language canonical, LP can control what happens to the translations when the canonical version changes.

Because LP translations are real Plone objects, you can "workflow" translations by making translations for content go through a workflow approval process, and if the canonical version of the content object changes, all of the translations can be automatically flagged to require an update to the canonical version.

LP works by translating individual schema elements on an object. You can also specify that certain schema elements are language independent and do not require a translation. Using Archetypes' interface generation framework, Lingua-Plone will generate all of your translation pages and navigation links for you, and it will attempt to present the most appropriate translation to you and your users based on the language settings of the various web browsers.

Figure 8.2: Different editing tabs for different languages

When your users look at your content objects, they will see the most appropriate translation for their browser settings. Alternatively, they can choose from familiar flag icons for the language in which they want to see the content.

LP only accommodates one-use case for translation, where a site displays in only one language at a time. In the case of a trilingual portal such as http://www.capegateway.gov.za/, this does not work. Cape Gateway presents the site navigation in one language, and content in the available languages. If a translation for your chosen language is available, that is what you will see. However, if there is only an English or a Xhosa version, you will see those instead. For this use case, I18NLayer and some customization work is required.

To install LP, go to http://plonesolutions.com/lp and download the LinguaPlonePack.

Install LP by linking or copying it into the instance home's *Products* directory. Once it is installed, you can begin to use it to internationalize your own content.

Warning: This package includes many packages that you may already have (like Archetypes), so installing this package might overwrite your other packages. You should only install LP into a non-production site if you are just experimenting with it.

Changing your existing Archetypes products to use LinguaPlone is a trivial four-line change to your product's import statements (see Listing 8.12):

Listing 8.12

```
from Products.ATContentTypes.config import *

if HAS_LINGUA_PLONE:
    from Products.LinguaPlone.public import *
else:
    from Products.Archetypes.public import *
```

The LinguaPlone API exactly mimics that of Archetypes, so once you have implemented the above code, all of your old code will continue to work perfectly with translations in place. This particular point is very important: LP works totally transparently. The above change is all you need to enable LP for your Archetypes-based content objects.

Because LP is based on the reference catalog, you can safely remove the above import statements and go back to using AT without LP. Nothing bad will happen to your objects or your translations. This is one of the great benefits of the reference catalog; you can easily add new functionality to objects without having to change them or damage them in any way. If you do go back to plain Archetypes, all your translations will still be there. They just won't be visible anymore.

To make your schema translatable, you need to specify to which fields in your schema are language independent, and which are language specific and require translation. For example, on an announcement, you might want to put a date, but the date should not be translated; it makes no sense to transform the date into any other language. The *format* of the date will change on a per-language basis, but not the *actual date itself.* Remember, LP is about translating content, not the UI of that content. See Listing 8.13.

Listing 8.13

```
ATEventSchema = ATContentTypeSchema.copy() + Schema((
    StringField('location',
                searchable=True,
                write_permission = ChangeEvents,
                widget = StringWidget(
    description = "Enter the location where the event
will take place.",
    description_msgid = "help_event_location",
    label = "Event Location",
    label_msgid = "label_event_location",
    i18n_domain = "plone")),

    LinesField('attendees',
        languageIndependent=True,
        searchable=True,
        write_permission=ChangeEvents,
        widget=LinesWidget(label="Attendees",
            label_msgid="label_event_attendees",

                description=("People which should attend "
                "the event."),
                description_msgid="help_event_attendees",
                i18n_domain="plone")),
```

This example comes from the `ATContentTypes.types.schemata` module. This module is the best place to look for examples of using Archetypes schematas. The important parts of the example are in bold.

An argument to the field defines that it is `languageIndependent`. This means that LP will not translate this field. As this field is a list of attendees to an event, this content should not be translated: it makes no sense to translate names.

For language-dependent fields, you do not need to specify anything. LP's default behavior is to translate all schema fields. Once again, if you do not wish to use this feature, or if you want to remove LP from your system, you can do so safely without breaking any of your canonical content objects.

TextIndexNG

TextIndexNG is a next generation text index for Zope. It has many improvements upon the ZCTextIndex that was used in Zope before Plone 2.1. It has several improvements, including these:

- ▶ **DocumentConverters** convert documents from various formats into a form suitable for cataloging.

- ▶ **SimilaritySearch** for English text looks for words that are similar to the query term. This is good for finding possibly misspelled query terms.

- ▶ **NearSearch** searches for terms that are in close proximity to each other.

- ▶ Extended **StopWords** filters out extremely common words to reduce "search noise."

- ▶ **Globbing** performs wildcard searches with ***** and **?**.

- ▶ **NormalizationSupport** reduces accented characters to their base form.

- ▶ **UnicodeAwareness** allows for multi-lingual text searching.

- ▶ **Relevance ranking** scores words in searches based on their frequency within a document.

- ▶ **HTML converter** uses Chris Withers' "Strip-o-Gram" module.

- ▶ **Range searches** use the **..** operator to provide a range of text values that should be searched.

▶ **Substring** searches for a substring within any of the words in the index.

Other than improved features and performance, the TextIndexNG works just like the older text indexes and requires no modification, nor does it change any user interfaces.

Users of Plone 2.0.5 can download TextIndexNG from the http://www.zopyx.com/OpenSource/TextIndexNG home page. To install it, link or copy it into your instance home's *Products* directory. Now when you restart Zope you can go to any ZCatalog object, create TextIndexNG indexes, and use them as drop-in replacements anywhere you would use the default ZCatalog text index.

KeywordManager

The PloneKeywordManager allows you to change, merge, and delete keywords in Plone, and it updates all corresponding objects automatically. You would want to merge keywords when one of your users creates a keyword that is semantically the same as one of your keywords but spelled differently. The PloneKeyword-Manager lets you merge these different spellings or synonyms into the same keyword.

It uses a similarity search to support you in identifying similar keywords. For example, users who have picked the keyword "subject" will be matched with others who picked "subject" or "subjects." The keyword manager allows you to discover and resolve these little inconsistencies.

PloneKeywordManager helps you to build an inductive vocabulary with several people working on the same Plone site. A site manager can clean up keywords from time to time to create a consistent vocabulary. As your users create new keywords, you can vet them to make them all consistent and match the keywords of other users.

The ZMI interface for the PloneKeywordManager contains an alphabetical listing for all of the keywords in your site and a selection box that allows you to select a keyword. Selecting a keyword allows you to see similar terms for that single keyword only. Otherwise, you can navigate a list of all keywords starting with the same letter. See Figure 8.3.

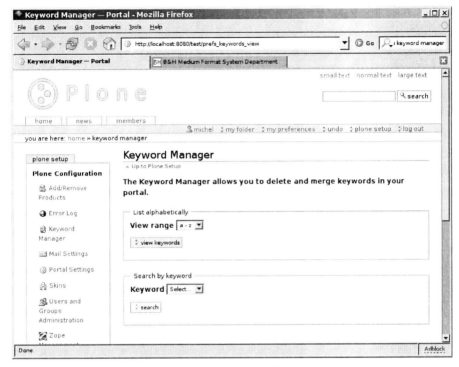

Figure 8.3: The PloneKeywordManager interface

The PloneKeywordManager will then search all keywords starting with that letter and will look for similar keywords. You can now select several keywords and delete them. If you only want to change a single keyword, select it, then enter the new keyword, and click on **Merge**. If you want to merge several keywords into one new one, select them, enter the new keyword, and click on **Merge**.

Summary

This chapter covered a variety of advanced Plone issues, including what is available on the "bleeding edge" of Zope and Plone software. Some of the software in this chapter is very new, making it riskier to use than software that has been in productions systems for years.

The open source world is fast-paced, and by the time many of you read this first edition of the book, Plone 2.1 will finally be released, and this chapter will change, possibly being expanded or split. It's an exciting future, and you can help in many ways to enhance Plone, Zope, Python, any of the myriad of associated open source products, and even this book by visiting PloneLive.com and leaving bug reports, suggestions, and blog entries for other book readers.

Plone and Relational Databases

Author: Munwar Shariff

Relational database are widely used in medium to large enterprises. Zope supports almost all the relational databases available in the market. This chapter highlights how Plone supports external databases to provide an enterprise-scale content management system.

Theory of RDBMS

A Relational Database Management System (RDBMS) stores data in the form of related tables. Prior to the relational system we use today, data was stored in flat-file format. In effect, this is as though data was stored with each record in one large table. The flat-file arrangement required redundant data, which produced large files. It was also extremely awkward to formulate ad hoc queries of flat-file data in an efficient way. In a nutshell, relational database theory was inspired by a problem: the expense and complexity of maintaining data and its associated programs.

The relational model solved the problem of redundant data. Once the theory existed, the tools followed. The solution appeared after Dr. E. F. Codd published a paper entitled "A Relational Model of Data for Large Shared Data Banks" in 1970[1]. In that paper, Dr. Codd introduced a set of rules intended to eliminate the need to store redundant data. These rule formed the genesis of relational database theory.

Many types of database management systems exist, ranging from small systems that run on personal computers to huge systems that run on mainframes. The following are examples of database applications:

▸ Computerized library systems

▸ Automated teller machines

▸ Flight reservation systems

▸ Computerized parts inventory systems

From a technical standpoint, databases can differ widely. The terms relational, network, flat, and hierarchical all refer to the way a database management system organizes information internally. The internal organization can affect how quickly and flexibly you can extract information.

---

1. Codd, E. F. "A Relational Model of Data for Large Shared Data Banks." *Communications of the ACM.* June 1970

Database Tables and Columns

A relationship is represented by a table that stores information about an entity—a conceptual collection of one type of data. Each row corresponds to one tuple (pronounced TUH-pul, which is an ordered set of values), and a column corresponds to an attribute. In this context, an attribute is simply a named column in a relation. In Table 9.1, each row contains information about an Employee in a company.

Table 9.1: Employee Table

Name	Department	Age	Salary	Contact Numbers
Amy	HR	25	$6000	111-222-1234
Michel	Engineering	30	$8000	111-222-1235
Munwar	Marketing	37	$5000	111-222-1236
Jean	Engineering	30	$7000	111-222-1237

Using special programs, you can store, modify, and extract information from a database. Users make requests for information from a database in the form of a *query*, which is a question expressed in a formal syntax. For example, the query in Listing 9.1 requests the list of employees (rows), who belong to the *Engineering* department (column).

Listing 9.1

```
SELECT * FROM Employee WHERE Department = "Engineering"
```

The set of rules for constructing queries is a *query language*. Different RDBMS support different query languages, although there is a standardized query language called *SQL* (structured query language). Few complete implementations of the most recent version of the SQL standard exist, and nearly every database implements its own extensions to the standard. Most databases also implement stored procedures that may be written in a variety of scripting or implementation languages.

Determining Your Database Needs

Eventually, you are going to need persistent objects, or some way to store and retrieve data. The approach you use depends on many factors:

- ▶ You have a lot of data to store (millions of records; Gigabytes and Terabytes of data).

- ▶ You need to quickly search and retrieve your data by joining information from various database tables.

- ▶ You need/want to have a traditional relational model so that you or your users can use standard report generating tools.

- ▶ You want to lock the record while updating information.

- ▶ You need support for ad hoc online queries, report generation, hot database backups, and heavy multi-user or transaction-intensive use.

- ▶ You have other applications that want to use your data.

If the answers to above questions are true, then you need a relational database to store and retrieve your data.

The relational data model allows you to eliminate redundant data, reduce data inconsistencies, and protect data integrity. A well-designed relational database is easy-to-use, flexible, and protects the validity of the data.

ZODB vs. RDBMS

Zope stores all objects in the Zope Object Database (ZODB). Table 9.2 highlights the advantages and disadvantages of ZODB.

Table 9.2: Advantages and Disadvantages of ZODB

Advantages	Disadvantages
It's Pythonic. Your Python data structure is persistent and automatically fetches itself from disk as necessary, and uncaches itself after a period of non-use. The "root object" is a dictionary containing any pickleable objects, which can themselves be lists, dictionaries, etc.	It's a modify-by-appending database. Rather than updating records in place, ZODB adds a new record and "forgets" the old one. This is good for safety, journal record, and undoing, but it's bad for fields that update frequently.
It supports transactions.	It backs up your database frequently. The default store puts everything in one flat file (*zope_instance/var/Data.fs*).
It stores various versions of scripts for each save, and it supports the undo feature.	It's Python-specific. One needs to use Python to query or otherwise manipulate the ZODB. There are a myriad of ways that one can manipulate data in a SQL database.
It supports heavy, primarily read-oriented loads, since many Zope sites rely entirely on it. It scales as needed, with ZEO.	

If you have lots of highly structured data that will be used by other systems, then go for a relational database and don't store them in the ZODB.

Tip: Using the *repozo* script, you can take either full or incremental backups of ZODB. For more information, go to http://www.zope.org/Wikis/ZODB/FileStorageBackup.

Zope Support for RDBMS

Zope supports almost all the databases available in the market as long as they're reachable using ODBC. ODBC (Open Data Base Connectivity) is a standard database access method developed by the SQL Access group in 1992. The goal of ODBC is to make it possible to access any data from any application, regardless of which database management system (DBMS) is handling the data.

You must install the appropriate database adapter to connect to them from Zope. Zope provides two objects to support RDMBS operations: a SQL connection object and a ZSQL Method. The following sections explain these objects in detail. Zope extends its transactional support to RDBMS transactions as well.

Transactions

Zope objects are stored in a high-performance transactional object database known as the Zope Object Database (ZODB). It treats each Web request as a separate transaction by the object database. If an error occurs in your application during a request, any changes made during the request will be automatically rolled back. The Zope framework makes all of the details of persistence and transactions totally transparent to the application developer. Relational databases which are used with Zope can also play in Zope's transaction framework.

A *transaction* is a group of operations that can be undone all at once. All changes done to Zope are done within transactions. Transactions ensure data integrity. When using a system that is not transactional and one of your web actions changes ten objects, and then fails to change the eleventh, then your data is now inconsistent.

For example, you have a web page that bills a customer for goods received. This page first deducts the goods from the inventory, and then deducts the amount from the customer's account. If the second operation fails, you want to make sure the change to the inventory doesn't take effect.

Most commercial and open source relational databases support transactions. If your relational database supports transactions, Zope will make sure that they are tied to Zope transactions. This ensures data integrity across both Zope and your relational database.

In this example, the transaction starts with the customer submitting the form from the web page and ends when the result page is displayed. It is guaranteed that operations in this transaction are either all performed or none are performed, even if these operations use a mix of ZODB and an external relational database.

Database Adapters

In Zope, database connections are made through Database Adapters (DAs), which are specific to the database. See Table 9.3.

Table 9.3: Zope Database Adapters for Common Databases

RDBMS	Description	Database Adapter
MySQL	MySQL is a fast open source relational database. You can find more information about MySQL at http://www.mysql.com.	ZMySQLDA (Zope adapter for MySQL) is available from http://www.zope.org/Members/adustman/Products/ZMySQLDA.
PostgreSQL	PostgreSQL is a leading open source relational database with good support for SQL standards, as well as object database concepts such as table inheritance. You can find more information about PostgreSQL at http://www.postgresql.org.	The newest and prefered DA is ZpsycopgDA, which is included in the psycopg package (http://www.zope.org/Members/fog/psycopg).
Oracle	Oracle is arguably the most powerful and popular commercial relational database. However, it is relatively expensive and complex. You can purchase or evaluate Oracle from http://www.oracle.com.	The DCOracle2 package from Zope Corporation includes the ZoracleDA (http://www.zope.org/Members/matt/dco2).
SQL Server	SQL Server is Microsoft's full-featured database for the Windows operating systems. For any serious use in Windows, it is preferable to Microsoft Access. You can find more information about SQL Server at http://www.microsoft.com/sql/.	mxODBC (http://www.egenix.com/) is written by Egenix and very well-maintained. ZODBC DA (http://www.zope.org/Products/DA/ZODBCDA) is written by Zope Corporation and is available for the Windows platform only. This DA is no longer actively maintained.
MS Access	Microsoft Access is a relational database management system that facilitates the storage and retrieval of structured information on a computer hard drive.	ZJetDA (http://zope.org/Members/jfarr/Products/ZJetDA) provides support for the Microsoft Access database object.

Table 9.3: Zope Database Adapters for Common Databases

RDBMS	Description	Database Adapter
DB2	DB2 from IBM is Oracle's main competitor. It has not only similar power, but similar expense and complexity. You can find more information about DB2 at http://www.ibm.com/software/data/db2/.	ZDB2DA (http://www.bluedynamics.org/products/ZDB2DAFolder/) is developed and maintained by Blue Dynamics.
SAP DB	SAP DB is an open source database developed by SAP. It has an Oracle 7 compatibility mode. You can find more information and downloads at http://www.sapdb.org/.	ZsapdbDA (http://www.zope.org/Members/jack-e/ZsapdbDA) is maintained by Ulrich Eck.
Sybase	Sybase is another popular commercial relational database. You can purchase or evaluate Sybase from http://www.sybase.com.	SybaseDA (http://www.zope.org/Products/DA/SybaseDA/) is written by Zope Corporation (but no longer maintained).
Interbase/ Firebird	Interbase is an open source relational database from Borland/ Inprise. You can find more information about Interbase at http://www.borland.com/interbase/. You may also be interested in FireBird (http://sourceforge.net/projects/firebird), which is a community-maintained offshoot of Interbase. The Zope Interbase adapter is maintained by Zope community member Bob Tierney.	A number of Das are available, including kinterbasdbDA (http://www.zope.org/Members/mwoj/kinterbasdbDA) and gvibDA (http://www.zope.org/Members/bkc/gvibDA).

Table 9.3: Zope Database Adapters for Common Databases

RDBMS	Description	Database Adapter
Gadfly	Gadfly is a relational database written in Python by Aaron Waters. Gadfly is included with Zope for demonstration purposes and small data sets. Gadfly is fast, but is not intended for large amounts of information since it reads its entire data set into memory. You can find out more about Gadfly at http://gadfly.sourceforge.net/. You should never use Gadfly for production systems because it is not thread-safe and does not scale.	The Gadfly Database Adapter is built into Zope.
Ingres	Ingres is Computer Associate's enterprise-level database, which they are open-sourcing and integrating with the ZODB using Shane Hathaway's APE product.	A database adapter is available at http://www.zope.org/Members/zeomega/Ingresda.

The mechanics of setting up relational database is different for each database, putting it beyond the scope of this book. All of the relational databases mentioned have their own installation and configuration documentation that you should consult for specific details.

Each Database Adapter will provide specific installation instructions; be sure to follow them carefully. Zope can connect to all the above-listed database systems; however, you should be satisfied that the database is running and operating in a satisfactory way on its own before attempting to connect it to Zope. An exception to this policy is Gadfly, which is included with Zope and requires no setup.

Installing MySQL and ZMySQLDA

For the rest of the chapter, assume the database is the MySQL database. You need three components for the installation:

▸ **MySQL Database**: Download and install the latest version of MySQL database from http://www.mysql.com.

▶ **MySQL Python adapter**: ZMySQLDA uses the MySQL-python package to connect to MySQL database. It is available at http://sourceforge.net/ projects/mysql-python. Download and install this package as per the installation instructions provided with the package.

▶ **ZMySQLDA**: Download ZMySQLDA from http://www.zope.org/ Members/adustman/Products/ZMySQLDA, unzip it, and move the ZMySQLDA directory to your Zope instance's *Products* directory. Restart Zope after installing the ZMySQLDA product.

Setting Up Database Connections in Zope

Once you install MySQL-python and the ZMySQLDA Product, restart the Zope server to recognize the new Product. In the ZMI (Zope Management Interface), the Z MySQL Database Connection will appear in the drop-down box.

The database connection object establishes and manages the connection to the database. Because the database runs externally to Zope, it may require you to specify information necessary to connect successfully to the database. This specification, called a *connection string*, is different for each kind of database. In ZMI of the Plone root folder, select and add Z MySQL Database Connection from the Products list. For example, Figure 9.1 shows the Add Z MySQL Database Connection form.

Add Z MySQL Database Connection

Id | MySQL_database_connection
Title | Z MySQL Database Connection
Enter a Database Connection String [1] | plonelive_db root
Connect immediately | ☑

[Add]

[1] Connection Strings

The connection string used for Z MySQL Database Connection is of the form:

```
[+/-]database[@host[:port]] [user [password [unix_socket]]]
```

or typically:

```
database user password
```

Figure 9.1: Add Z MySQL Database Connection form

In the **Enter a Database Connection String** field, enter values for the database to which you want to connect and your username. Since the MySQL database is on the same machine and the user has no password, the connection string contains only the database name and the username "root." See Figure 9.2.

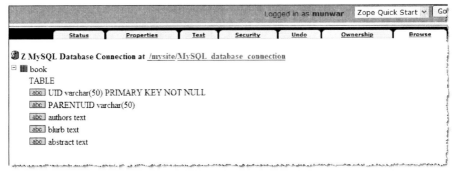

Figure 9.2: Z MySQL Database Connection object

Chapter 9: Plone and Relational Databases

Figure 9.2 illustrates the database connection object. The *Status* tab provides a button for opening and closing the connection. If connection is closed, no queries sent to this connection object will work. The *Properties* tab looks just like the Add Database Connection screen, and you can use it to edit the database connection string. The *Test* tab executes SQL statements on the database just like the console. The *Browse* tab enables you to browse through all the tables that exist in the database and to see the table definitions.

Z SQL Methods

Z SQL Methods are Zope objects that execute SQL code through a database connection. All Z SQL Methods must be associated with a database connection. Z SQL Methods can both query and change database data. Z SQL Methods can also contain more than one SQL command.

A Z SQL Method has two functions: it generates SQL to send to the database, and it converts the response from the database into an object called a *brain*. Brains wrap SQL result sets. This has the following benefits:

▶ Generated SQL will take care of special characters that may need to be quoted or removed from the query. This speeds up code development.

▶ If the underlying database is changed (for example, from MySQL to Oracle), then the generated SQL will, in some cases, automatically change too, making the application more portable.

▶ Results from the query are packaged into an easy-to-use object, which will make display or processing of the response very simple.

▶ Transactions are mediated.

See Figure 9.3.

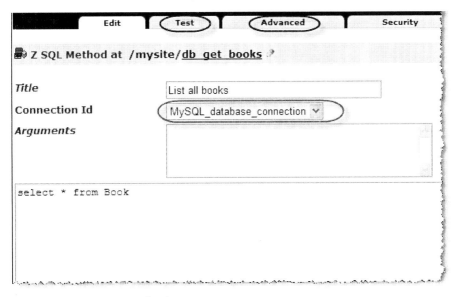

Figure 9.3: Z SQL Method

Figure 9.3 shows a Z SQL Method object. By default, the first database connection object in the acquisition path will be considered as the default database connection object for this Z SQL Method. The *Test* tab executes the Z SQL Method. The *Advanced* tab manages the advanced settings, such as caching and pluggable brains of a SQL method.

Note: For information on Z SQL Methods, refer to http://www.plope.com/ Books/2_7Edition/RelationalDatabases.stx.

Plone and RDBMS

Plone is an enterprise portal and content management system. You will need to integrate your Plone-based application with the existing enterprise databases. You will need to provide highly scalable RDBMS-based membership systems. You will need to store information to the backend RDBMS using Plone's content management framework such as workflow and security. Plone handles all these scenarios well, and the subsequent sections explain them in detail.

Database Applications in Plone

Using a SQL connection object and Z SQL Methods, you can create database applications in Plone.

Plone forms (Zope Page Templates) can capture the information from users on the web site and store the information directly in a backend database. It is always a good practice to submit the form information to a Python script, validate the information captured by the user, and store the information in backend relational database using a Z SQL Method. Plone comes with the portal_form_controller tool and supports special page templates called Controller Page Templates and special scripts called Controller Python Scripts. Controller Page Templates support extensive form validation and automatically redirects based on the result, as illustrated in Figure 9.4.

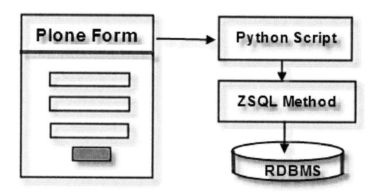

Figure 9.4: Storing form details in a relational database table

Similarly, you can use Z SQL Methods to extract the information from the backend database and send it to a Page template to display in Plone site, as illustrated in Figure 9.5.

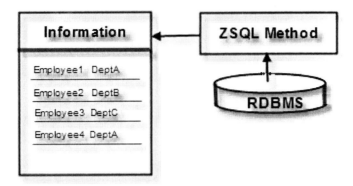

Figure 9.5: Displaying information which is retrieved from a relational database

Z SQL Methods on a File System

You can also create Z SQL Methods in skins out of files, just like scripts and templates. Any file in a skins layer directory with a .zsql extension is considered a Z SQL object. It is a good development practice to keep the SQL methods on disk.

Tip: Use the FSDUMP product to turn ZODB content into on-disk skins.

In order to have the Z SQL Methods in a file system (as skin objects in Plone product), you need a database connection object. In the *Install.py* file, include the appropriate connection details to create a Z MySQL Database Connection object, as in the example in Listing 9.2.

Listing 9.2

```
self.manage_addProduct['ZMySQLDA'].manage_addZMySQLConnection
    (plonelive_db', 'Z MySQL Database Connection', 'root', 'YES')
```

In the skins folder, create a file with the .zsql extension (for example, *zs_getEmployeeInfo.zsql*), as in the example in Listing 9.3.

Listing 9.3

```
<dtml-comment>
title:Provide employee information for the given first name
arguments: p_name
connection_id:plonelive_db
max_rows_:1000
max_cache_:100
cache_time_:0
class_name_:
class_file_:
</dtml-comment>

select * from employees
where
first=<dtml-sqlvar p_name type=string>
```

The parameters are set in a comment block, followed by the statement, all written exactly as in the web form. This Z SQL Method assumes the database connection object with the id *plonelive_db*.

Archetypes with MySQL Storage

In Plone, you usually work with objects that are stored in ZODB. You can store and retrieve information in the database as explained earlier in the "Database Applications in Plone" section. However, this approach has some issues:

▸ No workflow - you cannot associate workflow to the forms submitted

▸ No secure search

▸ No metadata, such as creator, modification time, or effective date

▸ No content management

Archetypes with SQLStorage will provide advantages for both Plone content management and database storage. You can map each archetype content type as a table, and you can map each field in a schema to a column in that table.

At the time of this writing, archetypes storage has some limitations.

▶ Archetypes provides storages only for MySQL and PostgreSQL. You must search and download storages for other databases.

▶ Archetypes reads one field at a time from the database. It reads each column with a single SQL select statement, creating a performance issue with content types that have many fields stored in the database.

Tip: Joel Burton has provided a HOWTO at Products/Archetypes/docs/ sqlstorage-howto.rst called "Using Archetypes SQLStorage and Advanced Tips."

SQLStorage

SQLStorage allows you to transparently store attributes of your Archetypes objects in an SQL-backed database. This is useful in many situations, such as:

▶ You have other applications that need simultaneous access to data in relational database format.

▶ You have a lot of existing data in a relational database format.

▶ You or your boss/client is more comfortable knowing that your data is accessible in a relational database format.

Schema

While defining schema, specify storage for each attribute that needs to be stored in the database, as in the example in Listing 9.4.

Listing 9.4

```
schema = BaseSchema +  Schema((
    StringField('authors',
                searchable=1,
                storage=MySQLSQLStorage(),
                widget=TextAreaWidget(),
                ),
```

Once you created the schema with storage, follow these instructions to make it work:

1. Go to ZMI, add a Z MySQL Database Connection and connect to an existing database or create a new one from MySQL and connect to it.

2. In ZMI, click on **archetype_tool**.

3. Click on the **Connections** tab in the archetype_tool, and select **MySQL Database Connection** as the connection type.

Using mysqlUserFolder with Plone

Plone provides a membership system so that individual users can have a specific identity within a site. This identity has many purposes: to make sure that only authorized people can read or change certain content, to provide a place for users to store documents, to track authorship and changes, and so on.

There are many advantage of using RDBMS-based membership compared to the built-in user folder. When you have thousands of users, it will take significant amount of time to search for members based on profile. You can get detailed reports with RDBMS membership, such as user login time, logout time, page access URL, etc.

This section discusses the *mysqlUserFolder* in detail, which uses the MySQL database to store user information.

Install mysqlUserFolder

mysqlUserFolder is a Zope user folder that uses the MySQL database to store user information and has the following functions:

▸ Authenticate users and set their roles based on data from the MySQL server.

▸ Keep track of sessions (including session logging).

▸ Read and write custom user data through the User object (which is returned by the User folder). It also keeps this information in a MySQL table. It supports custom session data.

▸ Use methods to allow users to modify their accounts. It also allows anonymous user creation (users create their accounts through the web). The folder's management interface allows user management.

mysqlUserFolder supports both HTTP and cookie authentication. Session support uses cookies only.

Download mysqlUserFolder from http://www.zope.org/Members/vladap/ mysqlUserFolder, and install it in Plone's Products folder and restart Zope.

Configure mysqlUserFolder

Read the scripts present in the product's *sql* folder and edit them as required. Create the MySQL database using the *create_tables.sql* script present in *sql* folder. Be sure to create non-transactional tables (this should be the default). mysqlUserFolder uses locking, and doesn't expect transactional support. Create a user with a Manager role. The *setup_manager.sql* script in the *sql* directory assumes that the user id and the role id is "1"; this might not be true. Check the tables. Repeat this for every realm that you are going to use.

You can use a number of alternative user (or group) sources in the Plone GRUF folder. Usually, they provide some means of importing users from another system. Using one of these Products is often a simple process:

1. Enter the ZMI screen for a Plone site's *acl_users* folder.

2. Navigate to the **Sources** tab.

3. Select the appropriate type of the new User Folder (mysqlUserFolder) from the drop-down box to either replace an existing source or to add a new user source.

4. Click on the name of the source to configure it.

The initial form will ask for default properties. After the instance is created, make your desired changes on the Parameters tab. Be sure to read the README.txt file, especially the "User Interface" section. Edit the DTML scripts in the mysqlUserFolder. If you wish, set up access for *act_ methods*.

Using the mysqlUserFolder object, you can map MySQL groups to Zope Roles. Similarly, you can create forms to search members and to add new members to the backend database.

Sample Product: ATmySQLPloneLive

ATmySQLPloneLive is a simple product to demonstrate the power of Archetypes with SQLStorage. This product provides two content types: Book and Chapter. Both the content types use archetypes with SQLStorage option, to store the content information in backend MySQL database.

The ATmySQLPloneLive product requires MySQL database and Archetypes. Download the product from http://www.plonelive.com/downloads/ and follow the given installation instructions:

1. In MySQL, create a new database called *plonelive_db* for testing purpose. The command to "create database" is shown in Figure 9.6. It is assumed that you already installed MySQL database and zMySQLDA adapters as specified in the "Installing MySQL and ZMySQLDA" section of this chapter.

```
C:\Program Files\MySQL\MySQL Server 4.1\bin>mysql
Welcome to the MySQL monitor.  Commands end with ; or \g.
Your MySQL connection id is 1 to server version: 4.1.7-nt

Type 'help;' or '\h' for help. Type '\c' to clear the buffer.

mysql> show databases;
+--------------+
| Database     |
+--------------+
| munwar_db    |
| mysql        |
| test         |
+--------------+
3 rows in set (0.08 sec)

mysql> create database plonelive_db;
Query OK, 1 row affected (0.04 sec)

mysql> exit
Bye
```

Figure 9.6: Create a sample database plonelive_db

2. Download and unzip the ATmySQLPloneLive product into Zope's *Products* directory and restart Zope.

3. In ZMI, create a new Plone site. In the Plone site, create a database connection object and connect to the plonelive_db database. Refer to the "Setting Up Database Connections in Zope" section and Figure 9.1 on

page 275 to create the database connection object. Once you create the MySQL database connection object, you will be able to see it in Plone's root folder as shown in Figure 9.7.

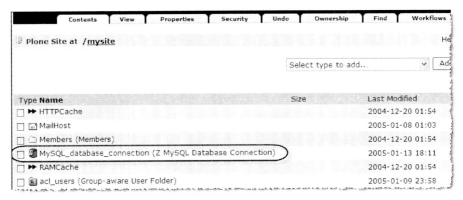

Figure 9.7: MySQL database connection object

4. In your Plone site, install Archetypes and ATmySQLPloneLive products using the **plone setup** menu item and the **Add/Remove Products** option. Install the Archetypes product first, then install the ATmySQLPloneLive product. Figure 9.8 shows the successful installation log details.

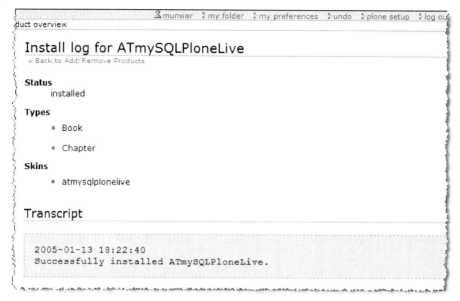

Figure 9.8: ATmySQLPloneLive installation log

5. In ZMI, click on **archetype_tool**, click on the **Connections** tab, and select **MySQL Database Connection** as the default connection type. The ATmySQLPloneLive product provides *Book* and *Chapter* content types, which use this connection object to store and retrieve data from the backend MySQL database. See Figure 9.9.

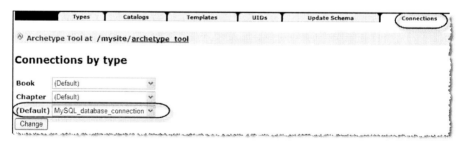

Figure 9.9: Linking the database connection object with the Archetypes tool

Now you can add Book and Chapter content to your Plone site, which will be stored in your backend database. Figure 9.10, Figure 9.11, and Figure 9.12 show the process to add Book content information and to see the backend MySQL database storage.

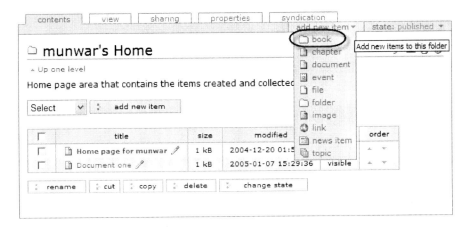

Figure 9.10: Add a new Book instance

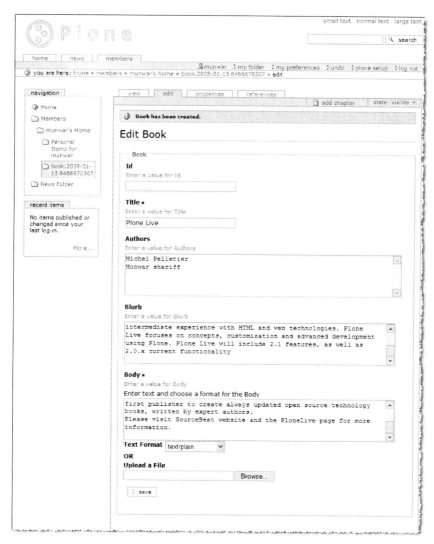

Figure 9.11: Add Book details using the Edit form

```
--------+
| book.2005-01-13.6466670307 | None        | Michel Pelletier
Munwar shariff | Plone Live by Michel Pelletier and Munwar Shariff is written for Zope, CM
nd Python developers familiar with web frameworks. The central purpose of this book is to
e developing Content Management Systems utilizing Plone. Readers should have at least a be
nderstanding of Python and intermediate experience with HTML and web technologies. Plone L
s on concepts, customization and advanced development using Plone. Plone Live will include
res, as well as 2.0.x current functionality
| PloneLive book is by SourceBeat. SourceBeat believes that the traditional publishing mo
ot work in rapidly changing environments such as open source software. Traditional books t
ng to go from author to bookshelf, and many times the books are outdated soon after releas
ow, SourceBeat is the first publisher to create always updated open source technology book
by expert authors.
Please visit SourceBeat website and the PloneLive page for more information.
|
--------+
1 row in set (0.00 sec)

mysql> _
```

Figure 9.12: Data in MySQL after adding book details

You can enhance the ATmySQLPloneLive product by adding your own schema and SQLStorage fields.

Summary

Plone (using its underlying framework Zope) supports transactions and connects with almost all the relational databases available in the market. Plone is an enterprise portal, which provides highly scalable database applications including membership systems. Using the Archetypes storage feature, you can store the content information in a relational database and take advantage of Plone's content management features such as metadata, workflow, secure search, and delegation.

Summary

## CHAPTER 10

Membership Using LDAP

Author: **Munwar Shariff**

In the earlier chapters, you have seen two different implementations of membership: the default built-in user folder, where membership data is stored in the ZODB, and the MySQL user folder where the membership data is stored in a MySQL relational database backend. This chapter explains how to leverage the Lightweight Directory Access Protocol (LDAP) to implement a highly scalable membership system on Plone.

Introduction

Here are some common problems in large web applications:

▶ "I have a very active user community with over 35,000 members, and I'm unable to access the user profile because it takes too long. Other than installing *BTreeUserFolder* (I did that, and it didn't solve the problem), how can I manage user accounts with large user folders?"

▶ "I work in the IT department of a large university. Over the years, the various departments have developed their own sites with local authentication and authorization. Our university has a directory-based central authentication system. How can I consolidate all the sites and provide a single point of authentication and authorization for all our sub-sites?"

▶ Our LDAP server contains both teachers and students. The requirement for us is to build a secure web site using the profile and group information available in our LDAP server. We have decided to use Plone as our content management system. How do I configure a Plone site to allow different levels of access to teachers and students?

It's common for large, consumer-oriented commercial sites and educational institutions to have large member communities. This chapter discusses how to use LDAP-based directories with Plone to solve such problems.

Theory of LDAP

LDAP stands for "Lightweight Directory Access Protocol," which evolved from X.500 OSI Directory Access Protocol. The biggest advantage of LDAP is that your company can access the LDAP directory from almost any computing platform, using any one of the increasing numbers of readily available LDAP-aware applications. It's also easy to customize your company's internal applications to add LDAP support.

The LDAP protocol is both cross-platform and standards-based, so applications needn't worry about the type of server hosting the directory. In fact, LDAP is finding much wider industry acceptance because of its status as an Internet standard. Vendors are more willing to write LDAP integration into their products because they don't have to worry about what's at the other end. Your LDAP server could be any one of a number of open-source or commercial LDAP directory servers (or perhaps even a DBMS server with an LDAP interface), since interacting with any true LDAP server involves the same protocol, client connection package, and query commands. In contrast, vendors looking to integrate directly with a DBMS usually must tailor their products to work with each database server vendor individually.

Directory

A *directory* is a hierarchical collection of objects along with their attributes, such as a file system with folders and files. Unlike a relational database with a fixed table structure, the objects in a directory can have different attributes and multiple occurrences of the same attribute. Directory servers are typically optimized for a very high ratio of searches to updates.

The directory is a service that provides information based on properties. An example is listings in the Yellow Pages. It is a data repository optimized for writing occasionally and reading frequently (unlike a database). In addition, a directory can be a centralized repository for information about resources in an organization, such as servers, printers, and other computer equipment. A directory is the central authentication engine for the enterprise. Some directories are specific, such as the Yellow Pages (telephone users), or a DNS (network hosts). Others are general, such as LDAP and X.500. You can configure them to store any type of data.

You can put almost anything into a directory:

▶ Text

▶ Photos

▶ URLs

▶ Pointers

▶ Binary Data

▶ Public Key Certificates

When applications access a properly designed, standard common directory, rather than using application-specific directories, they can eliminate redundant and costly administration, and security risks are more controllable. For example, the telephone directory, mail, and web applications shown in Figure 10.1 can all access the same directory to retrieve an e-mail address or other information stored in a single directory entry. The advantage is that you can keep and maintain the data in one place. Various applications can use individual attributes of an entry for different purposes, as long as they have the correct authority. New uses for directory information will be realized, and a synergy will develop as more applications take advantage of the common directory.

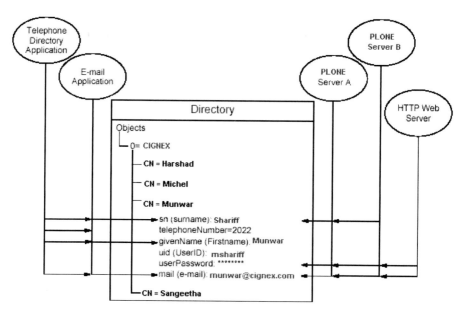

Figure 10.1: Several applications using attributes of same entry

LDAP Configuration

As mentioned previously, a directory is hierarchical and forms a tree structure. The root is a domain context (**dc**), country (**c**), or an organization (**o**); the branches are Organization Units (**ou**); the end is the leaf node, as identified by a Common Name (**cn**) or by a UID.

Listing 10.1 is an example of an LDAP configuration file:

Listing 10.1

```
Using domains:
dc=org, dc=com - top level
ou=People, dc=Cignex, dc=com
ou=Groups, dc=Cignex, dc=com  => intermediate nodes
cn=employee-x ,ou=People, dc=Cignex, dc=com => leaf node

Using organizations :
o=Cignex, c=US (X.500)
dc=foo.com
or
dc=foo,dc=com (RFC2247)
```

In order to use LDAP server, you will need to modify the configuration files. Configuration files location and format might be different for different LDAP servers. In order to use the OpenLDAP server, you will need to modify its configuration file, */etc/openldap/slapd.conf*. You must edit this file to specify the correct domain and server.

The suffix line names the domain for which the LDAP server will provide information, and you should change it from the code in Listing 10.2:

Listing 10.2

```
suffix          "dc=your-domain,dc=com"
```

to reflect a fully qualified domain name, such as the code in Listing 10.3:

Listing 10.3

```
suffix          "dc=example,dc=com"
```

The *rootdn* entry is the Distinguished Name (DN) for a user who is unrestricted by access controls or administrative parameters set for operations on the LDAP directory. You can think of the *rootdn* user as the root user for the LDAP directory. In the configuration file, change the rootdn line from its default value to something like the code in Listing 10.4:

Listing 10.4

```
rootdn          "cn=root,dc=example,dc=com"
```

If you intend to populate the LDAP directory over the network, change the *rootpw* line, replacing the default value with an encrypted password string.

Directory Schema and Organization

A *directory schema* specifies the types of objects that a directory may have and the mandatory and optional attributes of each object type. If you are using LDAP for storing and retrieving user records, then the schema specifies the attributes for each user record.

All entries stored in an LDAP directory have a Distinguished Name, or DN. The DN for each LDAP entry is composed of two parts: the Relative Distinguished Name (RDN) and the location within the LDAP directory where the record resides. The RDN is the portion of your DN unrelated to the directory tree structure. Most items that you'll store in an LDAP directory will have a name, and the name is frequently stored in the cn (Common Name) attribute. Since nearly everything has a name, most objects you'll store in LDAP will use their cn values as the basis for their RDNs.

LDAP Users

An LDAP user object contains information about the user such as attributes, password, and unique id to identify the user.

In a directory, a typical **user** object looks like the code in Listing 10.5:

Listing 10.5

```
dn: cn=Firstname Lastname, ou=People, dc=Cignex, dc=com
uid: fname
cn: Firstname Lastname
givenName: Firstname
sn: Lastname
mail: firstname@cignex.com
objectClass: person
objectClass: organizationalPerson
```

```
objectClass: inetOrgPerson
objectClass: account
objectClass: posixAccount
objectClass: top
objectClass: kerberosSecurityObject
userPassword:: e2NyeXB0fUNwLktlUi9vdG55UUU=
loginShell: /bin/csh
uidNumber: 780
gidNumber: 300
```

In this sample, the DN `ou=People, dc=Cignex, dc=com` identifies an organizational unit. This particular object has all the above Object Classes. The Object Classes are various predefined schemas. They contain one or more attributes. Some of these attributes are mandatory and some are optional. The Object Class schema is enforced on the object. In the above example, *givenName*, *sn*, and *mail* are schema attributes of the user object.

LDAP Groups

LDAP groups allow you to authorize a whole group of users that match the DNs of groups in an LDAP directory. If a group matches any of the groups in the LDAP directory server, the members of that group will be authorized to use specific applications or groups of applications.

In a directory, a typical group object looks like the code in Listing 10.6:

Listing 10.6

```
dn: cn=Member,ou=groups,dc=cignex,dc=com
objectClass: top
objectClass: groupOfUniqueNames
uniqueMember: cn=Manager,dc=cignex,dc=com
uniqueMember: uid=harish,ou=people,dc=cignex,dc=com
uniqueMember: uid=munwar,ou=people,dc=cignex,dc=com
uniqueMember: uid=andy,ou=people,dc=cignex,dc=com
uniqueMember: uid=rdasilva,ou=people,dc=cignex,dc=com
uniqueMember: uid=dick,ou=people,dc=cignex,dc=com
cn: Member
structuralObjectClass: groupOfUniqueNames
entryUUID: 8e01c4e6-e724-1027-9956-c050a9f337fd
creatorsName: cn=Manager,dc=cignex,dc=com
```

```
createTimestamp: 20040130040015Z
entryCSN: 2004040203:29:10Z#0x0002#0#0000
modifiersName: cn=Manager,dc=cignex,dc=com
modifyTimestamp: 20040402032910Z
```

In the sample given above, **ou=groups** represents the group object, **cn=Member** represents the name of the group, and **uniqueMember** represents the list of users who belong to this group.

Most of the LDAP directory servers provide tools to export the data into a text file and to bulk import data into LDAP directory. LDIF (The LDAP Data Interchange Format) is an ASCII text representation of LDAP entries. Files used for importing data to LDAP servers must be in LDIF format. Here are two of the tools provided by OpenLDAP for data import and export.

▸ **slapadd:** This tool adds entries from an LDIF file to an LDAP directory. For example, the command **/usr/sbin/slapadd -l ldif-input** will read in the LDIF file *ldif-input*, containing the new entries.

▸ **slapcat:** This tool pulls entries out of an LDAP directory in the default format (Berkeley Database) and saves them in an LDIF file. For example, the command **/usr/sbin/slapcat -l ldif-output** will output an LDIF file called *ldif-output*, containing the entries from the LDAP directory.

Security and Access Control

LDAP makes provision for complex and fine-grained access control to directory information. Because you can control the access on the server side, it's much more secure than securing data through client software.

With LDAP access control instances, you can:

▸ Grant users the ability to change their home phone number and home address, while restricting them to read-only access for other data types (such as job title or manager's login).

▸ Grant anyone in the group "HR-admins" the ability to modify any user's information for the following fields: manager, job title, employee ID number, department name, and department number. There would be no write permission to other fields.

▶ Deny read access to anyone attempting to query LDAP for a user's password, while still allowing a user to change his or her own password.

▶ Grant Managers read-only permission for the home phone numbers of their direct reports, while denying this privilege to anyone else.

▶ Via a web page, allow your sales people to selectively grant or deny themselves read access to subsets of the customer contact database. In turn, this would allow these individuals to download the customer contact information to their local laptops or to a PDA. (This is most useful if your sales force automation tool is LDAP-aware.)

▶ Via a web page, allow any group owner to add or remove any entries from groups they own. This would allow owners of mail aliases to add and remove users without having to contact IT.

This will give you an idea what's possible using access control with LDAP directories, but be aware that a correct implementation requires much more information than is given here.

Membership Scalability

Plone creates enterprise-wide web applications, intranets, and portals. These applications usually need to provide a customized and personalized view for a user, based on the user's credentials.

Usually, the user credentials are stored in an enterprise-wide repository (a database or a directory). In order to avoid the problems associated with replication and synchronization, it is always best to use the main authentication repository.

Plone supports various membership systems: the traditional acl_users folder based on the ZODB, a MySQL user folder, an LDAP user folder, and so on. The acl_users folder is the simplest, but does not scale efficiently beyond a couple of hundred users. Hence, it is not efficient for medium to large organizations. MySQL-based membership will provide more scalability and flexibility, especially if it is the main user repository for the enterprise.

However, many enterprises store their membership data in LDAP-based directory servers. In this case, using the *Plone LDAPUserFolder* to connect to this directory server becomes the best option. The directory scales easily to millions of objects. They can support partial replicas, which can contain just the information needed by Plone. The Plone-based application need not connect to main directory server, which may store information that is much more sensitive. Minimally, you can use the LDAP server to authenticate a user in an enterprise, allowing a single enterprise-wide password for a user. You can store the other details about the user's membership in a database used exclusively by the Plone application.

Installing LDAP on Linux

In order to use LDAP-backed membership in Plone, three components are necessary: the directory server itself (such as *OpenLDAP*), a *Python LDAP connector*, and the *LDAPUserFolder* product to connect to the directory server. You can use the LDAPUserFolder with any directory server, such as iPlanet, Novell's eDirectory, Microsoft's Active Directory, or OpenLDAP.

This chapter provides the installation procedure for *OpenLDAP*, as it is a free product in the true Linux, Apache, Zope, and Plone tradition. After that, you will install the *Python LDAP connector* and the *LDAPUserFolder* product. Skip the installation of OpenLDAP if you have an existing LDAP server.

Note: The installation instructions given in this section were tested on a Red Hat Linux 9.0 server. Please read the installation documentation of each product for your specific operating system.

Installing OpenLDAP-2.2.17

OpenLDAP requires the Berkeley Database (bdb). This comes with most Linux installations. However, the version needed for the OpenLDAP version installation may be different from the system-supplied one. The best way to find the version of bdb needed is during the configuration step of the OpenLDAP installation. It checks the version of bdb and gives an explicit error if it encounters the wrong version.

Installing the Berkeley Database

1. Download *db-4.2.52.NC.tar.gz* from http://www.sleepycat.com/download/db/index.shtml.

---

2. Untar the file using the command in Listing 10.7:

Listing 10.7

```
tar xvzf db-4.2.52.NC.tar.gz
```

3. Change the directory to *db-4.2.52.NC* (see Listing 10.8):

Listing 10.8

```
cd db-4.2.52.NC
```

4. To do a standard UNIX build of bdb, change to the *build_unix* directory and configure the source, using the commands in Listing 10.9:

Listing 10.9

```
cd build_unix (cd db_version/build_unix)
    ../dist/configure --prefix=/usr/local/bdb-4.2.52
```

5. Build the bdb library using the command in Listing 10.10:

Listing 10.10

```
make
```

6. To install the bdb library, enter the command in Listing 10.11:

Listing 10.11

```
make install
```

Following are the additional notes for bdb:

▶ To rebuild bdb, enter the commands in Listing 10.12:

Listing 10.12

```
make clean
make
```

▶ If you change your mind about how to configure bdb, you must start from scratch by entering the command in Listing 10.13:

Listing 10.13

```
make realclean../dist/configure --prefix=/usr/local/bdb-4.2.52
   make
```

▶ To uninstall bdb, enter the command in Listing 10.14:

Listing 10.14

```
make uninstall
```

Installing OpenLDAP-2.2.17

1. Download *openldap-2.2.17.tgz* from http://www.openldap.org/software/download/.

2. Untar the file using the command in Listing 10.15:

Listing 10.15

```
tar xvzf openldap-2.2.17.tgz
```

3. Change the directory to *openldap-2.2.17* (see Listing 10.16):

Listing 10.16

```
cd openldap-2.2.17
```

4. Copy the *db.h* file from the */usr/local/bdb-4.2.52/include* directory to the */usr/include* directory.

Note: This will ask you to overwrite the existing *db.h* file in the */usr/include* directory. You may want to back up that file before overwriting. Listing 10.17 is the command:

Listing 10.17

```
cp /usr/include/db.h /usr/include/db.h.original
    cp /usr/local/bdb-4.2.52/include/db.h /usr/include
```

5. Set bdb libraries and openldap libraries in the *ld.so.conf* file. Listing 10.18 is an example:

Listing 10.18

```
> echo /usr/local/bdb-4.2.52/lib >> /etc/ld.so.conf
> echo /usr/local/openldap-2.2.17/lib >> /etc/ld.so.conf
> ldconfig
```

6. Run the configure script (see Listing 10.19).

Listing 10.19

```
> env CPPFLAGS="-I/usr/local/bdb-4.2.52/include"
    LDFLAGS="-L/usr/local/bdb-4.2.52/lib"
    ./configure --prefix=/usr/local/openldap-2.2.17
    --without-cyrus-sasl --without-sasl
```

If it must use SASL, ensure that the corresponding version is properly installed. SASL (Simple Authentication and Security Layer) provides a number of methods for authentication, including plaintext passwords in a separate user database, GSSAPI, and external means such as SSL client certificate presentation.

7. Once you have run the configure script, the last line of output should be the code in Listing 10.20:

Listing 10.20

```
Please "make depend" to build dependencies
```

8. To build dependencies, run the code in Listing 10.21:

Listing 10.21

```
make depend
```

9. Build the software (this step will actually compile OpenLDAP). See Listing 10.22.

Listing 10.22

```
make
```

10. Once you have properly configured and successfully made the software, run the test suite to verify the build. See Listing 10.23.

Listing 10.23

```
make test
```

11. Once you have successfully tested the software, you are ready to install it. See Listing 10.24.

Listing 10.24

```
make install
```

12. Start OpenLDAP using the command in Listing 10.25:

Listing 10.25

```
/usr/local/openldap-2.2.17/libexec/slapd
```

13. To stop OpenLDAP, use the command in Listing 10.26:

Listing 10.26

```
kill -INT `cat /usr/local/openldap-2.2.17/var/run/slapd.pid`
```

Installing Python-LDAP Connector 2.0.3

Listing 10.27 contains the instructions to install Python LDAP connector. The installation instructions in this section were tested for Zope Version 2.7.2 and Python version 2.3.3.

Listing 10.27

```
> tar xzf python-ldap-2.0.3.tar.gz
> cd python-ldap-2.0.3
> vi setup.cfg
change the path on line 10
/usr/local/openldap-2.2.17/lib
change the path on line 11
        /usr/local/openldap-2.2.17/include
> /usr/local/python2.3.3/bin/python setup.py build
> /usr/local/python2.3.3/bin/python setup.py install
```

While building, you might get warning messages informing you that *Lib/ldap.py* and *Lib/ldap/schema.py* are not found (see Listing 10.28):

Listing 10.28

```
warning: build_py: file Lib/ldap.py (for module ldap) not found
warning: build_py: file Lib/ldap/schema.py
    (for module ldap.schema) not found
```

ldap and *ldap.schema* are both module packages (directories containing various sub-modules). DistUtils falsely produces the messages above. You can ignore these warnings.

Test your installation (see Listing 10.29):

Listing 10.29

```
/usr/local/python2.3.3/bin/python
>>>> import ldap
>>>> l = ldap.open("localhost")
>>>> l.simple_bind_s("","")
```

If you get an `ldap_first_first` reference error, edit the *setup.cfg* file, search for `ldap_r`, change it to `ldap`, and reinstall.

Installing LDAPUserFolder 2.5

The LDAP User Folder is a user folder replacement for Zope that authenticates Zope users against LDAP.

1. Download the LDAPUserFolder product from http://www.dataflake.org/ software/ldapuserfolder/.

2. Extract the LDAPUserFolder to your *Zope_instance/Products* folder and restart Zope.

Depending on your choice of Zope installation (that is, compiled from source or binary version), make sure that Zope can find the **python-ldap** module. Read the documentation provided by the LDAPUserFolder product (README.txt file and others).

Installing LDAP on Windows

This section provides a very high-level overview of LDAP options on Windows. Since the LDAP servers on Windows come with automatic installers, this section does not cover the installation instructions.

To use LDAP membership on a Windows platform, three components are necessary: the Directory Server, the python-LDAP Win32 binaries, and the *LDAPUserFolder* product. You can also mix-and-match, such as having an LDAP Directory Server running on a Windows platform and Plone running on a Linux platform, and vice-versa.

Various Directory Servers are available for the Microsoft Windows platform. Some common LDAP directory servers are:

▸ **OpenLDAP for Win32:** To download and compile OpenLDAP for the Windows platform, visit one of the many sites that provide binary packages for Windows, such as http://lucas.bergmans.us/hacks/openldap/.

▶ **Active Directory:** Active Directory is Microsoft's extended LDAP directory implementation for Windows domains. You can use an Active Directory server to authenticate users for your Plone site. However, you need to be a little careful with Windows authentication. Windows authenticates by both username and the domain to which they belong. Hence, it is possible to have duplicate user names in different domains. Plone differentiates users only by username. As an administrator, you need to make sure to use unique usernames. Also, check the LDAP port number. Some of the Active Directory servers use port 3268, instead of the standard port 389 for LDAP.

▶ **Exchange Server:** Microsoft Exchange Server runs LDAP service on port 389 by default. You can use the Exchange Server to authenticate users for your Plone site. Similarly, you can map the groups created in the Exchange server as Roles or Groups in Plone.

You can download Python-LDAP Win32 binaries (pre-compiled) from http://www.zope.org/Members/volkerw/LdapWin32.

The procedure to install *LDAPUserFolder* is the same for all operating systems. Refer to the installation steps provided for Linux platform.

Configuring the LDAP User Folder for Plone

When you install Plone, it has an acl_users folder in the root by default, which stores the user's credentials for the administrator. Plone uses these credentials to log into the ZMI for further configuration of the product.

Usually, using the ZMI, you will create one or more Plone sites. For implementing LDAP authentication for a Plone site, it uses the acl_users folder for the corresponding Plone site.

Warning: You should never use the root acl_users folder, since this will prevent even the administrator from logging in to the ZMI if LDAP is down for some reason.

LDAP Users Source

To configure LDAP as your default user source in Plone, follow these steps:

1. From the ZMI of your Plone site, click on the acl_users folder.

2. Click on the **Sources** tab. By default, the *User Folder* is the source for both the Groups and the Users.

3. Select **LDAPUserFolder** for User source.

4. Check the **I'm sure** box and click the **OK** button. If your pre-existing User Folder has users in it that you want to keep, you can add the LDAPUserFolder as an *additional* Users source.

Note: At this point, do not change the Groups source.

See Figure 10.2.

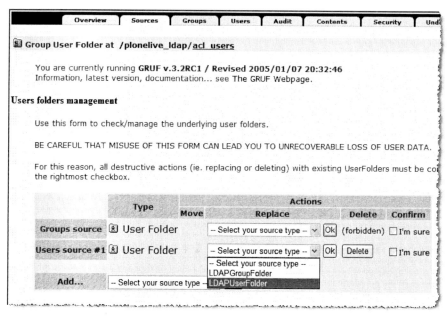

Figure 10.2: Adding LDAP users source to the Plone User Folder

LDAP User Folder Configuration

Once you add the LDAP User source, a form displays, where you will set up the LDAP configuration. See Figure 10.3.

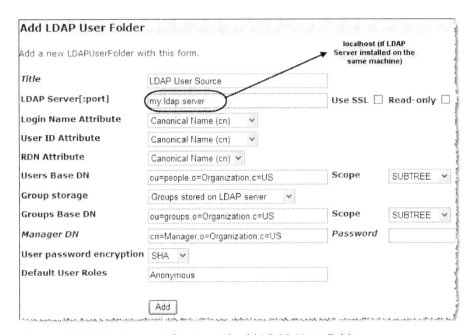

Figure 10.3: Form to configure and add LDAP User Folder

The details of the LDAP server are necessary to fill in the above form properly. You may need the help of the System Administrator to get the details.

▸ **LDAP Server:** Enter the IP address or DNS name for LDAP server. If you are using any port other than the default 389, you must specify it explicitly (for example, servername:portnumber).

▸ **Login Name Attribute**, **User ID Attribute**, and **RDN Attribute:** Select any one of the following LDAP attributes: Canonical Name (cn), UID, Surname (sn), or Distinguished Name (dn).

▸ **User Base DN / Groups Base DN:** Specify the distinguished name of a base folder where users / groups are stored. For each, you can further specify the scope as single level, base, or the entire sub-tree starting from base.

▶ **Scope:** Choose the depth for all searches. The options are BASE (searches only at base level), ONE LEVEL (searches base level and the first level sub-branch), and SUBTREE (searches base and all levels of sub-branches under the base). The default value is SUBTREE.

▶ **Group storage:** Specify whether your Plone roles and groups need to be stored in your LDAP directory or in your ZODB. You have to make a clear choice here - it's not possible to have *some* groups or roles in LDAP and *some* of them in ZODB.

▶ **Manager DN:** Enter the fully qualified name for the manager or any other account, which will be used to authenticate and make queries against the LDAP server. The **Password** is the Manager password.

▶ **User password encryption:** Specify the type of password encryption. If you want to use the LDAP bind for authentication, set the encryption to *clear*. Otherwise, select any method such as SHA, SSHA, MD5, or crypt.

▶ **Read-only:** Select this check box if you want to set a read-only access from Zope.

Click the **Add** button to save changes.

LDAP Schema

Adding or removing entries will not change your LDAP server schema or your records; it will only improve the LDAPUserFolder's knowledge of the schema you use for user records. In the acl_users (LDAPUserFolder), you can select the LDAP schema tab, associate LDAP schema attributes with friendly names, and map them to properties defined in portal_memberdata.

Some useful mappings are:

▶ cn to fullname

▶ mail to email

This automatically associates the properties with the actual data retrieved from the LDAP server. You can then access the LDAP data from Plone by using the Plone property APIs. See Figure 10.4.

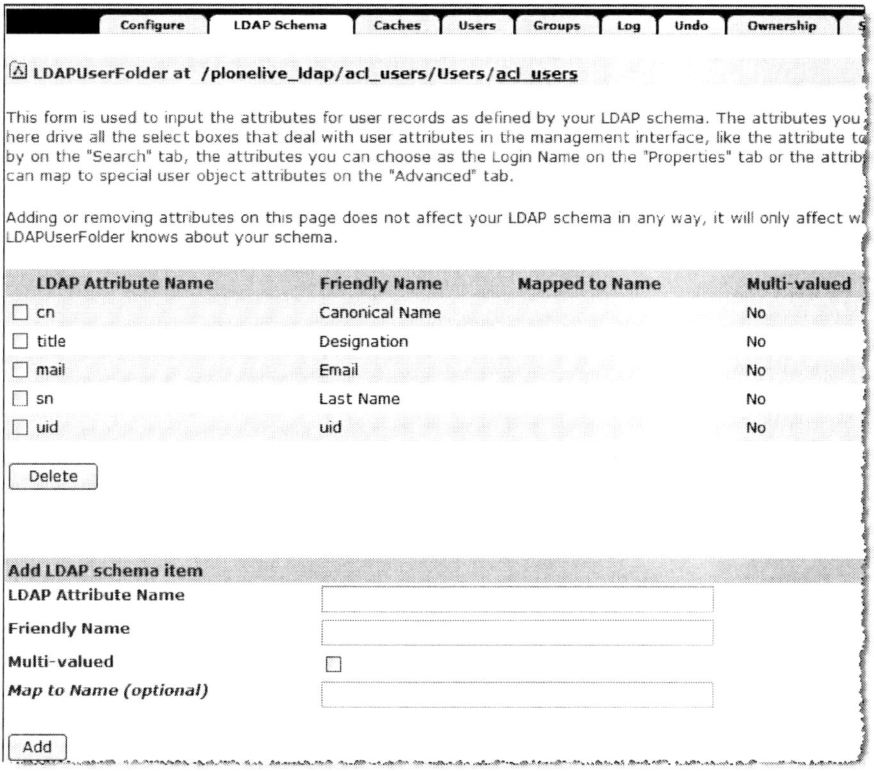

| Configure | LDAP Schema | Caches | Users | Groups | Log | Undo | Ownership | S |

⚠ LDAPUserFolder at /plonelive_ldap/acl_users/Users/acl_users

This form is used to input the attributes for user records as defined by your LDAP schema. The attributes you here drive all the select boxes that deal with user attributes in the management interface, like the attribute to by on the "Search" tab, the attributes you can choose as the Login Name on the "Properties" tab or the attribute can map to special user object attributes on the "Advanced" tab.

Adding or removing attributes on this page does not affect your LDAP schema in any way, it will only affect w LDAPUserFolder knows about your schema.

LDAP Attribute Name	Friendly Name	Mapped to Name	Multi-valued
☐ cn	Canonical Name		No
☐ title	Designation		No
☐ mail	Email		No
☐ sn	Last Name		No
☐ uid	uid		No

[Delete]

Add LDAP schema item

LDAP Attribute Name	[ ]
Friendly Name	[ ]
Multi-valued	☐
Map to Name (optional)	[ ]

[Add]

Figure 10.4: Adding Schema (attributes) to Users

Caches

Click the **Caches** tab of your *LDAPUserFolder*. This is a cache of currently authenticated users and the groups exposed by your LDAP server for authentication purposes.

Users that can be cached are created through "real" logins, where a physical user provided a login and password (these end up in the "authenticated" cache), or internal lookups that are done without passwords (these end up in the "anonymous" cache). Keeping separate caches for different kinds of users avoids intermingling and possible privilege escalation because no "anonymous" cached user object will ever perform actions that require real authentication and elevated privileges.

Every time an authenticated user makes a request to Zope, Zope verifies the username and password. Depending on site traffic and the number of users that log in through the LDAPUserFolder, this process can happen several times a second. Since a lookup on the LDAP Server can be quite slow, the product will cache the user information for 10 minutes. This is the duration of a typical session.

LDAP Users

The **Users** tab contains many forms to manage LDAP users. Based on the LDAP security, you can:

▶ Search for users in LDAP directory

▶ Add a new user

▶ Add a user to one or more groups

▶ Delete an existing user

▶ Edit the user attributes

▶ Reset the password for a user

Some of the important features are explained in the following sections.

Search LDAP Users

Choose the attribute and provide an appropriate search string to search users in LDAP directory as shown in Figure 10.5.

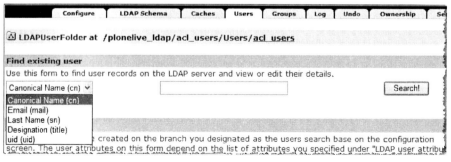

Figure 10.5: Search LDAP users through ZMI

Edit User Details

Search the results in the list of users who match the search criteria. Click on the user to edit the user details, as shown in Figure 10.6.

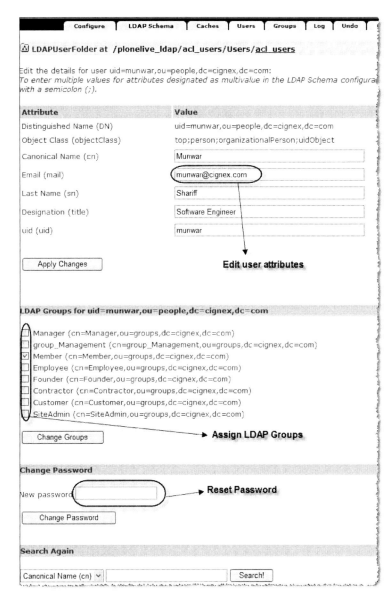

Figure 10.6: Edit LDAP user details through ZMI

LDAP Groups

The **Groups** tab contains many forms to manage LDAP groups. Based on the LDAP security, you can:

▶ View existing groups

▶ Add a new group

▶ Delete an existing group

▶ Map an LDAP group to a Zope Role

Some of the important features are explained in the following sections.

Create Users and Groups

The users and groups are visible if they are present in LDAP. You can create them in LDAP by using one of the following methods:

▶ Import an LDIF (LDAP Data Interchange Format) file.

▶ Use a generic LDAP browser to create users and groups at the proper location (User and Group base DN).

▶ In ZMI, use the Users or Groups tab of *LDAPUserFolder* to add users and groups.

Map LDAP Groups to Zope Roles

On the Groups tab, in the bottom portion, you can set the mappings of LDAP groups to Zope/Plone roles. Unless you do the mapping, the Plone roles won't work. Figure 10.7 illustrates the LDAP groups mapped to Plone roles.

Figure 10.7: Manage LDAP groups and map them to Zope roles

Although it seems painful, there are some inherent advantages to mapping the LDAP groups to Plone roles:

▸ If you are tapping into an enterprise-wide LDAP server, it will have many administrative groups (printers, servers, and other users like vendors), which should not appear in Plone. The manual mapping allows you to select the groups that you will need in Plone.

▸ By mapping, you can change the display names for groups, resulting in more user-friendly names (for example, Plone Developer's Group instead of Pln_Dev_Grp1).

Log

Click the **Log** tab of your LDAPUserFolder to see the log messages. A basic log entry has the following elements:

▸ The log level that produced this entry

▸ The entry timestamp

▸ The log message

You can specify what kinds of events to log using the **Log verbosity** setting on the **Advanced** management tab. The different log levels are:

▶ **0:** No logging entries will be made

▶ **1:** Catastrophes, like failures to connect to the LDAP server

▶ **2:** Major Events, like LDAPUserFolder property changes

▶ **3:** Minor Events, like initialization after Zope is restarted

▶ **4:** Authentication failures

▶ **5:** Successful authentications

▶ **7:** Authentication from cache

▶ **9:** Debugging, including extra debugging information

Configuring GRUF with LDAP

In versions of Group User Folder (GRUF) prior to version 3.0, you must have two *LDAPUserFolder* objects: one for users and another for groups. With GRUF 3.0 and above it is possible to use your LDAP groups directly instead of defining them locally in Zope. It is possible to set specific roles on Groups. (For more information on GRUF, see *Chapter 2*).

LDAP Groups Source

To configure GRUF with LDAP, follow these steps:

1. From the ZMI of your Plone site, click on the acl_user folder.

2. Click on the **Sources** tab. By default, the User Folder is the source for Groups.

3. Select **LDAPGroupFolder** for Groups source.

4. Check the **I'm sure** box and click the **Ok** button.

For more details, see Figure 10.8.

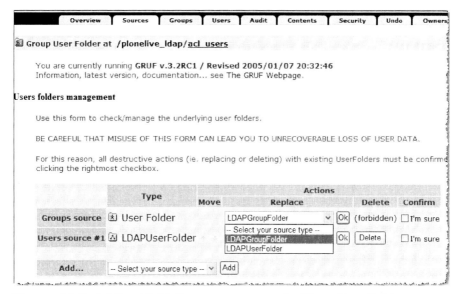

Figure 10.8: Adding LDAP Groups source to the Plone User Folder

After the brief configuration, make sure that the LDAPUserFolder source has defined the base DN of your LDAP groups. Then you can list all groups you have in LDAP and change their memberships and associated roles, just as for Users.

Plone Groups

Once you link the Groups source to LDAP, all the LDAP groups are automatically identified as Plone groups, as shown in Figure 10.9. You can remove the unwanted groups and map the Plone roles to groups as needed by your application.

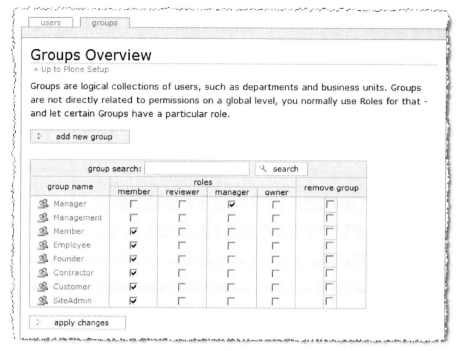

Figure 10.9: LDAP Groups in Plone

Customizing Plone Membership

After configuring the LDAPUserFolder for users and groups in Plone, the
default features of Plone (such as searching for Members, updating member
profile, replacing a forgotten password, etc.) won't function without some
configuration. You must customize certain scripts in Plone in order to view and
update the member data present in the remote LDAP directory server.

Search Members

Earlier, you learned how to use the ZMI to manage users and groups in a Plone
site. In a functional Plone site, the user management can be provided under a
secure administrative login. To do this, you must tap into the *ManageUsers* APIs
and provide the necessary screens to display and modify the user-related information.

An example is shown in Figure 10.10:

Figure 10.10: Members search screen customized for LDAPUserFolder

Listing 10.30 is the sample Python code to list groups in an LDAP server:

Listing 10.30

```
l_ret = []
l_userRoles = container.acl_users.Users.acl_users.getGroups()
for role in l_userRoles:
    l_ret.append(role[0])
return l_ret
```

Listing 10.31 is the sample Page Template code to list users in an LDAP server:

Listing 10.31

```
<span tal:define="l_users python:here.acl_users.Users.acl_users
    .getUserNames()">
  <p tal:repeat="l_user l_users"
    tal:content="l_user">
    Name
  </p>
</span>
```

Listing 10.32 is the sample Python code to find any users in the LDAP directory based on the schema attribute value. In this example, the users can be searched based on the login name, which is stored in the LDAP attribute called **uid**.

Listing 10.32

```
users = container.acl_users.Users.acl_users.findUser('uid', p_user)
```

With simple customizations, you can provide good user management screens in Plone.

Update Member Profiles

The "LDAP Schema" section explains the process to specify the member profile attributes. You can also use Plone to add new users to an LDAP directory and to update the existing user information. The sample APIs for some of the user management functions are listed in Table 10.1.

Table 10.1: User Management APIs

Feature	acl_users API
Add new users to LDAP directory	manage_addUser
Update existing LDAP user profile information	manage_editUser
Assign LDAP user to various groups	manage_editUserRoles
Reset user password	manage_editUserPassword

Figure 10.11 illustrates the sample user interface, which uses the User Management APIs to update user profiles, to assign specific roles to users, and to reset user passwords.

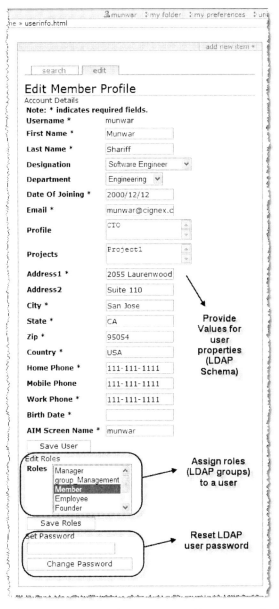

Figure 10.11: Update User Profile, Assign Roles, and Reset Password

Forgot Password Feature

Usually, the user passwords are encrypted and stored in an LDAP directory server. You can specify the encryption type in configuration. You can allow users to reset their passwords using the *acl_users.manage_editUserPassword* API. However, you cannot allow users to retrieve their password by e-mail, as the password will be in unreadable form.

There are different schemes you can follow to allow users to retrieve their forgotten password. We recommend the following secure scheme to handle forgotten password issue. It is a two-step process:

1. The member enters the user id to get a special code via e-mail.

2. The member enters this code to reset the password, and this new password is mailed to the member.

In both the steps, the user will receive e-mail at the e-mail address specified in his or her profile.

Summary

Plone supports highly scalable and secure membership systems by integrating with external LDAP directory servers such as openLDAP, Novell's eDirectory, Microsoft's Active Directory or Microsoft Exchange. Plone is effective as a centralized membership management system to retrieve, add, and manage users in the LDAP directory server. You can use LDAP group information to define a security model, business logic, and workflow process for the web applications developed using Plone.

## CHAPTER 11

Integrating with Non-Plone Systems

Author: Michel Pelletier

In an ideal world, there would be one operating system, one authentication system, and one content management system (which would be Plone, of course). However, the technology industry is not so ideal and many frameworks and technologies exist to accomplish similar goals. This chapter shows you how to integrate Plone with other important technologies that are in common use today.

Integration means many things, but with Plone it means using your Zope system with other frameworks. A simple Zope system keeps all of its data inside the object database and serves the content with its built-in server. A more complex system may need to keep its data on the file system, serve the data with Apache, or integrate with other languages, like Java. This chapter discusses the different protocols and tools used to integrate Zope with other systems.

File System Integration

So far, this book has focused on developing your code in the file system, but your data still typically gets stored in the ZODB. In many cases, however, you might not want your data in the ZODB. You might want to use a tool that requires your data to be in files on the file system, or perhaps you would like to use Apache to serve data that you manage directly in Plone.

One of the most common ways to integrate Plone with the file system is to add a file system *directory view*. This Zope folder looks like any other folder in the ZODB, but it is really backed by files in the file system and not by objects in the object database. A directory view object has all of the same look and feel in the ZMI as a standard Zope folder, but its contents come from a folder on your file system.

In order to use a file system directory view, you must first register your directory with Zope. This is a security feature to prevent users from viewing directories on your file system, through the web, without authorization. This technique appeared in *Chapter 5* when registering skins on a file system (see Listing 11.1):

Listing 11.1

```
from Products.CMFCore import DirectoryView
DirectoryView.registerDirectory('skins', globals())
```

You must place this code where Zope will execute it on startup, typically inside a Product's *__init__.py* file, although you can register a directory view at any time. Once you have registered the directory, it is easy to add a view of that directory in Zope. Go to the ZMI and add a File System Directory View object anywhere in Zope. This will display a screen where you can select your directory from the list of registered directories.

This action creates a new folder in your Zope instance, whose content is backed by the file system, not by objects in the database. Depending on each file's suffix, the system will treat them differently. For example, Image objects represent images, and .py files convert into Python scripts. The .pt files become Page Templates, and the .dtml files become DTML Methods.

PAGE **324**   **Plone Live**

This approach has a couple of disadvantages. First, file system directory view objects cannot have properties or other writable metadata. Second, you cannot edit file system content through the web using Zope's management interface (ZMI).

To work around this, use a more advanced product, such as ExtFile (http://www.zope.org/Members/MacGregor/ExtFile). This product maps files onto the file system and provides you with flexibility for editing and updating content and properties. ExtFile is more complex than using file system directory views when working with Zope's transaction machinery.

Apache Integration

If you have been following the examples so far, you have probably been accessing Zope though the ZServer, Zope's built-in HTTP server.

ZServer is fast and simple. It does one job very well, which is to funnel HTTP requests from the network into Zope and send a response back to the web client. ZServer is not a production web server; its only purpose is to serve up Zope content.

Many production environments work with a variety of software and have more robust requirements for their web servers. For many of these setups, it is much more productive to use a web server created for a production environment. While many such web servers exist, by far the most popular is the Apache open source web server (http://apache.org/).

Apache has nearly every possible feature you can imagine, including the proverbial kitchen sink. Unlike ZServer, which has one, very narrow, specific purpose, you can use Apache for almost any kind of web service feature you could ever need. For example, ZServer serves content only out of Zope, but Apache can serve content from many different sources, including Zope, the file system, or from a myriad of data sources. For more information on all that Apache can do, see the Apache web site.

Within the scope of this book, Apache is important because almost all production Zope sites run "behind" Apache. In other words, Apache handles all of the network level functionality of your site, while Zope still handles all of the dynamic content. While this setup is more complicated than using a straight Zope setup with ZServer, Apache has so many advantages that even low-traffic production Zope sites should always run behind Apache.

The following list describes several reasons for this:

▸ Apache is developed by many people all over the world. It is constantly evolving and usually includes state-of-the-art web technology. By using Apache with Zope, you can leverage what Apache does well in conjunction with what Zope does well.

▸ Apache has a powerful security framework that allows administrators fine-grained control over their web services. While Zope's advanced security framework makes it secure, ZServer does not offer the same level of security integration and control that Apache does.

▸ Running Zope behind Apache means that you can also use Apache to do things that it excels at, like serving content from the file system. The File System Directory View product can do this for Zope, but Apache performs much better at serving static content than Zope. Zope is a dynamic framework; it is not optimized to serve static content, while Apache is optimized fully for this use.

▸ Apache has hundreds of modules that let you plug in functionality that you may not be getting from Zope. For example, Apache has integration with Windows authentication, while Zope's Windows authentication features are rather poor. Apache has many more Windows users than Zope does, so it can provide more development resources and features in this area.

▸ Apache provides a much more powerful framework for logging auditing information, security, and access related information. Zope has a simpler logging framework that is not as flexible.

Apache and Zope, when configured properly, provide features in synergy that few other frameworks can claim to do better. This section describes how to set up Apache to serve Zope content. While there are several ways to do this, by far the most popular way to integrate Apache and Zope is to use the Apache **mod_proxy** module.

The mod_proxy module's job is to take HTTP requests that come into Apache and proxy them to some other HTTP server. Thus, if Apache is serving your

Zope site, it will proxy your web requests to the Zope server, and the Zope server will proxy the responses back through Apache. This provides a very powerful level of security for your Zope site because Zope is hidden behind Apache.

The mod_proxy module works transparently. You only need to configure Apache to know what kind of requests it should proxy to Zope. The simplest case is to configure Apache to proxy all web requests to Zope, but a much finer grain of control is possible. For example, you can proxy all of your web requests into Zope except those that have a special URL path. You could configure those special requests to serve static content from the file system. Your range of options in this regard is very wide; you can configure Apache in many ways.

Configuring Apache

To configure Apache to use with Zope, you must install Apache and make sure it works for you. Please refer to one of the many Apache books available to help you with installation. Once you install and properly configure Apache, you need to edit Apache's main configuration file to set it up as a proxy server front-end for Zope. The configuration file is typically *httpd.conf*, but its name and location may differ depending on how you installed Apache. Be sure to consult the documentation if you can't find your *httpd.conf* file.

The Apache configuration commands in Listing 11.2 and Listing 11.3 proxy Zope through Apache:

Listing 11.2

```
ProxyPass /visiblepath http://zopeserver:port/path...
```

This command intercepts any incoming requests whose URL location begins with /*visiblepath*. The command replaces this part of the request URL with *http://zopeserver:port/path....* Apache then forwards the request to *zopeserver:port.* Zope processes the request like it would any other, except it comes from Apache rather than a web browser. Zope then returns the result to Apache, which returns the result the client as though it had come from Apache itself.

To process outgoing responses, you must configure Apache so that requests coming back from Zope are "reversed" to make them look like they came from Apache. This is simple to do with the inverse directive for ProxyPass:

Listing 11.3

```
ProxyPassReverse /visiblepath http://zopeserver:port/path...
```

This directive tells Apache to watch for responses from the Zope server and replaces the *http://zopeserver:port/path...* part of the URL with */visiblepath*. Now the proxying process is complete in both directions; your Zope system is completely hidden behind Apache.

Configuring Zope

Now you must configure Zope to recognize that it is being proxied. This is because Zope does lots of dynamic generation of HTML and other content, including dynamically generated URLs. Without properly configuration, Zope will not rewrite the dynamic URLs it generates to look like they came from Apache, not Zope.

This is easy to do using the standard Zope SiteAccess product that comes with Zope 2.7. This product provides the VirtualHostMonster (VHM) object. Create a VHM object in any folder in Zope (typically the root folder) and configure the SiteAccess object. It requires two important configuration options: the site *VirtualHostBase* and the *VirtualHostPath*. The VHM object is documented in detail in the 2.7 Edition of *The Zope Book* (http://www.plope.com/Books/2_7Edition/VirtualHosting.stx#1-2).

The Base is the URL of the */visiblepath* prefix shown above, so if your Apache site is http://mysite.com/, then the Base URL for the Site Access is http://mysite.com/visiblepath. The Path value should always be just one forward slash (/) unless you are an advanced user and know how to use a SiteAccess object to access some other path.

To use the Zope Management Interface (ZMI) through the Apache proxy server, you must work around a small bug in the ZMI with the Apache configuration options in Listing 11.4:

Listing 11.4

```
ProxyPass /misc_ http://zopeserver:port/misc_ProxyPass /p_
    http://zopeserver:port/p_
```

It is not always wise to provide access to the ZMI through your production system, so you may want to include other Apache access rules to restrict access to your management interfaces to only trusted computers. This is an Apache configuration issue, and examples of this kind of configuration abound in the Apache books and documentation.

Now, you have a complete working Zope system running behind Apache. With more Apache experience, you can leverage many more of Apache's features in combination with Zope to make your site fast and robust.

WebDAV Support

WebDAV is a new protocol that extends HTTP with additional features that enable you to build high-level editing and version control functions for your online content. WebDAV is the basis for various advanced web editing frameworks, and is used widely in the Plone and open source worlds for its power and flexibility.

Zope provides some WebDAV support for editing files and content inside the object database from WebDAV aware tools. Many WebDAV-enabled tools are available, but this example will use one of the most common command-line clients called "cadaver" (http://www.webdav.org/cadaver/) for UNIX.

Windows users can use Novell Netdrive (http://support.novell.com/servlet/filedownload/uns/pub/ndrv41862.exe/) to mount Plone in Windows. Many other clients are available for Windows and UNIX that you can use to connect to your Zope system, just like the example in Listing 11.5 uses cadaver:

Listing 11.5

```
[michel@localhost michel]$ cadaver http://localhost:8080/
Authentication required for Zope on server `localhost':
Username: michel
Password: *******
```

```
dav:/> ls
Listing collection `/': succeeded.
Coll:   Control_Panel                       0   Nov 22 00:24
Coll:   archexample                         0   Dec  6 13:53
Coll:   one                                 0   Dec  6 13:23
Coll:   temp_folder                         0   Dec  6 13:09
        acl_users                           0   Nov 21 23:56
        browser_id_manager                  0   Nov 21 23:56
        error_log                           0   Nov 21 23:56
        index_html                         28   Nov 21 23:56
        session_data_manager                0   Nov 21 23:56
        standard_error_message           1227   Nov 21 23:56
        standard_html_footer               18   Nov 21 23:56
        standard_html_header               82   Nov 21 23:56
        standard_template.pt              282   Nov 21 23:56
        test1                             203   Dec  6 13:22
dav:/> cd one
dav:/one/> get remoteSearch
Downloading `/one/remoteSearch' to remoteSearch:
Progress: [==============================>]
    100.0% of 185 bytes succeeded.
dav:/one/>
Connection to `localhost' closed.
[michel@localhost michel]$ cat remoteSearch
[michel@localhost michel]$ ['http://localhost:8080/one/index_html',
    'http://localhost:8080/one/CustomizationLog',
    'http://localhost:8080/one/Members/michel',
    'http://localhost:8080/one/Members/michel/index_html']
[michel@localhost michel]$
```

The remoteSearch script queries the catalog and returns a list of URLs that match the query. The *results* of the script were called, not the script itself. This presents a common problem with protocols like WebDAV; there is no way for the client to indicate to the server that it wants the *source* of a script, and not the result of calling the script.

Zope's solution to this problem is to run two HTTP servers on different ports. One is the port on which you run normal web traffic (typically 80 or 8080), and the other is a port you reserve only for WebDAV traffic. This always edits the source of an object and never renders the object as it would on the normal web traffic port. You can enable this WebDAV-only port by adding the code shown in Listing 11.6 (or uncommenting the example that is in *zope.conf*):

Listing 11.6

```
<webdav-source-server>
  # valid keys are "address" and "force-connection-close"
  address 1980
  force-connection-close off
</webdav-source-server>
```

An excellent article by Jeffrey Shell (http://www.zope.org/Documentation/Articles/WebDAV) covers many of these details and explains how to use various clients to edit web content with other protocols, like FTP.

NetDrive uses WebDAV to show a remote Zope folder on your Windows desktop like it was any other folder. You can now treat the remote files like files on your hard drive, edit them with your applications, save them, and close them, without having to worry about uploading them when you are done.

Zope External Editor

The previous section explained how to use WebDAV to make remote files look like local files on your computer. Another technique is available through the Zope External Editor product (http://www.zope.org/Members/Caseman/ExternalEditor) to make your remote content in Zope appear like local content, although it works rather differently than WebDAV.

The ExternalEditor product works in conjunction with a "helper application" (which is included) that allows you to edit content in the ZMI using your native content editors. For example, if you uploaded a Word document into Zope, you normally cannot edit the document in Word; you must first download the Word file, edit it, and then upload the Word file again. The ExternalEditor product essentially automates this process.

ExternalEditor associates a special content type with your objects in Zope that causes your web browser to launch the helper application, which launches the appropriate editor for the type of object (for example, it will launch Word or OpenOffice for .doc files). You can now edit the file directly in Word, and when you save the document, the helper application kicks in again, saving the content back to the Zope server automatically. As the home page describes, it's one of those "have your cake and eat it too" products that is not essential to working with Zope, but can make your life a lot easier, especially if you use lots of non-web-based content like Word files and spreadsheets.

RSS and Syndication

Often, Zope sites present complex user interfaces, but do not provide that same information in a format that a computer can parse and understand. Consider a bulletin board site. The user can see the author, date, and content right on the screen, but a computer must translate the intent of the designer. For example, the HTML `<p>The author of this is Bob</p>` contains an important piece of data about the object, but there is no way for another system to know this. This information is not conveyed in the structure of the data (which is HTML) but instead in the words presented.

Getting a computer to "screen scrape" an HTML page for important data is one of the hardest things to do well, and you can never do it perfectly. To make it worse, as soon as you've managed it, the designer is sure to change the layout of his or her HTML. To solve this problem, web engineers have come up with a standard way for communicating information about web resources using a standard XML format that can be easily parsed by any framework. This protocol is Really Simple Syndication (RSS).

RSS is split into two major families. One major family is RSS 1.0, supported by the W3C standards body. The other major family is RSS 2.0, supported by the company UserLand. They are both open formats and solve the same problems, but do so in slightly different, incompatible ways.

Developers generally use RSS to "describe" a web resource. For example, if you have a document available on the web, you can use RSS to describe that document to another system that can access it. Typically, this other system is a search engine that records the description so that it can be searched for later.

Listing 11.7 is a simple RSS file:

Listing 11.7

```xml
<?xml version="1.0" encoding="utf-8"?>
<?xml-stylesheet type="text/xsl" href="/rss.xsl"?>
<rdf:RDF
  xmlns:rdf="http://www.w3.org/1999/02/22-rdf-syntax-ns#"
  xmlns:dc="http://purl.org/dc/elements/1.1/"
  xmlns:sy="http://purl.org/rss/1.0/modules/syndication/"
  xmlns="http://purl.org/rss/1.0/"
  xmlns:zopezen="http://rssnamespace.org/zopezen/ext/1.0"
>
<channel rdf:about="http://www.zopezen.org">
  <title>ZopeZen</title>
  <link>http://www.zopezen.org</link>
  <description>
    The Zen of Zope
  </description>

  <image rdf:resource="http://www.zopezen.org/logo.jpg" />
 <items>
    <rdf:Seq>
      <rdf:li rdf:resource="http://www.zopezen.org/Members/andy/
      news_item.2004-12-03.4938262015" />
      ...
    </rdf:Seq>
  </items>

</channel>

<image rdf:about="http://www.zopezen.org/logo.jpg">
  <title>ZopeZen</title>
  <url>http://www.zopezen.org/logo.jpg</url>
  <link>http://www.zopezen.org/</link>
</image>

<item rdf:about="http://www.zopezen.org/Members/andy/
    news_item.2004-12-03.4938262015">
<title>Plone vs Drupal</title>
<link>http://www.zopezen.org/Members/andy/
    news_item.2004-12-03.4938262015</link>
<description>
Chat on the &lt;a href=&quot;http://drupal.org/node/
    13733&quot;&gt;Drupal&lt;/a&gt; site. Pointed to me
    by Ofer (thanks).
</description>
<dc:publisher></dc:publisher>
<dc:creator>andy</dc:creator>
```

```
<dc:rights></dc:rights>
<dc:subject>
Plone
</dc:subject>
<dc:date>2004-12-03 11:43:22</dc:date>
</item>
```

This XML is the RSS syndication for Andy McKay's ZopeZen web site. This RSS is simplified so that it only shows one item in the syndicated stream. Using RSS clients like Mozilla and many others, you can track RSS sources by making live bookmarks and registering your client to update various feeds you are interested in at regular intervals.

You can make Plone generate RSS information for most of its content objects. For this to work, you must activate the plone_syndication tool inside your ZMI portal folder. To enable CSS, go to the **Properties** tab of the Syndication tab and click on the **Enable** button. This will display a screen with several options:

▸ **UpdatePeriod**: This argument lets you specify how often to update your RSS information channel. Clients use this information to determine how long they should wait before they check back for more recent information in your RSS feed. The options are Hourly, Daily, Weekly, Monthly, and Yearly.

▸ **UpdateFrequency**: The update frequency works in conjunction with the UpdatePeriod to define how often to update the RSS feed. For example, if the update period is hourly and the update frequency is two, then the channel is updated twice hourly.

▸ **UpdateBase**: This argument defines the base data used in conjunction with UpdatePeriod and UpdateFrequency to define the base publishing schedule of the syndicated information. This starts a feed at a particular time and follows an orderly update schedule.

▸ **Max Syndicated Items**: This option configures the maximum number of items in any one RSS feed you will syndicate out to a client. This not only prevents your client from downloading very old information, but also reduces the burden on clients that subscribe to very large RSS feeds.

Once you have enabled syndication and edited your options, you can view individual Zope folders as RSS syndicated feeds. Go to any Plone folder, click on the Syndication tab, and enable syndication for that particular object.

Now you can syndicate this folder by going to its syndication URL, which will return an XML description of the object in RSS. Remote news aggregators can display this folder by simply passing them the URL to the folder's syndication method.

XML-RPC

XML-RPC is a simple, lightweight, Remote Procedure Call (RPC) protocol for the web. An RPC is a way for one computer to call a program or other executable function on another computer. This is useful for providing web APIs that present a programmable interface over HTTP instead of the normal user interface one would expect from a web server.

Zope supports native XML-RPC calls into the object database. Any method or object that you can access through Zope's web scripting, for the most part, you can call from XML-RPC. See Listing 11.8.

Listing 11.8

```
## Script (Python) "remoteSearch"
##bind container=container
##bind context=context
##bind namespace=
##bind script=script
##bind subpath=traverse_subpath
##parameters=
##title=
##
results = []

for record in container.portal_catalog():
    results.append(record.getURL())

return results
```

You can call this script from any remote XML-RPC based framework. For example, Listing 11.9 is a Python session in another window accessing this script remotely via XML-RPC:

Listing 11.9

```
>>> from xmlrpclib import ServerProxy
>>> s = ServerProxy("http://michel:123@localhost:8080/")
>>> s.one.remoteSearch()
['http://localhost:8080/one/index_html',
    'http://localhost:8080/one/CustomizationLog',
    'http://localhost:8080/one/Members/michel',
    'http://localhost:8080/one/Members/michel/index_html']
>>>
```

XML-RPC has its limitations. First, it can only pass primitive data types as arguments or return values. You cannot pass other objects as arguments or expect them as return values, because XML-RPC is not sophisticated enough to transmit an object in XML. It can only transmit basic types like strings, integers, or arrays of such types.

Even with these limitations, XML-RPC is a great protocol for sending data back and forth from a Zope server, and given that there are dozens of implementations of XML-RPC in many different languages and platforms, it is an important and standard way for different frameworks and languages to communicate with each other.

SOA

Service Oriented Architecture (SOA) is a handful of newer XML-based technologies that allow you to create web services. Web services are web servers that serve up information using HTTP, but instead of serving HTML to a human using a web browser, they typically serve up XML to another system that parses that XML and uses it in some application-specific way.

SOA is a new and constantly evolving industry, so it is out of the scope of this book, especially since many of the technologies are so new that they may or may not see widespread adoption. However, many SOA protocols have gained popularity, especially SOAP.

SOAP

SOAP is the Simple Object Access Protocol. Its goals are very similar to those of XML-RPC, except SOAP allows you to communicate using high-level concepts like objects and methods. SOAP is one of the fundamental components of the SOA initiative.

SOAP is similar to distributed computing protocols like CORBA, and it relies on several accompanying protocols to form a complete SOA framework. While using all of these protocols in concert can be complex (and the subject of many large books itself), the SOAP protocol itself can be useful for Zope to call remote services on a Zope site using a local client.

Zope does not come with native SOAP support, but CIGNEX Technologies is currently funding an effort to include more SOAP and web services support for Archetype-based objects. This project is not yet complete, but it aims to create a way to publish Archetypes content objects using a simple SOAP interface.

As of this writing, CIGNEX is about to release an alpha version of this product, but for now you can experiment with using SOAP in Zope with a SOAP patch product from Petru Paler (http://www.ppetru.net/software/index.html).

Currently, this Zope SOAP product adds simple SOAP support to Zope in a way very similar to XML-RPC. This approach has its limitations, as it can't interoperate with other SOA systems fully, though it does provide some limited support.

Summary

This chapter covered many integration issues related to Plone: using and manipulating content from a file system, using Plone with Apache, accessing your content with authoring protocols like WebDAV, syndicating content with RSS, and integrating your framework with other frameworks using remote communication protocols like XML-RPC. The key to all of this is integration, and Plone is unique among many other frameworks in that it has many ways in which it can "play well with others."

Since the software market is continuously evolving, integration is a moving target. New products and protocols are developed constantly, so new software must be written to integrate old system with these new technologies. As these new events happen and new features are added, this chapter will be updated to include more examples and information on this important subject.

Summary

Mind Maps

Author: Munwar Shariff

Mind mapping is a powerful graphic technique that provides a universal key to unlock the potential of the brain. This appendix represents the key features of Zope and Plone as mind maps so that readers can remember them easily.

Mind Mapping

Tony Buzan developed mind maps in the late 1960s as a way of helping students make notes using only key words and images. They are much quicker to make than narrative descriptions, and they are much easier to remember and review because of their visual quality. The non-linear nature of mind maps makes it easy to link and cross-reference different elements of the map.

You can apply the mind map to every aspect of life where improved learning and clearer thinking will enhance human performance. Similar to a road map, a mind map will:

▶ Give you an overview of a large subject/area.

▶ Enable you to plan routes/make choices and let you know where you are going and where you have been.

▶ Encourage problem solving by showing you new creative pathways.

▶ Be enjoyable to look at, read, muse over, and remember.

▶ Attract and hold your eye/brain.

▶ Let you see the whole picture and the details at the same time.

Many tools are available in the market to help you create and use mind maps. The examples in this appendix are created using the commercial mind mapping software called *MindManager* from Mindjet.

Note: FreeMind is the premier free mind-mapping software written in Java. It is available at http://freemind.sourceforge.net/wiki/index.php/Main_Page.

Figure A.1 represents how to read a mind map. The Map Title (the central square box) is the main theme or concept of the map. First-level branches are the main topics related to the theme. Sub-branches are the sub-topics related to the main topic.

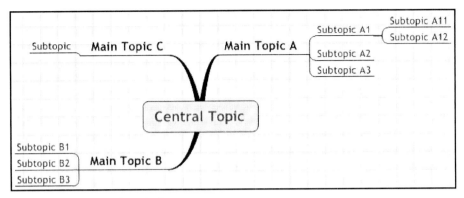

Figure A.1: Sample mind map

Zope Mind Maps

This section represents core Zope features as mind maps.

Zope

Figure A.2 represents the Zope server system. Zope provides various types of **interfaces** for client applications such as FTP, web browsers (HTTP and HTTPS protocols), and XML-RPC. Zope incorporates the Zope Object Database (ZODB), which may also be used standalone. Out of the box, Zope supports **objects** such as Folders, Images, Files, and Scripts. Zope is a very flexible application server, **interoperable** with any operating system providing Python and a C compiler, such as Linux, UNIX, Windows, and Mac. Zope also incorporates its own web server that is interoperable with other web servers such as Apache and IIS. Zope can be **integrated** with external systems such as Relational Databases and LDAP servers. It supports many **features** such as virtual hosting, session management and transactions. Important features (represented with small blue icon in Figure A.2) such as ZMI, Search, Security, and RDBMS are shown in detail in following sections. For detailed information about Zope, refer to *The Zope Book* at http://www.plope.com/Books/2_7Edition.

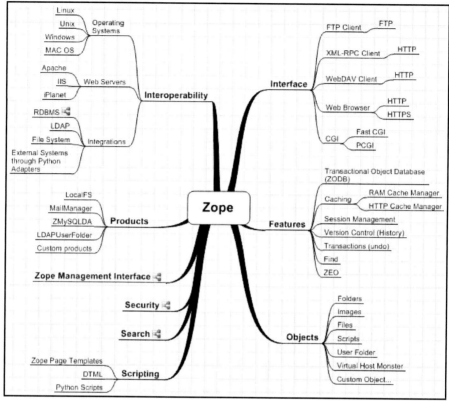

Figure A.2: Mind Map of Zope

ZMI

Figure A.3 represents the Zope Management Interface (ZMI), which is the administrative interface for programmers to inspect and manage applications and for site managers to perform configuration. For detailed information about ZMI, refer to *The Zope Book* at http://www.plope.com/Books/2_7Edition.

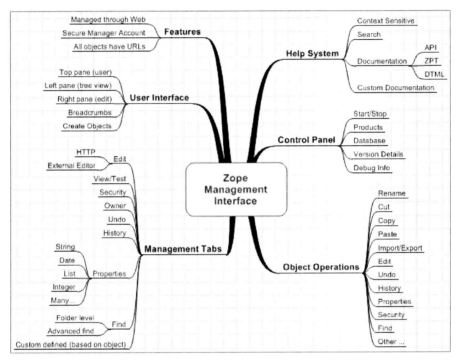

Figure A.3: Mind Map of ZMI

Zope Security

Figure A.4 represents Zope's security features. For detailed information about Zope security, refer to *Chapter 3*.

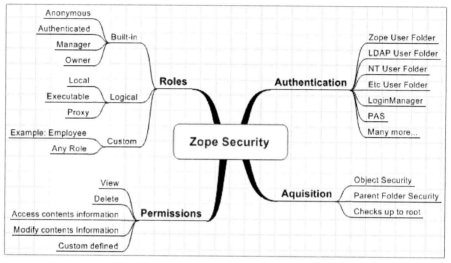

Figure A.4: Mind Map of Zope Security Features

Zope Search

Figure A.5 represents Zope's search features. For detailed information about Zope searches, refer to *Chapter 4*.

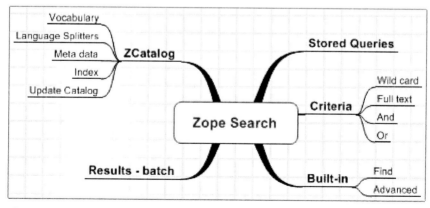

Figure A.5: Mind Map of Zope Search Features

Zope RDBMS

Figure A.6 represents Zope's RDBMS capabilities. For detailed information about Zope RDBMS, refer to *Chapter 9*.

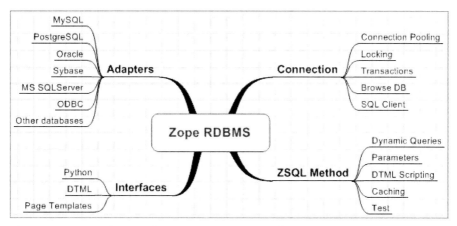

Figure A.6: Mind Map of Zope Integration with Relational Databases

Plone Mind Maps

This section represents core Plone features as mind maps.

Plone

Figure A.7 represents the features of Plone. Important features (represented with small blue icons in Figure A.7) such as Membership, Content Types, Search, and Workflow are shown in detail in following sections of this appendix.

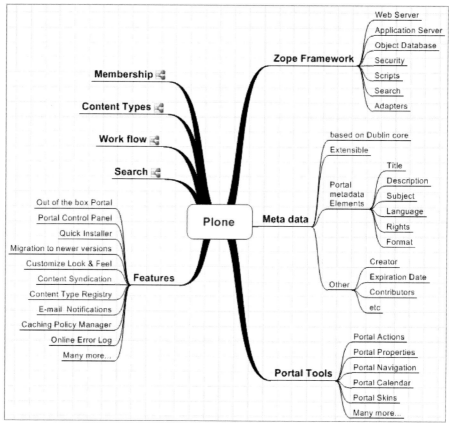

Figure A.7: Mind Map of Plone Features

Plone Membership

Figure A.8represents the various functions supported by Plone membership. For detailed information about Plone membership, refer to *Chapters 9* and *10*.

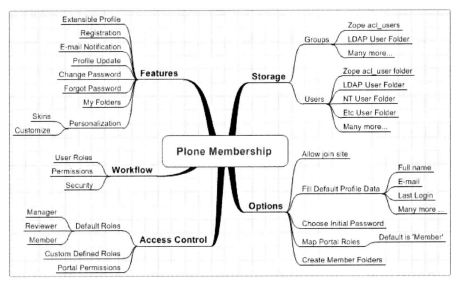

Figure A.8: Mind Map of Plone Membership Features

Plone Content Types

Figure A.9 represents the Plone content types. For detailed information about content types, refer to *Chapters 6* and *7*.

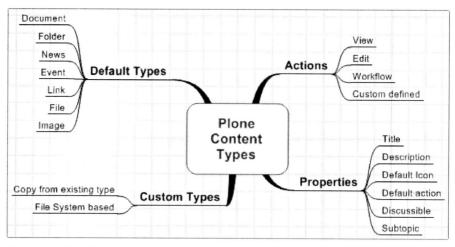

Figure A.9: Mind Map of Plone Content Types

Plone Workflow

Figure A.10 represents the features of Plone workflow. For detailed information about Plone workflow, refer to *Chapter 3*.

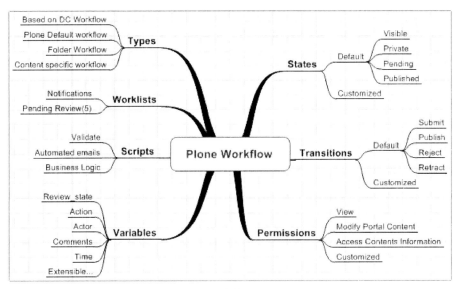

Figure A.10: Mind Map of Plone Workflow

Plone Search

Figure A.11 represents the high-level features of Plone's search functionality. For detailed information about Plone search, refer *Chapter 4*.

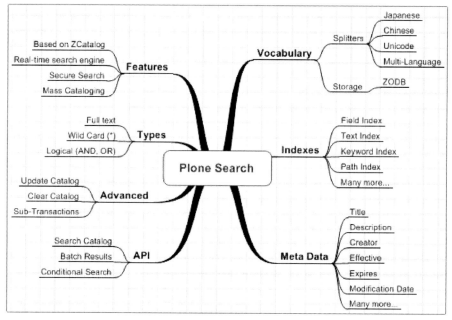

Figure A.11: Map of Plone Search Features

Page Template Reference

Authors: Michel Pelletier and Munwar Shariff

Most web application frameworks provide some means of dynamically generating HTML and other presentation formats, and Zope is no exception. In fact, it provides two different templating technologies. DTML, the Dynamic Template Markup Language, was the first, but in most areas Zope Page Templates (ZPT) has superseded it. ZPT has three components: the Template Attribute Language (TAL), the TAL Expression Syntax (TALES), and the Macro Expansions for TAL (METAL).

Page Template Languages

Page Templates are a web page generation tool. They help programmers and designers collaborate in producing dynamic web pages for Plone applications. Page Templates can create HTML pages and XML pages dynamically. This appendix is a reference for Zope Page Template (ZPT) standards: TAL, TALES, and METAL. This appendix also explains built-in Page Template variables in detail.

Variables

Zope Page Templates come with a number of built-in variables as described below. Built-in variables are the names of the objects that you can use in expressions.

template

The *template* variable is bound to the template object. Developers use it infrequently, but it is sometimes useful for accessing properties of the template object.

context

The *context* variable is the most commonly used one. A template is always rendered in some Zope context (for example, a template provides a "view" for a content object), and the template accesses this context via the *context* variable. The value of *context* depends on the context in which the template is rendered. Depending on how the template is called, this variable may be different objects at different times. This variable is synonymous with *context* used in Python scripts.

here

The *here* variable is synonymous with *context*; it is found in older templates.

container

The *container* variable is bound to the container that holds the template. You can use it to render the template in a context-independent way; in other words, while the context of a template may change, the container will always stay the same, provided you don't copy or move the template.

nothing

The *nothing* variable is the TAL equivalent to the Python built-in variable *None*. Use it in expressions to check for an *empty* condition, such as trying to access an object that does not exist.

options

If Python code calls a page template with parameters, or someone accesses a page template from the web via a URL that includes a query string with variables, those variables are placed into the *options* built-in variable. The *options* variable is a mapping, so if you are looking for the query string option *page*, you can write *options/page* (using path syntax) or *python:options['page']* (using Python syntax).

root

The *root* variable is bound to the root Zope folder object.

user

The *user* variable is bound to the current user object, which is accessing the page template.

request

The *request* variable is bound to the current request object if someone accesses a page template through the web.

modules

The *modules* variable provides access to Python modules that have been exposed to page template programmers.

TAL

Template Attribute Language (TAL) is a dynamic language that is expressed as attributes on HTML tags. TAL attributes are in the form `command="expression"`, where *command* is a tag in the TAL namespace (which is conventionally defined as "tal"). With the namespace, the tag looks like this: `tal:command="expression"`. There are eight TAL commands: `content`, `replace`, `condition`, `define`, `attributes`, `repeat`, `on-error`, and `omit-tag`. This appendix explains each command.

TAL commands define the dynamic behavior of a page template. You write them as attributes in the TAL namespace. You can indicate the namespace on the attribute itself (if the element tag is in the HTML namespace), or on the element (in which case all the attributes are in the element's namespace). If more than one TAL command exists on a single tag, they execute in the following order:

1. define

2. condition

3. repeat

4. content or replace

5. attributes

6. omit-tag

The *on-error* command is not in this list because it only executes when an error displays.

tal:define

The *define* command defines new variables. See Listing B.1.

Listing B.1

```
<html>
<head><title>...</title></head>
<body>
   <p tal:define="a_path  folder1/doc1;
                  x_value python:5">
</body>
</html>
```

This example creates two variables: **a_path**, which refers to the object whose path is **folder1/doc1**, and **x_value**, whose value is the Python integer **5**.

tal:condition

The *condition* command conditionally renders a document sub-tree (an element and everything nested inside it). If the condition is true, the tag is rendered into the output of the document; if the condition is false, it is not included in the output. See Listing B.2.

Listing B.2

```
<html>...
   <p tal:condition="visible">You might not see this.</p>
...
</html>
```

This example will only print the paragraph tag if the visible variable is true.

tal:content

The *content* command is perhaps the most common TAL command. It dynamically renders the content of a tag. See Listing B.3

Listing B.3

```
<html>...
   <p>The title of this document is:
      <b tal:content="here/Title"></b> and is bold.</p>
...
</html>
```

This example prints the document's title in bold.

tal:replace

The *replace* command works like the *content* command, except the result replaces the whole tag, not just the content of the tag. See Listing B.4.

Listing B.4

```
<html>
  <p>The title of this document is:
    <b tal:replace="here/Title">Placeholder Title</b> and isn't bold.
  </p>
</html>
```

This example does *not* print the document's title in bold, because the *Title* replaces the *bold* tag. In this case, why use the <b> tag? Viewing the unrendered template will show you the title (in this case, "Placeholder Title") in bold. This could be useful if you want to highlight text that will be replaced upon rendering. If you don't need this, then using an HTML tag might indeed be distracting and unnecessary. In this case, you can use an element in the TAL namespace, for example, `<tal:title replace="here/Title"/>`. Only the ZPT interpreter pays attention to anything in the TAL namespace, and it only looks at attributes; therefore, the `title` tag will be ignored, and is purely descriptive.

tal:repeat

The *repeat* command repeats over a sequence of data, rendering a chunk of HTML for each item. This is very useful for displaying rows of data that might come from a database or other query. See Listing B.5.

Listing B.5

```
<html>...
  <ul tal:repeat="item here/objectValues">
      <li tal:content="item/Title"></li>
  </ul>
  ...
</html>
```

The above example will repeat the contents of the **ul** tag for each item that the method **here/objectValues** returns.

tal:attributes

Often it is necessary to change not just the content of a tag, but also attributes on the tag. You can use the *attributes* command to alter the attributes of the current tag (see Listing B.6):

Listing B.6

```
<html>...
  <a href="."
    tal:attributes="href here/linkURL"
    tal:content="here/linkText>This is a dynamic link.</p>
...
</html>
```

This example creates a link whose **href** attribute is the value of the property or method **linkURL**, and whose content is the value of the property or method **linkText**.

tal:omit-tag

The *omit-tag* command takes an expression argument just like the *condition* command, but instead of optionally rendering the content of the tag, it optionally includes the tag in the output. In a way, you can simulate the *content* command and the *replace* command with the *omit-tag* command by passing either a true or a false value to the *omit-tag*. See Listing B.7.

Listing B.7

```
<html>
...
  <p tal:omit-tag="python: True">This is not a paragraph.
    It is some text that replaces the P tag.</p>
  <p tal:omit-tag="python: False">This is a paragraph.</p>
...
</html>
```

This command can be useful if you are rendering a navigation menu, where all the items are links except for the item that you are currently visiting. In this case, you could *omit* the **A** tag on the current item.

tal:on-error

The *on-error* command handles errors. You should usually handle errors in the application, not in a template, but in some cases, you can use this to handle errors (for example, if you do not have access to the application to change its code so that it handles errors itself). See Listing B.8.

Listing B.8

```
<html>
...
<p tal:on-error="string:Username is not defined!"
   tal:content="here/getUsername">Munwar</p>
...
</html>
```

In this example, a string *"Username is not defined!"* displays to the user instead of the standard page error, if there is an error occurs inside the paragraph tag page.

TALES Expressions

The "expression" component of a TAL attribute is written in the TAL expression syntax, TALES. There are different types of TAL expressions, the most common of which are path expressions and Python expressions. Applications can easily extend TALES to provide custom expression types. The expression type precedes the expression. The default type is path expressions, which is assumed when the type is omitted.

TALES expressions are the most dynamic part of a TAL command. While the TAL language itself is limited to only eight commands, you can write TALES expressions in a variety of ways by using one of the many different TALES expression types. In general, you will use only three expressions types (path, python, and string), but there are others. Here is a complete list:

path

Path expressions are the most common form of expressions in Zope. They define a path-style syntax that allows you to access Zope objects, methods, and properties. Path syntax works by starting from a well-known variable (such as **here** or **container**) and traversing a path until it finds an object. If the object is callable, the path expression calls it and returns the value returned by the call. Otherwise, it returns the object itself.

Path expressions may be followed by a pipe character (|) and an alternate expression. If the first expression returns a false value or raises an exception, it evaluates the alternate expression. The alternate expression can be any ZPT expression type, including **path**, **python**, **string**, etc. If the alternate expression is a path expression, alternates can also follow it.

This type of expression is the default, so it may leave out the **path:** prefix.

python

Python expressions are very straightforward Python code. Expressions allow most forms of Python and some standard Python modules. Note that *python* expressions run in a security-restricted environment, like Python Scripts, and therefore it does not allow users without permission to access objects.

string

String expressions are useful to replace scripts for simple string processing. See Listing B.9.

Listing B.9

```
<p tal:content="string:Copyright (c) $year by CIGNEX"> copyright </p>
```

This expression might be rendered as follows, depending on the value of the variable *year*. See Listing B.10.

Listing B.10

```
<p>Copyright (c) 2005 by CIGNEX</p>
```

---

not

The *not* syntax type is very simple: it negates the truth-value of any expression with which you use it.

nocall

The path expression machinery will call a callable object automatically, but sometimes you do not want this behavior. Consider the example in Listing B.11:

Listing B.11

```
<html>...
  <div tal:define="mtool nocall:portal/portal_membership"/>
...
</html>
```

If the *nocall* were not present, then the path expression machinery would attempt to call the portal_membership tool. The Plone tool objects aren't intended to be called directly. They generally provide methods and properties instead. With the *nocall* expression, it is possible to create a reference to a tool without calling it prematurely.

defer

The *defer* expression type is rarely used. For example, not one use of it exists in the Plone skins. However, in rare cases it can be handy. The defer expression type refers to a callable object but does not call it until it is used later. See Listing B.12:

Listing B.12

```
<html>...
  <div tal:define="logo defer:here/generateLogo">
    <span tal:content="logo"></span>
</div>
...</html>
```

In this example, the script *generateLogo* will not be called the first time the variable logo is defined, only when the variable logo is used. It is the equivalent of the snippet in Listing B.13:

Listing B.13

```
  <div tal:define="logo nocall:here/generateLogo">
    <span tal:content="python:logo()"></span>
</div>
```

METAL

Template *macros* allow shared presentation, and Template *slots* allow macro customization. METAL statements define macros and slots for using and customizing the look and feel of the page template. Each statement serves a particular purpose, and all statements must be used on HTML-style tags.

metal:define-macro

The *define-macro* statement defines element as a macro. Consider the example code of a page template called *page1.html*. See Listing B.14.

Listing B.14

```
<table metal:define-macro="sidebar">
....
</table>
```

This example defines a macro called **sidebar**, which begins with the **table** tag.

metal:use-macro

The *use-macro* statement dynamically inserts the macro. Consider the following example of a page template called *page2.html*, where the *use-macro* statement dynamically inserts the macro from *page1.html*. See Listing B.15.

Listing B.15

```
<table metal:use-macro="container/page1.html/macros/sidebar">
    </table>
```

metal:define-slot

The *define-slot* statement defines an element as a customization point. Consider the example code of the *page1.html* page template in Listing B.16:

Listing B.16

```
<table metal:define-macro="sidebar">
....
<tr><td>This will always render if the template is used.</td></tr>
   <tr metal:define-slot="links"><td>
   This will only render if you don't fill the 'links'
   slot with something when you use the 'sidebar' macro.
   </td></tr>
....
</table>
```

metal:fill-slot

The *fill-slot* macro overrides the slotted element. Consider the example in Listing B.17 of *page2.html*, where *fill-slot* dynamically overrides the slot defined in *page1.html*:

Listing B.17

```
<table metal:use-macro="container/page1.html/macros/sidebar">
   <tr metal:fill-slot="links">
      <td> <a href="link">link</a> </td>
   </tr>
</table>
```

Mind map

Figure B.1 highlights the TAL commands, METAL statements, and built-in variables of ZPT.

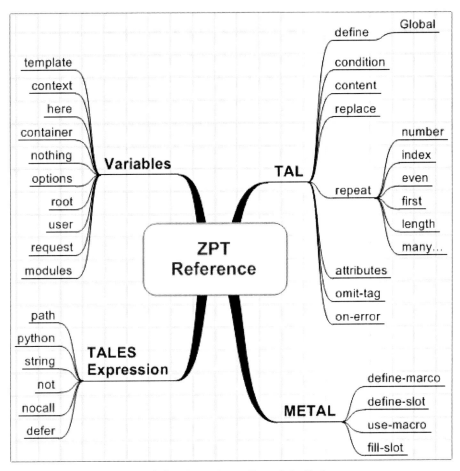

Figure B.1: Mind Map of the Zope Page Template Reference

Useful Resources

Authors: Michel Pelletier and Munwar Shariff

This appendix provides Plone, Zope, and Python related resources, as well as links to some useful Plone products that you can install and customize.

Recommended Reading

This section lists web sites, books, tutorials, mailing lists, white papers, and articles to find good online documentation about Plone and other useful products.

Web Sites

The central web sites of the community include:

▶ http://python.org/

▶ http://zope.org/

▶ http://plone.org/

Useful web sites by active community members include:

▶ http://zopezen.org/

▶ http://plope.org

The sites of the organizations (commercial entities, foundations, sponsors) behind Zope and Plone include:

▶ http://zope.com

▶ http://zope-europe.org/

▶ http://plone.org/foundation

Books

▶ *The Zope Book 2.7 Edition*, edited by Chris McDonough, based on the print edition by Michel Pelletier and Amos Latteier. http://plope.com/Books/2_7Edition/

▶ *The Definitive Guide to Plone* by Andy McKay. http://plone.org/documentation/books/definitive-guide. An online version of this book is available at http://docs.neuroinf.de/PloneBook.

▶ *Plone Content Management Essentials* by Julie C. Melonie. http://plone.org/documentation/books/cm-essentials

▸ *Building Websites with Plone* by Cameron Cooper. http://plone.org/documentation/books/building_websites

Tutorials

▸ The Python Tutorial (http://docs.python.org/tut/tut.html)

▸ The Zope Tutorial (http://zope.org/Documentation/Projects/Tutorial)

▸ Plone How-To and other documentation (http://plone.org/documentation/howto/).

▸ Training material (http://upfrontsystems.co.za/courses/)

▸ Raphael's tutorial (http://www.neuroinf.de/LabTools/MySite)

Mailing Lists

▸ Plone mailing lists (http://plone.org/documentation/lists)

▸ Zope mailing lists (http://zope.org/Resources/MailingLists)

▸ Python mailing lists (http://mail.python.org/mailman/listinfo)

White Papers and Articles

▸ *Zope Magazine* features monthly articles on Zope. (http://www.zopemag.com/)

▸ List of articles about Zope technologies. (http://zope.org/Resources/Articles/)

Overview of Useful Plone Products

This section contains some useful Zope and Plone products that you can install and customize. In no way is this a complete list; products are being developed and abandoned all the time, so be sure to check out the resources thoroughly before taking any of this as fact.

The Collective

The Collective is a collection of Plone developers who keep their community-contributed code in one CVS repository hosted at SourceForge.net. The Collective is home to lots of products, some very actively maintained, and others less so. Before using a product from the Collective it is best to find the status of that Product and who is maintaining it.

You can find more about the Collective, its products, and its maintainers by subscribing to the Plone users mailing list or logging into the #plone channel on the irc.freenode.net chat servers.

Note that most of the repositories have migrated to subversion, hosted at http://svn.plone.org. However, CVS at SourceForge still contains projects that might be dormant or where the developer preferred to continue using CVS. SourceForge still accommodates bug tracking and mailing lists.

Plone.org

Plone.org is a great place to find new products. Not only are there many products hosted on Plone.org, but also whenever a new product is released, the author invariably posts a news item to Plone.org about the event. It is easy to find a product from Plone.org's software center at http://plone.org/products, as products are categorized based on their functionality.

Zope.org

Zope.org has news items related to new Zope and CMF related products. Simply search through the products page (http://www.zope.org/Products/) to find products that might implement the behavior you're looking for.

Content Management Software

The web site http://www.contentmanagementsoftware.info/ provides a very long list of useful Plone products. Some of the important products are listed here for your reference.

SimpleBlog

The name says it all – this product provides a simple blog for your Plone site. This product categorizes blogs and provides a blog calendar.

http://sourceforge.net/project/showfiles.php?group_id=
55262&package_id=100573

PloneCollectorNG

The PloneCollectorNG product is a bug tracker. This product allows you to
track bugs in various software products that you may have and assign bugs to
Plone members for them to fix.

http://sourceforge.net/project/showfiles.php?group_id=
55262&package_id=96051

PloneMall

PloneMall is an e-commerce solution for Plone. The PloneMall framework is
flexible, pluggable, and extensible. PloneMall is not an out-of-the-box shop solution, but a developer with a grasp of Plone development can easily create a shop
with it.

http://plonemall.com/

PloneWebMail

PloneWebMail is a web-mail front end for Plone using the IMAP protocol. This
product is very useful for adding an inexpensive web e-mail system for your
users.

http://plonewebmail.openprojects.it

PloneQueueCatalog

This product changes the behavior of Plone catalog to defer cataloging of
content into a separate thread. This has a number of advantages, including faster
user interaction and more efficient cataloging performance. The downside is that
new content does not immediately show up in the Plone catalog.

http://sourceforge.net/project/showfiles.php?group_id=
55262&package_id=136417

HamCannon

Hamcannon is an open source, e-mail management service from ICP Europe. HamCannon provides management of outbound, opt-in e-mail marketing, with a complete subscription interface, bounce, open tracking, and personalization.

http://www.hamcannon.com/

CMFMember

The main purpose of CMFMember is to allow members to use Archetype-based objects, so that they can workflow and customize them.

http://sourceforge.net/project/showfiles.php?group_id=55262&package_id=118065

CMFBoard

CMFBoard adds forum support for CMF. This product adds chat boards or other discussion boards with file attachments to a web site.

http://www.cmfboard.org/

Link objects, 73
Linux
    installing LDAP, 300–306
    installing Plone, 8
local role
    defined, 154
local roles
    sharing, 163
Log tab
    LDAP, 315–316
login tools, 19–24
LP (LinguaPlone), 257–261

M

Macro Expansion Template Attribute
    Language (METAL)
    defined, 110
macros
    defined, 110
    main_template, 114–115
MailHost, 34
main_template, 110–115
    macros, 114–115
    slot definitions, 114
manager
    defined, 154
managing
    groups, 151–153
    member profiles, 172–175
    roles and permissions, 153–158
    users security, 148–149
marshaller
    defined, 216
marshalling
    defined, 213
member_search_form
    securing, 170
members
    adding Plone, 89–92
    adding properties, 172–173
    managing profiles, 172–175

searching Plone, 318–320
    updating profiles LDAP, 320–321
Members folder, 23–24
membership
    controlling in Plone, 175–177
    customizing Plone, 318–322
Membership framework, 150–151
membership scalability
    LDAP, 299–300
membership tools, 19–24
metadata
    adding custom, 30
    changing policies, 29–30
    defined, 5
    element fields, 30
    searching, 132–133
METAL (Macro Expansion Template
    Attribute Language)
    defined, 110
methods
    Archetypes reference, 234
migrating
    base software, 241–242
    Plone, 242–243
    with setstate, 245
migration
    ATCT, 237–238
    defined, 240
    scripts, 247–248
    to Plone 2.1, 240–249
migration tool, 39–40
MultiSelectionWidget, 231
MySQL
    and archetypes storage, 280–281
    installing, 273
mysqlUserFolder
    and Plone, 282–283

N

navigation_properties, 45
navtree_properties, 46

Index